EXCELLENCE IN EDUCATING THE GIFTED

JOHN FELDHUSEN, *Purdue University*
JOYCE VAN TASSEL-BASKA, *College of William and Mary*
KEN SEELEY, *Clayton Foundation, Denver, Colorado*

With Chapters By
GRAYSON WHEATLEY, *Florida State University*
LELAND BASKA, *Williamsburg, James City-
County Schools, Virginia*
LINDA SILVERMAN, *Gifted Child Development
Center, Denver, Colorado*

LOVE PUBLISHING COMPANY®
Denver, Colorado 80222

Library of Congress Catalog Card Number 88-82696

Copyright © 1989 Love Publishing Company
Printed in the U.S.A.
ISBN 0-89108-205-0

Contents

Figures

Tables

Preface

As we began writing this book and while it was in progress, we spent many hours clarifying our conceptions of giftedness and education of the gifted. We believe that gifted and talented youth have special characteristics that determine their educational needs. First and foremost, they need and want appropriately challenging learning experiences in school—most of the time within recognized academic disciplines. They need interaction with teachers who know the subject matter very well and who know how to engage them in generative learning experiences, probing and thrusting for deep understanding of complex concepts and searching for solutions to complex issues and concerns. They also need nurturing parents who support them emotionally and help them find stimulating experiences outside of school. Other people, notably intellectual peers and mentors, are also needed. Peers provide social-emotional support and intellectual stimulation. Mentors evoke and stimulate special talents and serve as role models of high-level achievement.

As an overriding proposition, we concluded that gifted and talented youth need high-powered learning experiences to challenge their minds and assure intellectual growth and achievement commensurate with their ability. The highest satisfaction in life comes to those who use their abilities and talents to the fullest extent and who create new ideas, inventions, or works of art. Thus, this book was conceived to delineate the many facets of gifted individuals and their learning patterns, so that they may be enabled to reach their greatest potential.

Our goal in writing the book was also to create a comprehensive introduction to the field of gifted education that will provide a strong base for understanding key issues and ideas. This book, we hope, provides a basic overview of the psychology and education of the gifted.

We have worked together for 7 years creating, developing, articulating, and critiquing the ideas presented in the following chapters. We intend this book to serve as a basic resource for those who view gifted education as a set of rigorous intellectual experiences for youth who exhibit aptitude and interest in matters of the mind.

1

Introduction

John F. Feldhusen

Bill is enrolled in an honors English class studying modern fiction writers. He is doing an in-depth study of the novels of Hemingway and will write an extensive report and make an oral presentation to the class. He loves the class and especially relishes the discussions in the class.

* * *

Mary is enrolled in a middle school seminar that is currently studying the impressionist painters. The group is fairly small, and the teacher is supplemented periodically by visiting speakers, the most recent being a professor of art history from a local college.

* * *

Terry is enrolled in a pullout class at the fourth grade level. The class meets 2 half-days a week. Terry has learned some library research and thinking skills in this program and is currently doing research on the history of transportation systems in her community.

* * *

Tommy is enrolled in a second grade self-contained class for highly gifted children. The class is taught by Mary Williams, a well trained teacher who has earned a special licensure in teaching the gifted. Class members are together for all their academic subjects, which are quite advanced, fast-paced, and individualized. The children are mainstreamed for art, music, physical education, and recess.

* * *

All of these students have been identified as gifted or talented. All are in specially organized services and differentiated programs for the gifted. These gifted and talented youth represent a tremendous resource for the future of our civilizations. A few of them will become the creators, inventors, artists, and Nobel Prize winners of the future, while many will become leaders at local, state, national, and international levels. The talent or ability of some will never be discovered or developed. Others will lose their motivation or drive along the way to adulthood, and they will suffer the anguish of knowing their potential but failing to exercise or realize it.

Many gifted and talented youth have abundant opportunities to realize their talent and abilities. They grow up in affluent and well educated families with parents who recognize their talents and are eager to foster its development. They attend schools in which the teachers expect and are ready to nurture academic and artistic ability. Although these teachers may not be well trained in the specifics of educating the gifted and talented, they are nevertheless very appreciative and supportive of youth who exhibit talent and motivation for school learning.

Some other youth, the "special populations," as we now call them, come from families who are far less certain about recognizing or nurturing talent or ability in their children. Among the poverty populations of the world there is despair and despondency, which severely limits educational and occupational goals. Populations the world over have long been assumed or accepted that girls would not enter science, engineering, or medicine, and that assumption still remains strong. Handicapped youth have also found that the focus in school programs is almost always on remediation of the handicap, not on discovery and nurturance of special talents and abilities.

We do not know the exact origins of talent or ability. It is partly derived from our genetic heritage and physical endowment. It seems to run in some families. But we also know that experiences from birth onward exert a profound influence on the emergence of talent and ability and on the personal, motivational factors that drive the development of talent and ability toward achievements. We are especially aware of the potential positive influence of mentors, coaches, and some special teachers who are sensitive to the presence of talent and inclined to make substantial personal efforts to nurture it. In many fields of human endeavor, a mentor, coach, guide, or special teacher is essential in the development of talent.

Society and schools remain somewhat ambivalent about their support for the gifted and talented. Their first commitment is to help all youth learn to function well in society. Helping the gifted and talented often seems frivolous or undesirable: "They can make it on their own." In the United States, we are deeply committed to helping the handicapped and the disadvantaged but question diverting funds for "advantaged" youth who are gifted and talented. There is also some suspicion in our egalitarian society of those who are markedly different or superior in some way, and we are sometimes extremely intolerant of those who are very "different." Among youth in particular there is a strong peer pressure to be like all the others, not to deviate. Thus, a variety of pressures in society and school militate against open acceptance and enthusiasm for the gifted and talented.

Parents also often seem ambivalent about potential talent or ability in their offspring. "I just want my child to be normal and happy like other children" is a frequent refrain. There seems to be a perception among many parents that giftedness may lead to a pressured and abnormal life. Research also suggests that the demands upon parents of gifted and talented youth may be very great if the parents embrace wholeheartedly the demands upon their time and financial resources to foster their children's talents (Bloom, 1985; Feldman, 1986). Thus, a variety of factors may cause genuine apprehension on the part of parents toward their children's giftedness.

What is the Historical Background of the Gifted Movement?

The movement to find and nurture the gifted has waxed and waned for many decades. The work of Lewis Terman and his colleagues during a period of approximately 40 years (Terman & Oden, 1959) laid the groundwork for scientific understanding of giftedness and paved the way for practical efforts to identify and nurture the gifted in schools. Beginning in 1921, Terman and his colleagues carried out a longitudinal study of 1,528 gifted youth with IQs greater than 140 who were approximately 12 years old. Terman died in 1959, but the study will continue until 2020, by which time the remaining subjects probably will have died. Results of the study debunked myths about the social and emotional abnormalities of gifted youth, showed that a large number went on to high level achievements, found that only one had achieved international eminence, and suggested that among those who were highly successful, a motivational or persistence factor and a capacity to get organized to accomplish tasks were present in youth.

Excellent research on the gifted was conducted by a number of other researchers in this same period, notably by Havighurst, Stivers, and DeHaan (1955), Hollingworth (1926, 1942), Passow, Goldberg, Tannenbaum, and French (1955), and Witty (1951). Their work extended our insights to the highly gifted and to a broader conception of giftedness as well as to trial efforts in educating the gifted.

Thus, the United States was ready to react in 1958 when the Soviet Union successfully launched *Sputnik*. That event was perceived as a huge educational failure on our part in the United States and especially as a failure to find and nurture scientific, engineering, and mathematical talent. Substantial research and development efforts were launched in the early 1960s to improve educational services for the gifted and talented with major support from the National Education Association (Bish, 1961). A flurry of publications from the association offered guidance to teachers on how to teach or counsel the gifted and talented. This thrust from the National Education Association and related research and development efforts in the 1960s led to sporadic programming for the gifted but no uniform service in all American schools. As the decade of the 1960s wore on, interest in the gifted was eclipsed by major legislation and funding to serve the handicapped and the disadvantaged.

But interest in the gifted continued, and in 1969 the Congress of the United States authorized the U.S. Commissioner of Education, Sidney Marland, to conduct a study of the status of educational services for the gifted in our schools. The report, completed in 1972, came to be known as the Marland Report. Its impact was immediate, and it set in motion events that continue to this day.

The report suggested that gifted youth were left to languish or go unserved in American schools and that one might even find school personnel who were antagonistic to the gifted. The report had a monumental effect in establishing a new definition of the gifted:

> Gifted and talented children are those identified by professionally qualified persons who by virtue of outstanding abilities are capable of high performance. These are children who require differentiated educational programs and services beyond those normally provided by the regular school program in order to realize their contribution to self and society.
>
> Children capable of high performance include those with demonstrated achievement and/or potential ability in any of the following areas:
>
> 1. General intellectual ability
> 2. Specific academic aptitude
> 3. Creative or productive thinking
> 4. Leadership ability
> 5. Visual and performing arts
> 6. Psychomotor ability. (p. 2)

Thus, the older monolithic view of giftedness simply as high intelligence began to be displaced in favor of a multifaceted view of talents and abilities. That view would later be extended and modified in a seminal and influential theoretical analysis of giftedness by Joseph Renzulli (1978). This latter work extended the conception of giftedness to motivational aspects and creativity.

In 1974, with small appropriations from the U.S. Congress, an office was established in the U.S. Office of Education to support the development of programs for the gifted in American schools. Two leadership training institutes were organized, one in Reston, Virginia, and the other in Los Angeles, to work with state education agencies and with school districts and develop systematic plans for programs to serve the gifted and talented. The institutes, consolidated into one center in Los Angeles in 1977, were extremely influential in bringing about an awareness of the educational needs of gifted and talented youth and in establishing sound guidelines for program services.

Throughout the remainder of the 1970s and during the 1980s, in spite of the closing of the Federal Office for the Gifted in 1981, programs for the gifted grew and prospered, supported increasingly by state educational funding. Every state in the United States established some kind of leadership effort with at least a part-time consultant or coordinator guiding the effort. In some states, the support was so strong that an extensive staff was employed and budgets reached as high as $80 million annually (in Florida).

How Can We Identify the Gifted and Talented?

Throughout the effort to develop programs for the gifted, schools also were developing new, formal, and often intricate methods for finding the gifted and talented. Identification systems tended to search for *the* gifted child, an approach seemingly based on the assumption that giftedness was a stable, internal condition, either present or absent, and never likely to appear later if not present at the time of assessment. Identifiers indeed were likely to use multiple measures such as IQ, achievement test scores, rating scales, and creativity tests, but the assessment often was ill-conceived, and tests often were used inappropriately (Richert, Alvino, & McDonnel, 1982). Although psychological research suggested that human abilities are plastic and emerge in response to environmental variation (Fischer & Silvern, 1985), identification of the gifted proceeded as though giftedness were a homunculus embedded in the body of the gifted child.

This conception of a fixed and stable giftedness led to a promiscuous labeling of identified children as "gifted." In spite of the cautions from special education about the risks of explicit labeling, educators of the gifted readily selected and named certain children as "gifted," "creative," and "talented" (see, for example, Colangelo & Brower, 1987; Cornell, 1983; Guskin, Okolo, Zimmerman & Ping, 1986). A more appropriate approach, as we shall suggest in chapter 7, is to view the identification process at any age level as providing tentative indications of a level of functional ability at that age but to recognize also that giftedness, talent, or high ability may emerge later if the educational and motivational conditions are effective. This is to say that some teachers, some schools, some mentors, some coaches, some educational environments and resources may be more effective at times than others, not just in teaching new skills and concepts but also in evoking growth in intelligence or ability (Detterman & Sternberg, 1982).

The identification process also should be viewed as a matching process. That is, identification is a diagnostic process through which we delineate the special talents and abilities of the gifted and use that information to select appropriate educational experiences. Identification is not an end in itself; it is a means to the end of appropriate educational programming.

What Do the Gifted Need?

There is widespread agreement that gifted and talented youth should receive special educational services but considerable disagreement about the direction those services should take.

Enrichment

One argument is that the educational services should be essentially supplementary or (euphemistically) *enrichment oriented*. This usually means opportunities to study additional topics not covered in the regular curriculum, but not necessarily advanced topics. Thus, a gifted child is encouraged to do supplementary study of robots while the rest of the class works on the basic science curriculum. Furthermore, there is often a suggestion that such special enrichment study for the gifted should be done *in depth*, although the concept of "in depth" is puzzling and difficult to define. Does it mean dealing with the subject's conceptual complexity . . . the ideas? Does it mean doing library research in more reference sources than is typical for the grade level? Or does it mean spending more time in certain types of cognitive activity such as observing, analyzing, problem solving, or evaluating? There is much talk in schools about enrichment for the gifted, but it is often difficult to get a clear picture of what purpose it serves.

Acceleration

An alternative special educational service is called *acceleration*. This typically refers to any or all the ways we permit, encourage, or help gifted students engage in study of new material that is typically taught at a higher grade level than the one in which the child is currently enrolled and speed up instruction to cover more material in a shorter time. Accelerated learning experiences are more easily defined than are enrichment experiences. Condensing a 1-year algebra course to 1 semester or allowing gifted children to take algebra in seventh grade are two examples of acceleration.

Enrichment approaches often are based on the assumption that *more*—more in depth or more activity at higher cognitive levels—will meet the gifted child's needs. In contrast, acceleration assumes that gifted children, who, by most identification schemes, are seen to be achieving or operating at advanced skill levels, should be studying new material at levels commensurate with their levels of ability. Perhaps the best resolution is the suggestion that gifted students need both enriched and accelerated learning experiences.

Individualization

A third approach to meeting the needs of the gifted is to *individualize* instruction by presenting new learning tasks at the next higher level of difficulty or progression. In many ways this approach is similar to the acceleration approach, but individualization stresses tailoring instruction to the individual gifted child. The tailoring also might use criteria other than achievement level as guides. In particular, the individualization might be based on the child's interests, learning styles and modalities, and special talents. Although few totally individualized classrooms can be found, many teachers do at least small amounts of individualization, such as permitting children to select reading books at levels commensurate with their reading achievement levels and their special interests.

Remediation

A fourth approach to serving the gifted is to focus on *remediating* their weak areas. It may seem contradictory to suggest that the gifted have weaknesses, but a broad spectrum evaluation reveals both strengths and comparatively weaker areas of functioning. Thus, on an achievement test a mathematically gifted adolescent scores at the 99th percentile in math concepts and math problem solving but at the 80th percentile in math computation and only the 70th percentile in language usage and punctuation skills. Shall we now focus instruction exclusively on the math conceptual and problem solving ability and press on to even greater heights of accomplishment or instead emphasize math computations and language arts skills? Or shall we try to do both? Popular judgment would support doing both. The child should be allowed to fly, to soar in the areas of strength in math concepts and problem solving, and educators should try to bring up the basic skills in the context of further learning of concepts and problem solving.

Identification of Special Talents

Still another approach to serving the gifted and talented is to place major emphasis on the identification of their *special talents* (Gagné, 1985) and do all possible to foster the development of that talent. This approach is similar to the acceleration approach, which focuses on strong areas of achievement. The focus on talent, however, usually means focusing on a more general area such as artistic ability, creative writing, musical talent, or athletic prowess. Recent research (Bloom, 1985) seems to suggest that the best approach to assure high-level achievement is to identify talent early and to concentrate resources, excellent teachers, and parent commitment to its development.

Focus on Social and Emotional Needs

Still another way to serve the gifted and talented is to focus on their *social and emotional needs*. Some researchers argue that gifted and talented students may experience unique social and emotional problems and that they have somewhat unique social and emotional needs because of their giftedness (Webb, Meckstroth, & Tolan, 1982). Counseling programs are being organized in many schools to help the gifted deal with their problems (Betts, 1986; Perrone, 1986; VanTassel-Baska, 1983). Such programs often offer both individual counseling and small group discussion sessions. In addition to focusing on the social-emotional problems of the gifted, such programs are also likely to deal with vocational planning (Hoyt & Hebler, 1974), goal setting, and time management.

To what end should we serve the gifted? One major goal may be to help them realize or achieve their full potential development, as we wish to help all youth to achieve. Another end may be that our nation needs the best human resources so that we may enhance life for all American citizens. Or it may be that, as in special education, we feel obligated to meet the special needs of individual children (VanTassel-Baska, 1988). Finally, it may be a combination of all those goals that drives our special efforts for the gifted and talented.

Current Status of Gifted Education in the United States

Where are we in our efforts to identify and nurture the gifted in the United States? Three major surveys provide some indication of our current status. Research by Richert et al. (1982) indicated that while there may be many shortcomings in the way we address the task, there is nevertheless a huge effort in progress in all states to identify the gifted and talented. Research by Gallagher, Weiss, Oglesby, and Thomas (1983) found that programs to nurture giftedness have grown up throughout the United States and that the resource room/pullout model or part-time approach predominates at the elementary level while separate classes prevail at the secondary level. Finally, research by Cox, Daniel, and Boston (1985) confirmed the prevalence of the pullout model but concluded that it does not serve the gifted well. The latter project offered instead a pyramidal model with a base of enrichment experiences for all youth and an apex of full-time intensive classes for the highly gifted.

Teacher training in education of the gifted and graduate programs for leaders in gifted education also have grown apace, as documented by Parker and Karnes (1987). Thus, there seems to be an awakening to the need for special educational services for the gifted and talented throughout the United States. Furthermore, gifted education seems to be growing throughout the world, as evidenced by the appearance of two international journals, *Gifted Education International* and *Gifted International*, the latter a publication of the World Council for Gifted and Talented Children.

The Plan for This Book

This book offers a comprehensive introduction to major topics and issues in gifted and talented education. Seven chapters focus on the general nature of giftedness; specific gifted subpopulations such as underachievers, gifted girls, the disadvantaged, and the handicapped; and the process of identifying the gifted. Four chapters deal with aspects of developing programs for the gifted. Six chapters are devoted to the organization of curriculum and instruction for the gifted. Finally, three chapters turn to the facilitators (teachers, counselors, mentors) and their training, counseling the gifted, and a general philosophical position on helping the gifted achieve excellence. Overall, our goal is to provide a basic introduction to the key issues and ideas in educating the gifted and talented.

Summary

The United States and the world are awakening to the needs of gifted and talented youth and to a recognition that these youth are a priceless human resource who can help all citizens of the world surmount their problems and lead rich and fulfilling lives. Great progress is being made in the science of identification and education of the gifted and talented, but much remains to be done to make an excellent education available to all gifted and talented youth. The purpose of this book is to present a comprehensive overview of the current status of the field.

References

Betts, G.T. (1986). Development of emotional and social needs of gifted individuals. *Journal of Counseling & Development, 64*(9), 578–589.

Bish, C.E. (1961). The academically talented. *National Education Association Journal, 50*(2), 33–37.

Bloom, B.S. (1985). *Talent development*. New York: Ballantine Books.

Colangelo, N., & Brower, P. (1987). Gifted youngsters and their siblings: Long term impacts of labeling on their academic and personal self concepts. *Roeper Review, 10*(2), 101–103.

Cornell, D.G. (1983). Gifted children: The impact of positive labelling on the family system. *American Journal of Orthopsychiatry, 53*, 322–335.

Cox, J., Daniel, N., & Boston, B.O. (1985). *Educating able learners*. Austin: University of Texas Press.

Detterman, D.K., & Sternberg, R.J. (1982). *How and how much can intelligence be increased?* Norwood, NJ: Ablex.

Feldman, D.H. (1986). *Nature's gambit*. New York: Basic Books.

Fischer, K.W., & Silvern, L. (1985). Stages and individual differences in cognitive development. In M.R. Rosenzweig & L.W. Porter (Eds.), *Annual Review of Psychology* (Vol. 36, pp. 613–648). Palo Alto, CA: Annual Reviews.

Gagné, F. (1985). Giftedness and talent: Reexamining a reexamination of the definitions. *Gifted Child Quarterly, 29*(3), 103–112.

Gallagher, J.J., Weiss, P., Oglesby, K., & Thomas, T. (1983). *The status of gifted/talented education: United States survey of needs, practices and policies*. Los Angeles: Leadership Training Institute.

Guskin, S.L., Okolo, C., Zimmerman, E., & Ping, C.Y.J. (1986). Being labelled gifted or talented: Meanings and effects perceived by students in special programs. *Gifted Child Quarterly, 30*(2), 61–65.

Havighurst, R.J., Stivers, E., & DeHaan, R.F. (1955). *A survey of education of gifted children*. Chicago: University of Chicago Press.

Hollingworth, L.S. (1926). *Gifted children: Their nature and nurture*. New York: Macmillan.

Hollingworth, L.S. (1942). *Children above 180 IQ*. New York: World Book.

Hoyt, K.B., & Hebler, J.R. (1974). *Career education for gifted and talented students*. Salt Lake City: Olympus.

Marland, S.P. (1972). *Education of the gifted and talented* (Report to the Subcommittee on Education, Committee on Labor and Public Welfare, U.S. Senate). Washington, DC: U.S. Government Printing Office.

Parker, J.P., & Karnes, F.A. (1987). A current report on graduate degree programs in gifted and talented education. *Gifted Child Quarterly, 31*(3), 116–117.

Passow, A.H., Goldberg, M.L., Tannenbaum, A.J., & French, W. (1955). *Planning for talented youth*. New York: Teachers College Press.

Perrone, P. (1986). Guidance needs of gifted children, adolescents and adults. *Journal of Counseling & Development, 64*(9), 564–566.

Renzulli, J.S. (1978). What makes giftedness? Reexamining a definition. *Phi Delta Kappan, 60*, 180–184.

Richert, E.S., Alvino, J.J., & McDonnel, R.C. (1982). *National report on identification: Assessment and recommendations for comprehensive identification of gifted and talented youth*. Sewell, NJ: Educational Improvement Center—South.

Terman, L.M., & Oden, M.H. (1959). *The gifted group at mid-life*. Stanford, CA: Stanford University Press.

VanTassel-Baska, J. (Ed.). (1983). *A practical guide to counseling the gifted in a school setting*. Reston, VA: Council for Exceptional Children.

VanTassel-Baska, J., Feldhusen, J., Seeley, K., Wheatley, G., Silverman, L., & Foster, W. (1988). *Comprehensive curriculum for gifted learners*. Boston: Allyn & Bacon.

Webb, J.T., Meckstroth, E.A., & Tolan, S.S. (1982). *Guiding the gifted child*. Columbus: Ohio Psychology Publishing.

Witty, P. (1951). *The gifted child*. Boston: Heath.

Study Questions

1. What are some major arguments for special educational services to meet the needs of gifted and talented youth?

2. What are some arguments against special provisions for the gifted and talented?

3. Does the historical development of interest in and provision for the gifted and talented suggest a steady growth or intermittent surges of interest?

4. In your view, what is giftedness? What is talent?

5. What do you think the gifted need—enrichment or acceleration, or both?

6. What special social and emotional needs do the gifted and talented have?

7. How would you characterize the current status of gifted education in the United States?

THE GIFTED
AND THEIR
INDIVIDUAL
DIFFERENCES

2

Characteristics
and Needs
of the Gifted

Leland K. Baska

Much of the foundational work in creating a field of gifted education has been based on articulation of the characteristics and needs of gifted children. Early pioneers of this movement, such as Lewis Terman (1925) and Leta Hollingworth (1926), did much to aid our understanding of these children in the context of behavioral characteristics, and case study research has additionally refined our understanding. Witty (1930), Benbow and Stanley (1983), Tannenbaum (1983), and others also have sought to identify differences within the gifted population with respect to family backgrounds, special aptitudes, ability levels, and temperament. In recent years, scales for rating behavioral characteristics (Renzulli, Smith, White, Callahan, & Hartman, 1976) have attempted to quantify the relative presence or absence of some of these key behavioral indicators.

Characteristics and needs also have played an important role in defining appropriate interventions for gifted learners in schools. Classroom teachers frequently make inferences about curriculum that flow directly from the observation of a stated behavior (see Table 2.1). In this way, an "optimal match" might be made between the learner's strength area and a curricular opportunity.

This chapter discusses some of the most significant characteristics and needs of the gifted child so the reader can more readily come to appreciate the nature of

TABLE 2.1
Characteristics of Gifted Learners and Curriculum Implications

Characteristics of the Gifted Learner	Curriculum Implications
Reads well and widely	Individualize a reading program that diagnoses reading level and prescribes reading material based on that level Form a literary group of similar students for discussion Develop critical reading skills Focus on analysis and interpretation in reading material
Has a large vocabulary	Introduce a foreign language Focus on vocabulary building Develop word relationship skills (antonyms, homonyms, and so on)
Has a good memory for things heard or read	Present ideas on a topic to the class Prepare a skit or play for production Build in "trivial pursuit" activities
Is curious and asks probing questions	Develop an understanding of the scientific method Focus on observation skills
Is an independent worker and has lots of initiative	Focus on independent project work Teach organizational skills and study
Has a long attention span	Assign work that is long-term Introduce complex topics for reading, discussion, project work
Has complex thoughts and ideas	Work on critical thinking skills (analysis, synthesis, evaluation) Develop writing skills
Is widely informed about many topics	Stimulate broad reading patterns Develop special units of study that address current interests
Shows good judgment and logic	Organize a field trip for the class Prepare a parent night Teach formal logic
Understands relationships and comprehends meanings	Provide multidisciplinary experiences Structure activities that require students to work across fields on special group/individual projects

Organize curriculum by issues and
examine from different perspectives (for
example, poverty—economic, social,
personal, education views)

Produces original or unusual
products or ideas

Practice skills of fluency, flexibility,
elaboration, and originality
Work on specific product development

Note: From *Comprehensive Curriculum for Gifted Learners* (pp. 158-159) by J. VanTassel-Baska, J. Feldhusen, K. Seeley, G. Wheatley, L. Silverman, & W. Foster, 1988, Boston: Allyn & Bacon. Reprinted by permission.

these children. Furthermore, the chapter addresses characteristics and needs in the framework of both cognitive and affective domains and then draws implications for educational practice.

Characteristics of Gifted Children

Cognitive Characteristics

Gifted children display atypical behaviors in the cognitive arena from an early stage of development. If proper nurturance occurs in the environment, these characteristics continue to expand as the children grow older. When nurturance is not present, however, many of these characteristics can act as negative forces to learning or can be hidden because of a gifted child's vulnerability. These characteristics must also be apprehended in light of the following:

1. Not all gifted children will display all of the characteristics.
2. There will tend to be a range among gifted children in respect to each characteristic.
3. These characteristics may be viewed as developmental in the sense that some children may not display them at early stages of development but may at later stages. Others may manifest the characteristics from a very early age.
4. Characteristics of the gifted tend to cluster and thus constitute different profiles across children as the combination of characteristics varies.

Some of the most important differences found in a gifted population are discussed in the remainder of this chapter.

Ability to Manipulate Abstract Symbol Systems

The gifted child exhibits a greater facility for learning systems such as language and mathematics at an earlier age than is typical. Children with gifted potential usually become known to parents and teachers by their skills in manipulating language or numbers. Less apparent are abilities to solve puzzles and to use figural analogies or other kinds of nonlanguage systems. Available resources that enhance those skills early on are crucial to the development of superior talent. Thus, prodigies such as Bobby Fisher, who benefited from mentoring at the Manhattan Chess Club, and Wolfgang Mozart, who inherited a genetic and environmental predisposition for music from Leopold Mozart, are examples of talent and a supportive milieu that resulted in eminence.

Power of Concentration

The absentminded professor has become synonymous at the adult level with the gifted child who is absorbed by a science project or other arcane subject. Both display a high degree of concentration and ability to focus on a problem for a considerable period of time. The reality is that long-term application and concentration in an area of interest are important components for gifted children to cultivate. An enduring interest or curiosity in some field that produces expert-level knowledge may be satisfying for its own sake as an avocation or may become the foundation of a career. The MacArthur fellows (Cox, Daniel, & Boston, 1985) represent persons who have been rewarded for the kind of contribution that does not necessarily have commercial value but does promote knowledge.

Unusually Well Developed Memory

Memory is the sine qua non for the acquisition of information. Unfortunately, memory can be trivialized into spelling contest activity or other demonstrations and feats that have fewer long-term implications and less usefulness. Memory of events that are connected by historical significance related to other social, economic, and cultural change, for example, has more meaning than does a series of dates with little connection.

History texts, for example, tend to focus on dates of battles, which subsequently are translated into test items because of ease of scoring. But societal changes and causative issues related to the dates usually are more important for the gifted curriculum. Although testing for this kind of knowledge requires a more sophisticated set of questions, it also may raise philosophical issues that publishers and school districts wish to avoid. Thus, dates should be considered mnemonics for relating and connecting events from a myriad set of historical documents and not an end to be pursued for a game of trivial pursuit.

Early Language Interest and Development

The gifted child often exhibits precocious development in language and has a strong interest in reading from an early age. Cases of early reading from as young as 2½ years are not uncommon. One study documented that early reading was apparent by age 5 in 80% of children later identified as gifted learners (VanTassel-Baska, 1983). The early reader has become less of an anomaly in our society in recent years for a number of reasons, some related to decreasing family size, others to older parents who are career-established and able to devote more time and attention to home teaching. Television programming that includes "Sesame Street" and the "Electric Company" also may positively influence the reading skills children bring to school. Thus, this characteristic alone may be less predictive of gifted behavior than it once was.

Curiosity

The gifted child displays a strong need to know and to understand how the world works. From early childhood on, this child craves to make sense of the world, and adults who treat these questions with respect and information appropriate to the needs of the child help build in him or her a personality orientation that seeks to discover the world. Reconstruction of the world or internalization of personal knowledge that comes about in learning is a long-term process that can be damaged by insensitive parents or teachers. Thus, the teacher who "turns on" the child's curiosity is likewise remembered long afterward as part of a pivotal educational event. A tragedy for children of gifted potential occurs when there is no early connection of this type that would improve their motivation and orientation to academic pursuits.

Preference for Independent Work

The gifted child has a natural propensity for working alone, for "figuring out" things on his or her own. This trait reflects enjoyment in constructing an internal schema to solve problems rather than any tendency toward antisocial behavior. At age 13, Robert attended one of the Eastern summer talent search programs at a major university. On entering the class, the instructor asked each of the students what he or she hoped to accomplish. Robert answered that he wished to complete algebra and trigonometry so as to take Advanced Placement (AP) calculus in the fall. The instructor's reply was that all Robert needed to do was to finish two math books, whereupon Robert said, "Give me the books." He finished both algebra and trigonometry with a 97 + grade average for the summer. He then took AP calculus as a high school freshman and, because of a tragedy in the instructor's family, stepped in to teach the last 10 weeks of the course. Needless to say, Robert's independent work habits contributed significantly to his early accomplishments.

Multiple Interests

The gifted child has a large storehouse of information that interacts with good memory skills as well as with wide-ranging interests. Adrienne was a 5-year-old child in first grade who appeared highly able, so it seemed reasonable for the teacher to discuss with Adrienne the concept of birds as linear descendants of dinosaurs. Even so, the girl's response, "Oh, you mean like Archaeopteryx," did come as a surprise. Similarly, after she was given an aquarium for her fourth birthday, she became an "icthyologist" who could explain differences between skates and other fish to her older brothers. When asked about her favorite books, she spoke of an interest in science fiction and in H. G. Wells's *War of the Worlds*, which Adrienne had read four times. This was the same child who was criticized by her teacher for being inattentive to the spelling lesson from the second-grade curriculum. Thus, this characteristic may be missed or go unappreciated in gifted children if activities used with them are not open-ended in nature.

Ability to Generate Original Ideas

The gifted child can generate new ideas and products. In some children this ability is manifested predominantly in one area, but for others the creative response is marked in several types of endeavor. John was a published poet in fourth grade partly because of his teacher's encouragement and partly by virtue of the writing talent search in a large school system. His science fair project was an example of programming subtleties with numbers. Such originality displayed at the elementary level bodes well for future individual insights and contribution.

Affective Characteristics

Sense of Justice

Gifted children display a strong sense of justice in their human relationships. At later ages they are quite attracted to causes that promote social equality. This characteristic reflects a general concern for others and also a concern that the world work in a humane way.

The sense of justice and need for fair play in these children can lead to classroom problems when the teacher is unable to justify rules that govern school procedures. The interpretation of such rules and procedures in the context of social good and fairness to all is not typically easy, but in the long run is the best strategy for teachers to employ.

Altruism and Idealism

Gifted children in general display a helping attitude toward others that may manifest itself in wanting to serve, to teach, to tutor other children. The altruism and idealism that gifted children exhibit frequently lead to involvement in service organizations or leisure activities that can consume large amounts of energy. This is a socially desirable direction when balance is maintained with the child's growth and when those activities promote goals that the parents can appreciate or at least accept.

Sense of Humor

Gifted children often have the ability to recognize or appreciate the inconsistencies and incongruities of everyday experience. The relatively large knowledge base they possess allows them to perceive those instances more quickly than their agemates do. A sense of humor and a playfulness with ideas attest to the gifted child's ability to interpret the world in what may be a less threatening manner. Humor can defuse many painful experiences and subtly point up foibles with less damage to the self-esteem of the child or of others.

Emotional Intensity

Just as gifted children are more able cognitively, they frequently experience emotional reactions at a deeper level than their age peers do. The ability to emote within a dramatic framework makes gifted children good candidates for theater productions. Their sensitivity to nuances of expression and use of language is an asset in that activity. That same asset can become a liability when other children find they can provoke a reaction that brings negative attention to the child. The hypersensitivity of gifted children in the regular classroom is a phenomenon that troubles many parents. The grouping of high-ability children academically and socially potentially places them in a more accepting environment that reduces the temptation for attack by their agemates. The sharing of experiences for these children and the reduction of the isolation they may have felt in a regular classroom should be viewed as some of the more important benefits of the grouping/identification process.

21

Early Concern About Death

A concern with death or mortality often emerges early in the thoughts of gifted children. Helping them understand and accept the life-cycle process has to be approached and treated with maturity. Using their cognitive strength to view the natural process apart from the emotional impact and stress that accompany the death of loved ones will be an important part of emotional growth. Respect for and celebration of life should be part of this process. The discovery of intergenerational relations through tracing the family tree and coming to know the events in the lives of forebears also offers a good perspective and a sense of identity for the child.

Perfectionism

Many gifted children display characteristics of perfectionism. These children focus undue energy on doing everything perfectly and become disturbed if they or others in their environment make mistakes.

In our enthusiasm to encourage a child to do his or her very best work, we may cross a line that becomes internalized as perfectionism. A realistic acceptance of error in the world and of the imperfection of our knowledge should temper the judgments a child is likely to make. The unrealistic fear and anxiety that can accompany perfectionism may hinder growth or result in guilt that works against the child's maximal development. Growth toward excellence, not perfection, is a subtle distinction that teachers and parents must appreciate when working with the gifted child.

High Levels of Energy

Gifted children often display high energy in the conduct of play and work. This energy can be observed in the ability to accomplish a great deal of work in a short time or in highly tuned verbal or psychometric activity.

The high energy levels that gifted children bring to school tasks can be misinterpreted as hyperactivity by teachers who are not sensitive to rapid learning styles. Using the child's energy for productive purposes requires a channeling into meaningful tasks and an encouragement of persistence in working toward short- and long-term goals. The resulting motivation for achievement and success then will reinforce the child's identity and self-esteem. Positive use of high energy is a critical part of children's emotional development so that boredom, frustration, and a tendency toward hostile outlets for the energy do not develop.

Strong Attachments and Commitments

The gifted child frequently forms strong attachments to one or two friends who may be a few years older, or to an adult figure. And these children, as they develop, form equally strong attachments to their work.

Role modeling of an ego ideal or hero can help the child begin to formulate a long-range focus toward adult life goals. Mentors can provide a view of the adult world that will help a gifted child understand the commitment required for vocational success. Gifted children tend to form unusually strong attachments to "the idealized self" that have to be balanced with knowledge of the steps to that goal.

Aesthetic Sensitivity

The gifted child's appreciation of complexity often is expressed through aesthetic sensitivity. The "unity in variety" that is integral to works of art provides intellectual and emotional satisfaction in ways that are surprisingly comprehensible to young gifted children. The multilayered analysis required for interpreting works of art appeals to the child and presents an excellent opportunity for demonstrating an interdisciplinary view of knowledge. Enhancement of perceptual processes through music and art is an appropriate way to stimulate gifted children and address their needs in this area.

Needs of Gifted Children

An important way to view the needs of the gifted child is through the lens of behavioral characteristics. In so doing, we can translate these characteristics into a set of educational needs that schools might address. Tables 2.2 and 2.3 summarize the linkage of key cognitive and affective characteristics, respectively, to learning needs and to curriculum interventions for the gifted.

Many times gifted children appear to be "out of sync" for their age when we consider the normal development expected at any given age in cognitive, emotional, and physical realms. The mythical "norm" has become a benchmark that schools use; it may fit very few students in any case, but it is especially pernicious when applied to the gifted. The ceiling effect of regular grade curriculum and the distorted notion of the child's ability based on the narrow range sampling of standardized testing obscure a realistic view of gifted children. This is compounded by the fact that gifted children share many characteristics with all children; they may excel intellectually but be more typical in respect to physical or emotional development.

23

TABLE 2.2

The Relationship of Characteristics, Learning Needs, and Curriculum for the Gifted (Cognitive)

Characteristic	Learning Need	Curriculum Inference
Ability to handle abstractions	Presentation of symbol systems at higher levels of abstraction	Reorganized basic skills curriculum Introduction of new symbol systems (computers, foreign language, statistics) at earlier stages of development
Power of concentration	Longer time frame that allows for focused in-depth work in a given area of interest and challenge	Diversified scheduling of curriculum work "Chunks" of time for special project work and small-group efforts
Ability to make connections and establish relationships among disparate data	Exposure to multiple perspectives and domains of inquiry	Interdisciplinary curriculum opportunities (special concept units, humanities, and the interrelated arts) Use of multiple text materials and resources
Ability to memorize and learn rapidly	Rapid movement through basic skills and concepts in traditional areas; organization of new areas of learning more economically	Restructured learning frames to accommodate capacities of these learners (speed up and reduce reinforcement activities) New curriculum organized according to its underlying structure
Multiple interests; wide information base	Opportunity to choose area(s) of interest in school work and go into greater depth within a chosen area	Learning center areas in the school for extended time use Self-directed learning packets Individual learning contracts

TABLE 2.3

The Relationship of Characteristics, Learning Needs, and
Curriculum for the Gifted (Affective)

Characteristic	Learning Need	Curriculum Inference
Need for justice, fair play	Understanding of the complexity of issues associated with justice	A course study curriculum of humankind Study of court cases (judicial opinion) Bill of Rights/Constitution as sources of understanding
Altruism	Opportunities to help others matched with understanding needs of family and personal needs	Work with younger gifted children Study of the role of religion in televangelism from newspaper and presidential campaigns Study of Puritans and early American religion
Humor	Opportunity to appreciate various forms of humor; use of humor for positive and negative purposes	Political cartooning in perspective Satire in Greek drama Clowns; pathos/bathos
Interest in death and mortality	Appreciation of human life cycle	*Roots* model for genealogy Use of curriculum that takes a life span perspective
Perfectionism	Acceptance of human fallibility as a natural event	Heisenberg principle of indeterminism Understanding of statistical probability Safe risk-taking activities that allow students to fail
High energy	Focus of attention to make best use of that energy	Psychomotor outlets for sublimation Gradual lengthening of learning increments Variety of experiences

Commitment	Realistic assessment of talent and process necessary to achieve	Mentoring Counseling toward goal in systematic fashion
Aesthetic sensitivity	Development of skills as an observer or performer	Exposure to the fine arts from various periods of history Opportunities for inter-related arts curriculum

The match of ability to a curriculum that maximizes opportunities of choice and development has ostensibly become the cornerstone of educational planning for all students. Gifted students have a right to an optimal match of curriculum and ability without having to justify their performance against the class average. A free and appropriate education is a principle in law that has been compelling for school districts but at the same time has created resentment when parents exercise those legal rights. The school's resources and priorities often become ordered on the basis of "obvious need," which usually means failure or some other negative attribute. Because gifted students do not have trouble with the core curriculum, they are ignored while others are served, and when the problems of mismatch become troubling, the home or parents are blamed.

Arguments against providing for the gifted are many, but they usually constitute excuses to maintain the status quo and reduce parental and legal attacks. Gifted children often have large variability in their profiles, which leads to attacks on their "weak" or average areas as evidence of "ungiftedness." Overlooking the strengths of these children and the implications for change is a much easier strategy because there already are mechanisms in place to give additional time to the "weaknesses." Another strategy consists of making the criteria for identification so cumbersome or restrictive that only a few children are found to qualify. This solves the problem of having an identifiable program for public relations and keeps the number of students small enough to maintain the status quo. A common problem related to the peaks and valleys of development for the gifted is the contrast of rapid cognitive development with less rapid physical maturation. Accelerating students as an accommodation to rapid mental growth by placing them with older students is a common school strategy that has been employed during the years. Because cognitive and physical maturation rates operate separately, this acceleration can highlight the differential in unrealistic, and harmful, ways. Thus, the child who can think through problems but not write them fast enough for the final test is penalized for writing and not thinking.

The narrow-range, grade-level, standardized test that schools use for accountability also has become a problem for the gifted. Little diagnostic/teaching infor-

26

mation is to be derived from 95th percentile scores, and gifted children are characteristically in this group on such measures. The school explanation of these scores usually points to the excellence of their teaching and programs rather than to the problem inherent in a test that was too easy to provide useful information. The rush to improve scores "on the average" by administrators, and the willingness of publishers to provide tests that will serve that end, has done a disservice to gifted children in particular. A more realistic testing procedure should be developed that helps tailor the curriculum to the child's needs rather than support the idea of a mythical average that fits everyone.

Summary

Important issues are associated with the characteristics and needs addressed in this chapter. These issues may be summarized as follows:

1. The gifted student has learning needs that require a special education program, just as other populations that deviate significantly from what we call the norm for learning. Characteristics such as varied interests, intense curiosity, and the ability to manipulate abstract symbol systems all point to the need for a responsive school environment.
2. Most gifted learners will not develop their potential commensurate with their capacity without careful nurturance—some of which must be provided by the home and greater community and some by the schools. Data on dropout rates among the gifted, the lack of funding and servicing of low-income students who have promise, and serious problems with underachievement among that population all point to areas of need.
3. A general education program does not respond adequately to such specialized needs because of an undue emphasis on basic skills taught from basal texts.
4. Change in schools is slow and reactive in nature, and innovative efforts are frequently diffused. Consequently, seeking positive change with a targeted group of learners whose performance outcomes can have the greatest impact provides a safe testing ground for efforts ultimately to be used with larger segments of the school population.

Gifted education seeks to enable and empower exceptional learners to engage in meaningful experiences that will help develop their initial promise, both for the sake of themselves and of society. Gifted education also seeks to use what is learned from successful work with the gifted to make positive changes in schools for all learners.

References

Benbow, C. P., & Stanley, J. (1983). *Academic precocity.* Baltimore, MD: Johns Hopkins University Press.

Cox, J., Daniel, N., & Boston, B.O. (1985). *Educating able learners: Programs and promising practices.* Austin: University of Texas Press.

Hollingworth, L. (1926). *Gifted children.* New York: World Press.

Renzulli, J. S., Smith, L. H., White, A. J., Callahan, C. M., & Hartman, R. K. (1976). *Scales for the rating of behavioral characteristics of superior students.* Mansfield Center, CT: Creative Learning Press.

Tannenbaum, A. (1983). *Gifted children.* New York: Macmillan.

Terman, L. (1925). *Genetic studies of genius* (Vol. 1). Stanford, CA: Stanford University Press.

VanTassel-Baska, J. (1983). Profiles of precocity: The 1982 Midwest talent search finalists. *Gifted Child Quarterly, 27*(3), 139–144.

Witty, P. (1930). *A study of one hundred gifted children.* Lawrence, KS: Bureau of School Service & Research.

Study Questions

1. How do the particular needs of gifted children pose special challenges for schools?

2. What approaches could teachers reasonably explore when gifted children are not producing or flourishing in school?

3. What are some of the problems inherent in labeling children as gifted? How might sensitive educators deal with these problems?

4. How can we involve parents more effectively in recognizing and acting on the observed characteristics of their children?

5. How might the affective characteristics of gifted children be supported in the home? In the school? In society?

6. Individual profiles of gifted children typically reveal differential mixes of cognitive and affective characteristics. What might we infer from this situation with regard to identification and programming in schools?

3

Underachieving and Handicapped Gifted

Ken Seeley

T he term *gifted underachiever* is an ambiguous one. Gifted underachievers can be identified at all academic levels, although more frequently at the secondary level. To teachers, these students may seem to be lazy, uninterested, bored, rebellious, or generally irksome. They often are described in report cards as "capable of doing much better." The case can even be made that most gifted students could be identified as underachievers because they rarely are challenged sufficiently to match their potential level of achievement.

To begin our discussion of this topic, we should review the definitions found in the literature. Table 3.1 lists sample definitions ranging from general to specific. Most authors agree that gifted underachieving students show significant discrepancy between academic performance (in class or on achievement tests) and tested intellectual ability in the upper range.

What Are the Causes of Underachievement?

The research on underachievement has been inconsistent because a variety of definitions have been used and there has been no control of variables from study to

TABLE 3.1
A Sample of Definitions of Underachieving Gifted Students

Authors	Definitions
Bricklin & Bricklin (1967)	Student whose day-by-day efficiency in school is much poorer than would be expected on the basis of intelligence
Fine, B. (1967)	Student who ranks in the top third of intellectual ability but whose performance is dramatically below that level
Finney & Van Dalsel (1969)	Student who was in the top 25% of the Differential Aptitude Battery (DAT) in verbal-numerical score and whose GPA was below the mean for all students at the DAT level
Gowan (1957)	Student who performs 1 sd or more below his or her ability level
Newman (1974)	Student achieving significantly below the level statistically predicted by his/her IQ (GPA of C or below considered as significant)
Pringle (1970)	Student with IQ of 120 or above having educational or behavior difficulties
Shaw & McCuen (1960)	Student in upper 25% of the population on the Pinter General Ability Test (IQ over 110) who had earned a GPA below the mean of his/her class in grades 9–11
Thorndike (1963)	Student whose underachievement is measured in relation to some standard of expected or predicted achievement
Whitmore (1980)	Student who demonstrates exceptionally high capacity for academic achievement but is not performing satisfactorily for levels on daily academic tasks and achievement tests
Ziv (1977)	Student with a high IQ who has low grades in school

study. Sample selection has also varied widely. Tannenbaum (1983) summarized the research on underachievement by stating that:

> Underachievement should be regarded as a single symptom representing diverse etiologies. One type of underachiever fails to measure up to expectations because of overestimated general abilities; a second type possesses inadequate special aptitudes of any kind; a third type does not have the necessary drive, mental health, meta-learning habits or any other personality supports; a fourth type lacks the proper nurturance at home, at school and in the community; and a fifth type sinks into mediocrity through a series of misfortunes or distractions beyond anybody's control. Thus, the five factors that serve as links between potential and fulfillment are also clues to potential and failure. But it would be a mistake to assume that all underachievers suffer from all five handicaps. Each kind of deterrent can by itself make the difference between success and failure. (p. 224)

Whitmore (1980) described some of her research in a special program for underachieving gifted students in Cupertino, California. Student self-reports of the causes of their underachievement were used. The students indicated that the following factors at school contributed to their underachievement:

1. Perceived lack of genuine respect from teachers
2. A competitive social climate
3. Inflexibility and rigidity
4. Stress on external evaluation
5. The "failure syndrome" and criticism predominated except for those who were achieving and conforming
6. Constant adult/teacher control of the class
7. An unrewarding curriculum of textbook learning. (pp. 192–193)

In a more recent study, Seeley (1987) interviewed 128 high-ability high school students (upper quartile on nonverbal intelligence test). These students were at risk for dropping out of school because of poor attendance, low grades, or behavior problems. Many already had dropped out but had returned to alternative schools. He also statistically analyzed the academic records of 2,000 middle school students who were in the upper quartile in nonverbal intelligence. Middle school high-ability students were studied to give a broader understanding of some of the causes of the at-risk conditions seen in the high school sample. The data analysis used structural equation modeling (Joreskog & Goldberger, 1975) to develop a causal model to predict risk of dropout.

Of particular interest is the finding that behavior had a reciprocal relationship with grades. Not only did behavior problems cause poor grades, which was not surprising, but grading practices produced behavior problems. This vicious cycle caused underachievement for many students who failed in school not because of lack of mastery but, rather, lack of conformity to school rules. The factor model appears in Figure 3.1.

FIGURE 3.1

Schematic of the Causes of Dropout Risk Among Upper Intellectual Quartile in Grades 7, 8, 9, 10 (N = 2065)

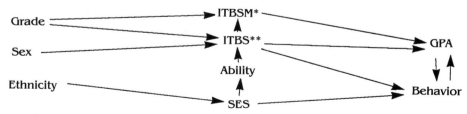

* Iowa Test of Basic Skills—Math
** Iowa Test of Basic Skills—Composite

The interview data clustered in five areas of concern: home/family, school environment, teachers, peer/social, and racial minority. Some of the more pertinent findings are as follows:

1. 90% of the at-risk group were middle or youngest in their families.
2. Frequency of school change was a major factor in being at risk.
3. Teen pregnancy and drug use were not significant factors in the lives of these interviewees.
4. Teacher indifference was a major factor in poor achievement.
5. Competition with peers or family members was not influential.
6. Uneven academic performance was common.
7. The school treated minority students with behavior conflicts different than the majority students, even though the characteristics of both groups were the same overall.
8. Family disruption (divorce, remarriage, separation) was twice as common as the normal expectancy.

The causes of underachievement are obviously multifaceted in scope and intensity. This discussion merely presents an overview of the problem. The final section looks at intervention.

What Can We Do to Help Underachievers?

In planning intervention it seems appropriate to abandon the medical model. If we were to address all of the research on causes of underachievement, we would have to find specific prescriptions to ameliorate each cause. Although this is a laudable goal, public education likely cannot provide the level of intensity necessary to achieve that goal. Rather, we should consider approaches to the general problem by suggesting that schools be an inviting place, rather than a source of alienation and indifference, for underachievers. Alternative schools provide such an opportunity in many locales, but they should start earlier than high school—middle school level at a minimum.

To address the feelings of alienation and isolation among underachievers, a sense of "community" must be developed at school. Many students in the school's mainstream experience this feeling. Like most adolescents, these underachieving students want to feel that they count in someone else's life. Their desire to find a caring environment at school also is tied to their need to be caring and giving about something important. School-sponsored community service options are an excellent way to involve students who might not choose pep club, football, or chorus as a means of feeling a part of the school community. Service projects within the school or nearby community might offer an excellent opportunity for involvement.

If the goal is prevention of underachievement rather than remediation, we should begin at the preschool level. Head Start programs have made a positive difference in preventing school failure for disadvantaged children, but more is needed for all young children with above average potential. Early intervention as a means to address most educational problems has proven to be the best preventive approach. It is cost-effective and provides benefits for a smaller investment compared to the major remediation tasks later.

Creating alternatives for middle school students is also a good place to intervene. It may be the last chance for many of those students who become mediocre and just "get by" for the remainder of their secondary school years.

Overall, intervention programs for underachievers should focus attention on improving the self-esteem of these students regardless of age. This was nicely summarized by Whitmore (1980):

> Supportive strategies are those which affirm the worth of the child in the classroom and convey the promise of greater potential and success; yet to be discovered messages of the classroom environment that communicate to the child promises of belonging, finding acceptance, being affirmed as a valued and respected member of the group and being free to become the person he wishes to become—to realize his potential and develop his gifts. (p. 257)

Who Are the Gifted Handicapped?

To be called "handicapped," children must meet specific state and federal guidelines. And to do this usually means extensive assessment and a determination that the child needs special educational services in order to benefit from education. Handicapped children are different from underachievers in two ways. First, some handicapped children are achieving appropriate to their potential so could not be considered underachievers. Second, some handicapped children are underachieving, but the cause of underachievement is clearly attributable to the handicap, and they are receiving special education services for compensatory or remedial skills.

The concept of gifted handicapped may appear to be an oxymoron. Educators particularly view these two types of children as opposite ends of the education spectrum. That the characteristics of each type could reside in one child seems incongruous. But it is a phenomenon that has received long overdue attention in the past 10 years.

How Do We Find the Gifted Handicapped Student?

The special education obsession with the medical model approach to children has resulted in a focus on deficits rather than a search for strengths among the handicapped. As such, there are important obstacles to finding these children. Whitmore and Maker (1985, pp. 14-21) discussed four of these major obstacles in identification:

1. Obstacle 1: stereotypic expectations that disabled persons are below normal.
2. Obstacle 2: developmental delays, particularly in verbal areas among handicapped children, so their high intellectual ability usually goes undetected when using verbal tests with them.
3. Obstacle 3: incomplete information about the child, which results in overlooking areas of strength that might be displayed in nonacademic settings.
4. Obstacle 4: no opportunity to evidence superior ability because of the highly verbal nature of school tasks and ability testing used in special education.

Given these obstacles, it is a wonder that gifted handicapped children are discovered at all. Greater use of nonverbal intellectual measures and tests of adaptive behavior have helped to some extent. Also, many handicapped children whose verbal ability is intact, such as the blind or emotionally disturbed, can demonstrate superior intellect. But giftedness in the vast pool of learning disabled, deaf, and physically disabled is obscured by the handicap. Specialized testing procedures are needed to find these children. These procedures usually bring into play nonverbal measures of intellectual ability. Tests such as the Raven's Progressive Matrices or the performance section of the Wechsler Intelligence Scale for children–Revised (WISC–R) can be used to identify abilities often masked by handicapping conditions that limit verbal ability.

Each school district is required to have a "child-find" program to screen all children for handicapping conditions as they enter school in kindergarten or through transfer. The child-find mechanism is also a good way to search for gifted handicapped children. Early identification is crucial so that intervention can begin. Teachers of the gifted should call attention to this area of concern with their school's child-find coordinator and look for high-potential children among those considered at risk in the screening process.

How Do We Serve the Gifted Handicapped?

The nature and extent of services needed for gifted handicapped children will vary according to the child. Federal and state laws require that an individualized education program (IEP) be formulated for each child placed into special education. This IEP follows the assessment and staffing of the child and involves parents, special educators, and the building principal.

Teachers of the gifted should become resources to the team that develops the IEP. An intensive evaluation of the child's strengths serves as a vehicle for addressing the disabilities imposed by the handicap. In a team effort, the special education staff and the teacher of the gifted can work together in planning and implementing the IEP. The child who is visually, hearing, or physically handicapped and also gifted can use her or his intellectual strengths to learn compensatory skills. Gifted children with learning disabilities or behavior disorders also can use their superior intelligence to learn problem solving or metacognitive strategies to help themselves cope with academic and social tasks required to be successful in school.

Learning disability is perhaps the most complex handicapping condition to impact on high potential ability. Its causes are not known, and appropriate treatments are still evolving with mixed success. Generally, the approach to gifted students with learning disabilities involves a thorough academic task analysis to find strengths and weaknesses. The strengths are used to help compensate for the weak areas. These students need a lot of organizational skills, such as time management, note taking, tape recording of lectures, sequencing of topics, basic writing skills, and so on.

Conventional approaches in special education often focus on remediating weaknesses rather than on developing compensatory strengths. Teachers of the gifted can supplement specialized instruction by using these strengths as a means of capturing the interests of the students and motivating them toward advanced study and task persistence.

The special education program typically has far more resources than does the gifted program and therefore has the potential to offer more extensive services to the gifted handicapped than might be available to gifted underachievers. Social work services can be applied to the families to help them work at home with improving self-esteem in the child. Special education specialists can provide intensive individual services to teach remedial and compensatory skills. Finally, teachers of the gifted can provide the child with enriched and accelerated learning experiences to make learning both challenging and enjoyable. The old adage that "nothing succeeds like success" certainly holds true for these students. Teachers of the gifted can provide success experiences for gifted handicapped learners by focusing on strengths and acknowledging and rewarding their advanced conceptual ability.

Summary

This chapter has discussed the complex problem of gifted underachievers and gifted handicapped children. It is an introduction to an often overlooked condition that deserves attention from gifted educators and special educators. These children pose a serious paradox for education. By virtue of their giftedness, they often are not identified for any special services. To provide the most appropriate education, we must deal with this paradox through staff development, modified screening techniques, and team planning.

References

Alexander, P., & Muia, J. (1982). *Gifted education*. Rockville, MD: Aspen Systems.

Baum, S. (1984). Meeting the needs of learning disabled gifted students. *Roeper Review, 7*(1), 16–19.

Bricklin, B., & Bricklin, P. (1967). *Bright child—poor grades: The psychology of underachievement*. New York: Delacorte.

Fine, B. (1967). *Underachievers—How they can be helped*. New York: Dutton.

Finney, B. C., & Van Dalsel, E. (1966). Group counseling for gifted underachieving high school students. *Journal of Counseling Psychology, 16*, 87–94.

Goertzel, V., & Goertzel, M. (1962). *Cradles of eminence*. Boston: Little, Brown.

Gowan, J. C. (1957). Dynamics of the underachievement of gifted children. *Exceptional Children, 24*, 98–101, 122.

Jackson, D. (1980). *Foundations of gifted education*. Guilford, CT: Special Learning Corp.

Joreskog, K. G., & Goldberger, A. S. (1975). Estimation of a model with multiple indicators and multiple causes of a single latent variable. *Journal of the American Statistical Association, 70*, 631–639.

Karnes, M. (1979). Young handicapped children can be gifted and talented. *Journal for the Education of the Gifted, 2*(3), 157–172.

Maker, C. (1977). *Providing programs for the gifted handicapped*. Reston, VA: Council for Exceptional Children.

Newman, R. (1974). *Groups in schools*. New York: Simon & Schuster.

Pledgie, T. (1982). Giftedness among handicapped children: Identification and programming development. *Journal of Special Education, 16*(2), 221–227.

Pringle, M. L. (1970). *Able misfits: A study of educational and behavior difficulties of 103 very intelligent children (IQs 120–200)*. London: Longmans.

Schiff, M., Kaufman, A., & Kaufman, N. (1981). Scatter analysis of WISC–R profiles for learning disabled children with superior intelligence. *Journal of Learning Disabilities, 14*(7), 400–404.

Seeley, K. R. (1987). *High ability students at risk*. Denver: Clayton Foundation.

Shaw, M. C., & McCuen, J. T. (1960). The onset of academic underachievement in bright children. *Journal of Educational Psychology, 51*, 103–108.

Sternberg, R. (1982). Lies we live by: Misapplication of tests in identifying the gifted. *Gifted Child Quarterly, 26*(4), 157–161.

Tannenbaum, A. J. (1983). *Gifted children*. New York: Macmillan.

Thorndike, R. L. (1963). *The concepts of over and underachievement*. New York: Columbia University, Teachers College, Bureau of Publications.

Whitmore, J. (1980). *Giftedness, conflict, and underachievement*. Boston: Allyn & Bacon.

Whitmore, J., & Maker, J. (1985). *Intellectual giftedness in disabled persons*. Rockville, MD: Aspen Systems.

Ziv, A. (1977). *Counselling the intellectually gifted child*. Toronto: University of Toronto.

Study Questions

1. How might we identify giftedness among deaf or blind children through cooperative efforts with special education personnel?

2. What effect might underachievement have on the emotional development of gifted learners?

3. How can parents help overcoming underachievement in their children?

4. How could you find strengths in a learning disabled gifted child that could be used to help capture and maintain his or her interest in academic areas?

5. How might you develop a team approach to intervention with gifted handicapped learners with special education personnel?

4

Gifted Girls

Joyce VanTassel-Baska

Much has been written about women as a special population to be singled out for attention under the rubric of gifted education (Callahan, 1979; Kerr, 1985; Reis, 1987; Silverman, 1986). Yet very little has been attempted in the way of differentiation for this group of learners. In that sense, gifted women suffer the same neglect as do other populations with atypical needs among the gifted.

Who Are Gifted Girls?

Who are these gifted girls? Basically, they comprise half of the academically able population (VanTassel-Baska, 1983) and many times a disproportionate share of students who receive top grades and honors at the elementary and secondary levels in our schools. Evidence exists to suggest, however, that we lose many of these able women between high school and college as well as between a baccalaureate degree and advanced work leading to a professional career (Denny, 1987). Thus, although the talent pool of gifted girls is relatively equal during the school years, there is a reduction of their numbers at each successive level of schooling and in high-level professional careers.

How Do We Identify Gifted Girls?

Generally, the identification of gifted girls is not differentiated by gender. Instead, traditional measures are used, including intelligence tests, achievement and aptitude batteries, and nomination forms, completed by teachers, parents, and others. Grade records also are frequently considered.

We also might ask if female students are being identified in equal numbers for gifted programs. Some available data indicate that females are not being identified in equal numbers to males for special programs (Richert, 1982). Regional talent search data also support the conclusion that female students are underrepresented in secondary-level talent search programs and that even fewer choose to participate in on-campus programs. Among talent search participants in residential summer programs at one university, for example, during a 5-year period fewer than 40% of the attendees were women (VanTassel-Baska & Olszewski, in press). At the elementary level, where more emphasis may be placed on achievement and grades, girls tend to outnumber boys in gifted program identification.

When we examine and compare achievement outcomes for girls versus boys in specific areas of the curriculum, however, we tend to see significant differences in patterns of achievement based on gender. In the area of mathematics, boys and girls achieve at similar rates through fifth grade level. Beyond that level, however, boys outperform girls on math achievement and aptitude measures on an incremental basis (Maccoby & Jacklin, 1974). This differential achievement pattern is a fact, but its underlying causes are somewhat unclear. Some researchers have viewed the issue primarily in terms of participation in math programs; specifically, girls have a much lower participation rate in advanced math classes (Fennema & Sherman, 1977; Fox, 1977).

In today's society, participation in mathematics classes through the level of calculus is perceived to be an important base for mathematical competence for many professional careers, including many in the social sciences. Therefore, gifted girls who do not pursue this course-taking pattern are inadvertently opting out of career opportunities in many potential fields of interest. Clearly, this tendency also negatively affects the number of gifted girls who pursue science course taking and related careers as well. Another related area of concern is gifted girls' seeming avoidance of involvement with computers and computer science coursework (Lockheed & Frakt, 1984). Again, a lack of preference and participation in coursework leading to computer competence creates a serious gap in the preparation of gifted girls for later professional opportunities.

Other accounts of causes for these mathematical differences also have been proposed by researchers. Benbow and Stanley (1980) argued that biological differences between the sexes may account for differential achievement patterns in mathematics. Waber (1977) explored the idea that the early maturation of girls in comparison to boys may account for differences in mathematical abilities, particu-

40

larly those of a spatial nature. Eccles (1984) advanced the idea that girls' self-perception of not being good at math, even when achievement data confirm excellence in mathematics coursework, interferes with their ability to persevere with mathematics and its career paths. As Fox (1980) found, this perception is particularly acute among gifted girls.

Regardless of the explanations put forth to explain the phenomenon of gender differences in math achievement, it seems appropriate to examine potential interventions that can positively affect the development of mathematical potential among gifted girls. As educators, we are in a position to help young gifted girls develop that potential because strong evidence links confidence in learning mathematics to both math achievement and math course selection (Fennema & Sherman, 1977). Intervention might ameliorate the current situation and reduce the discrepancy between the sexes on this important dimension. Some evidence also exists that in schools where a conscious effort has been made to work with changing the attitudes of gifted girls, their parents, and counselors, differences in math and science achievement scores are negligible (Brush, 1980; Paulsen & Johnson, 1983).

Other research on gender differences has revealed key areas of concern in terms of gifted girls. Dweck (1986) noted a tendency toward low expectancies, avoidance of challenge, ability attributions for failure, and debilitation under failure as characteristics of bright girls when compared to boys. Thus, gender differences in motivational and personality patterns are also central issues in designing an effective intervention plan for gifted girls. Bandura and Dweck (1985) reported that measures of children's actual competence do not strongly predict their confidence in future attainment—a finding of particular relevance to gifted girls whose discrepancy between actual and perceived competence was the greatest of any of the groups examined.

What Differential Interventions Would Work with Gifted Girls?

The ability of the individual girl to monitor her own learning, to be an autonomous learner, appears to be a key variable in much of the gender research currently being done. If we can affect the motivation pattern of gifted girls and their often faulty perceptions of their own abilities, we can make progress in helping girls develop their potential at appropriate levels. It is also useful to consider Zinker's (1977) list of blocks to creativity, as they have a great deal of relevance to the plight of gifted girls noted in the research. Key blocks that relate to gifted girls include:

1. Rigidity-stereotyped reactions; overemphasis on traditions and on necessary conformity

41

2. Fear of failure and the unknown
3. Avoidance of frustration
4. Low self-evaluation—failure to see their own strengths

In planning interventions, it is important to view the problem of gifted girls as complex, which means that multiple interventions may prove important. Various general approaches to effective interventions in a school setting to counteract the low aspiration level of many gifted females, as well as the blocks to development of their full potential, may be in order.

Early and Consistent Identification and Programming

One of the problems we have with many special populations of the gifted is a late recognition of the problem and a mild intervention to combat it. This "too little, too late" model certainly applies to gifted girls. We should begin at the primary level to work on the identified areas of need already delineated in this chapter. We cannot assume that outward displays of confidence in gifted girls at any stage of development mirror inward feelings of self-worth. Modifying such perceptions of self is a long-term process, better begun early and integrated into the ongoing educational process in key domains of learning. Silverman (1986) suggested several general approaches for parents in rearing gifted girls:

- Holding high expectations for their daughters
- Not purchasing sex-typed toys
- Avoiding overprotectiveness
- Encouraging high levels of activity
- Allowing them to get dirty
- Instilling beliefs in their capabilities
- Supporting their interests
- Getting them identified as gifted during preschool years
- Finding gifted playmates for them to identify with and emulate
- Fostering interest in mathematics outside of school
- Considering early entrance and other opportunities to accelerate
- Encouraging them to take every mathematics course possible
- Introducing them to professional women in many occupations
- Having mother acknowledge her own giftedness
- Having mother work at least part-time outside the home
- Spending alone-time with father in "masculine" activities
- Sharing household duties equally among the parents
- Assigning chores to siblings on a nonsexist basis

- Discouraging the use of sexist language or teasing in the home
- Monitoring television programs for sexist stereotypes and discussing these with children of both sexes
- Encouraging siblings to treat each other equitably, rather than according to the traditional sex-role stereotypes they see outside the home

Counseling

Providing small-group and individual counseling sessions for gifted girls has been suggested by Fox (1980) as a strategy to encourage girls to take more mathematics courses before puberty. It also may be useful as a generalized strategy for developing female potential in other areas as well. Ascertaining the level of confidence that girls have of their ability and then working to bolster it in such sessions may provide them with a valuable service. The counseling may be conducted by a teacher, a school counselor, or even a parent. Group counseling hopefully can provide a strong sense of group identity among girls that would build toward an important networking function during the adolescent years. Silverman (1986) has recommended the use of support groups or seminars for gifted women beyond the high school years. Topics of consideration for such a counseling model include:

- Dealing with multiple interests and desires
- Entering a predominantly masculine profession
- Deciding whether to marry
- Deciding whether to have children
- Determining how to combine a career and a family
- Maintaining ego strength when their choices bring censure from family or friends
- Supporting each other's achievements
- Understanding the impact of keeping one's own name or taking a married name in establishing one's professional identity
- Recognizing and appreciating the multipotentiality of their giftedness
- Developing a big sister support system for younger gifted women
- Overcoming fears of success and fears of failure
- Combatting dependency and conformity
- Believing in their own abilities
- Learning that they can be successful without risking the loss of femininity
- Learning assertiveness-training techniques
- Learning to appreciate their own work cycle and to judge their accomplishments according to internal standards that take into account the many demands of their multifaceted lives

Mentors as Role Models

Using successful females as adult role models is another strategy worthy of implementation. Women in professional life can provide elementary and high school gifted girls with aspirations in line with their potential rather than in line with their family background and the roles their mothers play. These professional women also can provide assistance in thinking through the issues of how to balance a career and family life—still a major stumbling block for many gifted girls in thinking about long-term careers. Mentors can help girls set long- and short-term goals and make career decisions in light of the advantages and disadvantages of particular options.

In addition to adult role models, older gifted girls may be recruited to work with younger girls in various models and program configurations. High school female gifted students could be wonderful role models for the prepuberty group of gifted girls in respect to course-taking issues as well as socialization and self-perception problems.

Career Development

Career development as an active intervention for gifted girls is an essential part of their schooling, probably from kindergarten through graduate school. Girls need to recognize their capacity and competence in a multitude of career areas. They also need to envision themselves engaging in such careers. Consequently, internships, as a part of career exploration, should prove very useful to them, as should career models that stress options for serial careers, concurrent careers, and the creation of new careers. Recognizing gifted girls' concerns about having a family and balancing a career also has to be addressed. Citing research on gifted women and what has contributed the most to life satisfaction for them may be a useful tool in exploring these issues.

The Sears and Barbee research (1977) on gifted women in the Terman sample at age 60 revealed an interesting pattern of life satisfaction as it related to career. The happiest women in the Terman group were those who had a career and were single. The least satisfied were women who were housewives and did not have a career. Thus, gifted girls must understand the long-term impact and importance of finding a suitable career.

Female-Only Groupings, Classes, and Schools

Some evidence exists that female-only programs, especially in adolescence, can have a positive effect on gifted girls' attitudes toward themselves and their capacity for leadership in the future. Such programs can delay the social conflict about finding a mate or at least reduce its primacy in girls' thinking. The Program for Exceptionally Gifted Girls at Mary Baldwin College, for example, stresses advanced academic work that is challenging but also provides a nurturing context for developing leadership in the young women who attend. Programs for collegiate women at female-only colleges demonstrate excellent track records for placement of graduates in leadership positions. Undertaking within the gifted program a careful grouping strategy that encourages gifted girls working together on various aspects of learning can facilitate the positive development of leadership capabilities. This strategy is particularly important when done prior to puberty so that girls learn the strengths they possess devoid of the socialization pressure to hide them. In that sense, these strengths must be made manifest in order to realize their presence.

Use of Teaching Models That Stress Connectedness, Independence, Creativity

Some research evidence indicates that teachers can influence the development of cooperative learning structures and independence among students, which can positively enhance girls' education (Serbin, 1984). Findings also support the contention that teachers give more attention, both of a positive and a negative nature, to boys (Good, Sikes, & Brophy, 1973). Working with teachers to stress individualized attention models can counteract such tendencies, and using such strategies can clearly benefit both sexes in their development. Some examples of desired teacher strategies, juxtaposed with undesirable approaches to the same situation, are given in Table 4.1.

Use of Discipline-Specific Models That Value the Contributions of Women

The teaching of all subject matter can be handled in such a way as to recognize the achievements of women while stressing the problems women have encountered in being able to contribute at particular stages in our history or in particular areas of the world. The nature and extent of actual contributions are also important, particularly in male-dominated subjects such as math and science. Girls need to know that women have excelled in these areas—if not in equal numbers to men, at least in the level of the contribution made, including the Nobel Prize. Having girls read biographies of famous women, instituting career days that reflect equal achievement by the two sexes, and selecting texts that treat gender issues in a balanced way can all contribute to classrooms in which girls can thrive. Use of reading mate-

45

TABLE 4.1
Desirable and Undesirable Teacher Strategies

Desirable Teacher Strategy	Undesirable Teacher Strategy
Emphasis on utilizing all thinking skills (convergent, divergent, evaluative)	Emphasis on *only* convergent thinking with one right answer
Emphasis on problem-finding and problem-solving behavior	Emphasis on getting *the* answer
Emphasis on presentation of organizing concepts and ideas in each discipline of study	Emphasis on individual problems, isolated facts, or parts of a knowledge system
Use of concept mapping to encourage alternative ways of organizing information	Use of one process model for understanding an area of study

Use of teaching behavior that values thinking, such as:
    wait time
    students processing of information
    follow-up questions that probe issues at a deeper level
	Use of teacher behavior that *discourages* thinking, such as:
	    ending discussions on right answer formats
	    using right answers as the cue to proceed
	    rewarding quick response from a few students

rials that have girls as heroines, leaders, and inventors further enhances the possibility for positive self-image.

Family Education and Counseling

If we are serious about effecting changes in gifted girls' perception of self and in the development of self-esteem and confidence, intervention approaches must involve the girls' families. Mothers and fathers need to understand their roles in the process of helping young girls develop their potential. Only when the family begins to understand these issues can the collaborative effect of home and school begin to work on behalf of girls. Family needs are typically of two types: *information* needs and *strategy* needs. Parents need to know what the issues of subtle sexism are and how these can affect their gifted daughters. Parents also need to know what to do to combat bias and stereotyping, particularly within their own family.

Early Systematic Intervention in Mathematics and Science Programs

Additionally, the issue of early intervention for gifted girls in critical areas such as mathematics and science cannot be overestimated. In a study conducted among members of the Association for Women in Mathematics, more than one third of the respondents indicated interest in mathematics as a career preference by age 11 (Luchins & Luchins, 1980). Consequently, prepubescent girls should be provided with career information and opportunities in math-related areas. Table 4.2 depicts major interventions that key individuals in the lives of gifted girls can make to effect positive self-perception and to provide the nurturance needed to continue with mathematics.

In a major summary of research and recommendations on influences in math achievement, Bearvais, Mickelson, and Pokay (1985) recommended that parents, teachers, and school personnel undertake the following actions to encourage girls in mathematics:

1. Provide more information and discuss the value of mathematics in careers and in society at large.
2. Attribute girls' success in math to ability and interest, not just to hard work.
3. Be aware of one's own potential sex bias in regard to one's daughters' math abilities and expectations and openly encourage daughters to pursue math endeavors.

TABLE 4.2
Roles of Significant Others Influencing Gifted Girls

Teachers Can	Counselors Can	Parents Can
Proactively talk about females who are mathematicians or mathematics-prone	Proactively counsel girls before puberty to take advanced math coursework	Set high expectations for female children regarding course taking and success in mathematics
Assure girls they *can do* mathematics	Lay out detailed courses of study in mathematics to serve as a model	Seek information on excellent mathematics programs for girls and enroll daughters in them
Discourage stereotyping of math as a male subject	Discuss math anxiety issues with girls if/when they arise	Stress the competence of females in mathematics
Teach math in the context of social science experimentation	Provide career data that emphasize the central role of mathematics competency	
Teach math from a more conceptual framework, with linkages to other domains of inquiry		

47

4. Employ cooperative learning models in mathematics classes; use real-world problems to illustrate math concepts; and employ discovery learning techniques.
5. Consider math courses that promote the understanding of mathematics as a skill and stress the need for 4 years of mathematics in high school.

Use of Spatial Reasoning Strategies from K to 12

Studies have found differences between boys and girls in the area of spatial reasoning ability, with boys scoring higher on tests of this ability (Hyde, 1981). Teaching strategies that provide gifted girls with concrete experiences in visual spatialization tasks from an early age can address this issue. Such strategies include having girls play with building blocks, LEGOs, mechanical toys, and trucks. Given that studies of toy preference still support a tendency among girls to gravitate away from experiences like these, it is important to ensure their inclusion in a preschool program. In the early elementary years, girls should have ample opportunity to experience the following kinds of spatial task:

- Manipulating Cuisenaire rods and other materials to create models, solve problems, and so on
- Learning a typewriter/computer keyboard
- Learning LOGO on the computer
- Working matrices problems
- Learning visual patterns in math, science, art, poetry, and the like.
- Manipulating shapes and colors in progressively more complex ways (tangrams)

By the time girls are ready to take geometry, they should have had myriad experiences that would ready them for dealing with three-dimensional figures, rotation of figures in space, and manipulation of patterns and designs for a desired effect. Without systematic intervention in this area, however, many gifted girls will not feel competent to handle geometry, a key course in the path to advanced mathematics and science training. Additionally, lack of competence in visual-spatial reasoning will continue to cause problems in other areas of endeavor as well.

Summary

Only when interventions such as those described in this chapter are undertaken are we apt to improve the number of gifted women obtaining the highest levels of education, commensurate with their ability. Currently only 1 in 300 gifted women do so (Groth, 1969).

Aiding in the development of underutilized potential can be one of the most rewarding acts that educators can undertake. Clearly, gifted girls fall into this category, as do other special populations that are not likely to succeed in representative numbers without personalized support. Given the nature of what gifted girls face as they move toward adulthood, it behooves educators to intervene appropriately to ensure that gifted girls develop their abilities commensurate with their potential. If this means providing a differential model of intervention, it should be done to the extent necessary to effect the desired results.

References

Bandura, M., & Dweck, C. (1985). *Self-conceptions and motivation: Conceptions of intelligences choice of achievement goals, and patterns of cognition, affect, and behavior.* Manuscript submitted for publication.

Bearvais, K., Mickelson, R., & Pokay, P. (1985). *Influences on sex equity in math achievement: Summary of research and recommendations.* Ann Arbor: University of Michigan, Bush Program in Child Development & Social Policy.

Benbow, C., & Stanley, J. C. (1980). Sex differences in mathematical ability: Fact or artifact? *Science, 210,* 1262–1264.

Brush, L. R. (1980). *Encouraging girls in mathematics.* Cambridge, MA: Abt Books.

Callahan, C. (1979). The gifted and talented women. In *NSSE Yearbook on the Gifted and Talented.* Chicago: University of Chicago Press.

Denny, T. (1987). *A study of Illinois valedictorians.* Presentation at AERA, Washington, DC.

Dweck, C. (1986). Motivational processes affecting learning. *American Psychologist, 41*(10), 40–48.

Eccles, J. (1984). Sex differences in mathematics participation. *Advances in Motivation & Achievement, 2*(2), 93–137.

Fennema, E. (1977). Influences of selected cognitive, affective, and educational variables on sex-related differences in mathematics learning and studying. In *Women and mathematics: Research perspectives for change* (NIE Papers in Education and Work No. 8). Washington, DC: National Institute of Education.

Fennema, E., & Sherman, J.A. (1977). Sex related differences in mathematics achievement, spatial visualization, and affective factors. *American Educational Research Journal, 14,* 51-71.

Fox, L. H. (1977). The effects of sex role socialization on mathematic participation and achievement. In *Women and mathematics: Research perspectives for change* (NIE Papers in Education & Work No. 8). Washington, DC: National Institute of Education.

Fox, L. H. (1980). Conclusions: What do we know and where should we go? In L. H. Fox, L. Brody, & D. Tobin (Eds.), *Women and the mathematical mystique* (pp. 195–208). Baltimore, MD: Johns Hopkins University Press.

Fox, L. H., & Turner, L. (1981). Gifted and creative female: In the middle school years. *American Middle School Education, 4,* 17–23.

Good, T. L., Sikes, J. N., & Brophy, J. E. (1973). Effects of teacher sex and student sex in classroom interaction. *Journal of Educational Psychology, 65,* 74–87.

Groth, N. (1969). *Vocational development for gifted girls: A comparison of career needs of gifted males and females between the ages of ten and seventy years.* Paper presented at American Personnel & Guidance Association.

Hyde, J. (1981). How large are cognitive gender differences? A meta-analysis using w2 and d. *American Psychologist, 36,* 892–901.

Kerr, B. (1985). *Smart girls, gifted women.* Columbus: Ohio Psychology Press.

Lockheed, M. E., & Frakt, S. B. (1984). Sex equity: Increasing girls' use of computers. *Computing Teacher, 11*(8), 16–18.

Luchins, E. H., & Luchins, A. S. (1980). Female mathematicians: A contemporary appraisal. In L. H. Fox, L. Brody, & D. Tobin (Eds.), *Women and the mathematical mystique* (pp. 7–22). Baltimore, MD: Johns Hopkins University Press.

Maccoby, E. E., & Jacklin, C. N. (1974). *The psychology of sex differences.* Stanford, CA: Stanford University.

Paulsen, K., & Johnson, J. (1983). Sex role attitudes and mathematical ability in 4th-, 8th-, and 11th-grade students from a high socioeconomic area. *Developmental Psychology, 19*(2), 210–214.

Reis, S. (1987). We can't change what we don't recognize: Understanding the needs of gifted females. *Gifted Child Quarterly, 31*(2), 83–89.

Richert, E. S. (1982). *National report on identification: Assessment and recommendations for comprehensive identification of gifted and talented youth.* Sewell, NJ: Educational Improvement Center-South.

Sears, P., & Barbee, A. (1977). Career and life satisfactions among Terman's women. In J. C. Stanley, W. C. George, & C. H. Solano (Eds.), *The gifted and the creative: A fifty-year perspective* (p. 180). Baltimore, MD: Johns Hopkins University Press.

Serbin, L. (1984). Teachers, peers, and play preferences: An environmental approach to sex typing in the preschool. In S. Delamont (Ed.), *Readings on interaction in the classroom.* New York: Methuen.

Serbin, L., O'Leary, K., Kent, R., & Tonick, I. (1973). A comparison of teacher responses to the preacademic and problem behavior of boys and girls. *Child Development, 44*, 796–804.

Silverman, L. (1986). What ever happened to the gifted girl? In J. Maker (Ed.), *Critical issues in gifted education* (pp. 43–89). Rockville, MD: Aspen Publications.

VanTassel-Baska, J. (1983). Profiles of precocity. *Gifted Child Quarterly, 13*(4), 183–185.

VanTassel-Baska, J. (1987). The case for acceleration. In J. Maker, *Critical issues in gifted education* (pp. 179–196). Rockville, MD: Aspen Publications.

VanTassel-Baska, J., & Olszewski, P. (Eds.). (In press). *Patterns of influence: The home, the self, and the school.* New York: Teachers College Press.

Waber, D. P. (1977). Sex differences in mental abilities, hemispheric lateralization, and rate of physical growth at adolescence. *Developmental Psychology, 13*(1), 29–38.

Zinker, J. C. (1977). *Creative process in gestalt therapy* (pp. 62–67). New York: Brunner/Mazel.

Study Questions

1. What are some of the factors in the larger society that may interfere with gifted girls as they attempt to develop their talents?

2. What approaches to program intervention might be most effective with gifted girls at various stages of development? How might you defend your perspective?

3. What issues must gifted girls consider in choosing a career?

4. What if you had a 12-year-old daughter who was good at mathematics but superior in the humanities and enjoyed writing poetry more than anything else? How would you counsel her in regard to mathematics course-taking?

5. Evaluate the costs and benefits of providing single-sex classes or schools or both.

6. What is the appropriate role for the schools in addressing the needs of gifted girls? For parents? For others in the community?

5

The Disadvantaged Gifted

Joyce VanTassel-Baska

One of the most neglected populations among the gifted is the disadvantaged gifted. This population is frequently overlooked for special programs by school districts whose identification procedures fail to find these students or whose standards for program entry are above the tested levels achieved by many of them. Furthermore, even when such students are found and placed in programs, little attention is given to the background socioeconomic factors that may seriously affect their performance in special programs and their future achievements beyond the programs. Consequently, educators must focus more precisely on these questions: (1) Who are the disadvantaged gifted, and how do we find them? (2) What common and differential provisions should be made for them in schools? (3) What types of additional facilitation of talent development would be most useful to them?

Why Focus on the Disadvantaged Gifted?

Many educators and politicians would question the wisdom of targeting resources for such a small-incidence population. Studies have shown, for example, that the majority of gifted learners come from higher socioeconomic backgrounds (Sears & Sears, 1980; VanTassel-Baska & Willis, 1988). Thus, we are looking for a minority within the already limited population of gifted learners. There are important reasons, however, to pursue this issue:

1. Our sense of a low incidence rate is not substantiated, for the most part, by data. It is limited by the restrictions we place on the meaning of the term *gifted*. Historically, more students who came from advantaged home and school backgrounds were identified as part of the gifted population. Yet, even when we look within restricted definitions based on standardized testing protocols, we find sizable numbers of students, such as 15.5% of an eight-state region talent search, or some 2,800 students in seventh and eighth grade (VanTassel-Baska & Chepko-Sade, 1986). The incidence rate of disadvantaged gifted learners may be far greater than we have assumed.
2. There is a clear underrepresentation of minority students, particularly blacks, in gifted programs at the K–12 level of schooling. The disparity between minority representation in the general population and in gifted programs is an issue that must be addressed in a pluralistic society.
3. Colleges and universities, as well as selected professions, are still experiencing an underrepresentation of minorities capable of meeting entry standards.
4. The gap between low socioeconomic status (SES) and higher SES levels is widening, and, contrary to popular opinion, upward mobility rates of lower SES levels is less than 3% (Sennett & Cobb, 1972).
5. The plight of the black family, which is experiencing an increasing rate of single parentage, teenage pregnancy, and high unemployment, points to a need for increased interventions for the children of these families that constitute the new poor. These children will comprise a sizable segment of tomorrow's adult population.
6. Many have called gifted education "elitist," concerned with a group of learners not in need of special services given their advantaged status as students with high ability. Although such charges clearly do not appreciate the importance of attending to individual differences in schooling regardless of the nature or type of difference, gifted educators should be cognizant of the charge. As a field, we must focus attention and resources on finding talented learners whose need may be more readily understood and then clarify the importance of providing a needs-based education to all who show exceptional promise.

Disadvantaged gifted learners do not, in fact, have the family or community resources to "make it on their own." This population of learners has the greatest need of programs and services that can help optimize their human potential and has the greatest risk of being forgotten in the context of both gifted and general education.

Who Are the Disadvantaged Gifted, and How Do We Find Them?

A recent 3-year study of key demographic features of disadvantaged gifted learners in the Midwest defined disadvantaged in purely economic terms (VanTassel-Baska & Willis, 1988). Other research efforts have focused on a consideration of father's education and occupational status as the key variables (Jencks, 1972). Other efforts within the field of gifted and general education have focused on minority status and cultural difference as the preconditions for being considered (Frasier, 1980). No one definition appears to be clearly accepted by the field. Perhaps the state of California has the best approach; the state's definition is an amalgam that takes into account any or all of the following factors: environmental, economic, linguistic, and social.

Most studies on disadvantaged gifted populations have focused in four need areas related to identification and service:

1. The need to use nontraditional measures to identify them (Bernal, 1974; Bruch, 1978; Frasier, 1979; Torrance, 1971)
2. The need to recognize subcultural attributes and factors in deciding on identification procedures (Gay, 1978; Miller, 1974; Samuda, 1975; Witty, 1978)
3. The need to focus on the student's strengths in nonacademic areas, particularly in creativity and psychomotor domains (Bruch, 1975; Torrance, 1977)
4. The need to create programs that address noncognitive skills and that enhance motivation (McClelland, 1978; Moore, 1978)

Efforts to find these students have been further complicated by the confusion over whom to look for with what instrument. Several techniques have been tried with varying degrees of success. Yet the need to identify gifted students from disadvantaged populations—including culturally different, minority, low SES, and rural—is great. Some educators tend to focus on the debilities rather than the strengths of these populations. Others tend to view the job of the public school as that of raising skill levels to a minimum standard only and do not concern themselves with the larger job of educating to levels of potential ability.

Selection and programming for gifted students in these categories should be a priority for all school districts because the discrepancy between their current instructional program and one that is appropriate to their ability is probably greater than for other populations of gifted students, perhaps with the exception of the highly gifted, some of whom also fall into these categories.

Some disadvantaged students undoubtedly will be chosen for a gifted program as a matter of course, because they will fall within the selection criteria. But much depends upon what criteria are used and how they are applied. If the criteria focus strongly on test scores and use rigid cutoffs, students from economically deprived or "culturally different" streams may be at a disadvantage because of the mainstream cultural bias of many of the instruments. One alternative is to make the cutoff level more flexible to include students who are highly able but are within a standard deviation below the established cutoff on test scores. Many more disadvantaged learners probably will be included if this procedure is followed.

This alternative frequently becomes important after initial screening. If the community is 30% minority, and if, after screening procedures for a gifted program have been completed, only 2% of the students selected are minority, the screening committee may wish to adjust the cutoff standards so that a larger proportion of minorities will be included.

A second alternative is to augment identification procedures with parent, teacher, or community checklists that include special characteristics that have been noted for culturally different students who have been identified as gifted. Torrance (1969) listed 18 creative positives to look for among this group:

1. Ability to express feelings and emotions
2. Ability to improvise with commonplace materials and objects
3. Ability to articulate well in role playing, sociodrama, and storytelling
4. Enjoyment of and ability in visual arts such as drawing, painting, and sculpture
5. Enjoyment of and ability in creative movement, dance, dramatics, and so forth
6. Enjoyment of and ability in music, rhythm, and the like
7. Use of expressive speech
8. Fluency and flexibility in figural media
9. Enjoyment of and skills in group activities, problem solving, and so forth
10. Responsiveness to the concrete
11. Responsiveness to the kinesthetic
12. Expressiveness of gestures, body language, and so forth and ability to interpret body language
13. Humor
14. Richness of imagery in informal language
15. Originality of ideas in problem solving
16. Problem centeredness or persistence in problem solving
17. Emotional responsiveness
18. Quickness of warm-up

Moreover, Bernal (1974) identified specific characteristics of gifted Chicano children:

- Rapidly acquires English language skills once exposed to the language and given an opportunity to use it expressively

- Exhibits leadership ability, be it open or unobtrusive, with heavy emphasis on interpersonal skills
- Has older playmates and easily engages adults in lively conversation
- Enjoys intelligent (or effective) risk-taking behavior, often accompanied by a sense of drama
- Is able to keep busy and entertained, especially by imaginative games and ingenious applications, such as getting the most out of a few simple toys and objects
- Accepts responsibilities at home normally reserved for older children, such as supervising younger siblings or helping others do their homework
- Is "street-wise" and is recognized by others as a youngster who has the ability to "make it" in the Anglo-dominated society

Still another alternative is to state that every building in a school district will select the upper 3%, 5%, or 10% of its most talented students and then assume that the "levels of giftedness" from building to building will vary. Thus, a building that draws upon a group of economically deprived youngsters may identify a group of relatively "less gifted" (as indicated by standard test scores) youngsters than would a building that draws upon a more affluent population.

Frasier (in press) has delineated key ideas in the identification of minority students for gifted programs. They include:

1. Using multiple criteria that include inventories and checklists corresponding to traits found in gifted black populations
2. Using the diagnostic-prescriptive teaching approach to improving test performance, popularized by Feuerstein's notion of test-teach-test.
3. Broadening the data-finding procedures for students including approaches such as peer nomination, self-nomination, and assessments by personnel in addition to teachers
4. Considering broader ranges of scores for entrance into programs
5. Using standardized tests that have a history of effectiveness in identifying disadvantaged students

What Differential Provisions Are Needed?

Whether we are talking about minority students or poor white students from rural areas, one factor remains common to the members of each group—they reside outside the mainstream networks that provide knowledge about how to access educational advantage. This knowledge is crucial to the conversion of high aspirations into creative, productive achievement at various stages of development, particularly in providing families with the resources necessary to gain their own access, and thereby mobilize a community of parents to take responsibility for linking their high-potential children to available resources. Although schools can provide direct service programs for such atypical gifted learners, they typically are not in a position to act as strong resource linkers or to deliver knowledge about the process of talent development.

At their best, in-school programs have provided rigorous coursework comparable to the kind advantaged learners in the best school settings receive. At the same time, other school programs have focused on remediating skill deficits or offering programs in nonacademic areas such as the performing arts. Almost no data exist on the prevalence of such efforts or their perceived impact, and almost no efforts have been undertaken to counsel families of disadvantaged learners on the route to developing talent in their children.

Based on regional incidence data, VanTassel-Baska (1986) outlined some major initiatives for disadvantaged gifted learners in several arenas. These include:

1. Providing opportunities for scholarship assistance for special lessons and programs at the elementary and middle school years
2. Offering a counseling program for students and parents no later than the middle school years
3. Establishing a peer tutoring model of older and younger disadvantaged gifted students to enhance role-modeling effects and responsiveness to individual needs
4. Developing appropriate policies and procedures at state and local levels to encourage early identification and appropriate program provisions for such learners
5. Involving resources beyond the school (universities, laboratories, foundations, and so on), to target these students for special programs and services

Some of these ideas, such as peer tutoring, have been used on a limited basis, but no data are available from outcomes of such interventions. Even where differential provisions have been put in place, no evidence exists to support the effectiveness of the effort. But successes have been recorded for disadvantaged gifted learners in traditional gifted programs that employ common treatments across populations (Baska, in press).

What Do We Know About Effective Interventions?

Bruch (1978) reviewed the available literature on culturally different gifted children and concluded that there were many gaps and "no consistent plan for development of the culturally different gifted has been encompassed to date" (p. 383). In the same issue of *Gifted Child Quarterly*, devoted entirely to the disadvantaged and handicapped gifted, Torrance challenged his audience, "It is time we did some genuine, serious research concerning the identification and development of the creative positives of minority/disadvantaged children" (p. 306).

Nevertheless, in 1987, studies on how disadvantaged gifted students are best served were relatively few. Progress is being made, however. One method of gaining insight into "what works" with the gifted disadvantaged is to broaden the concept to examine effective strategies for educating the disadvantaged in general.

For our purposes here, the term *disadvantaged* refers to economically disadvantaged, which includes large numbers of minority students. In 1985, minority groups made up nearly 20% of the population of the public schools in the United States. In that same year, approximately 31% of blacks and 29% of Hispanics were considered below poverty level (U.S. Bureau of the Census, 1987). Although highly visible in dropout, teen pregnancy, and special education counts, disadvantaged students continue to be underrepresented in programs for the gifted and college bound.

Early Intervention

Early intervention has been influential in reducing later academic problems for disadvantaged students (Ramey, Yeates, & Short, 1984; Seitz, Rosenbaum, & Apfel, 1985). Lazar (1981) reviewed the progress of children in Head Start programs. He concluded that participants in the preschool programs were significantly more likely to finish high school, stay out of special education, and complete school careers without retention. Similar findings were noted by Royce, Lazar, and Darlington (1983) in a study of children in preschool programs in the 1960s and 1970s. Lazar determined that the following characteristics related to positive outcomes: "the earlier the better," small adult-child ratio, parent participation, and service to families rather than just to the child.

Although it has been demonstrated that early intervention is effective, this does not imply that later intervention is useless. Kagan (1976) reminded us that even in a situation where slowing of development has taken place because of environmental factors, this can be reversed if "the environment after infancy is beneficial to growth" (p. 103).

School and Classroom Environment

How then can a beneficial environment be best provided in the schools? Research on school and classroom environment is extensive, and there is no reason to assume that effective school literature would not apply to disadvantaged learners as well as to the general population. In fact, much of this effort has centered on

59

schools with sizable populations of lower SES students (Lezotte & Bancroft, 1985; Mann, 1985; Maskowitz & Hayman, 1976; Ornstein, 1983).

In an extensive review of what we know about educating disadvantaged learners, Ornstein (1983) included many controversial points of view. But he did cite several studies to indicate that the quality of school is an important factor in outcomes for disadvantaged students. He listed leadership, supervision of teachers, teacher morale, emphasis on reading instruction, and communication with parents as important factors.

Murphy (1986) saw structured learning environments, emphasis on math and reading, staff development, parental involvement and again, active, motivated leadership as more likely to be found in schools that are successful in teaching the disadvantaged. To these criteria, Mann (1985) added matching of instruction to the child's learning style and ensuring overlap between what is taught and what is tested. These issues get theoretical support from other studies as well (Lezotte & Bancroft, 1985).

Effective Teachers

Maskowitz and Hayman (1976) took us into the classroom for a look at the difference in styles between "best" teachers and first-year teachers of mostly lower SES junior high students in a large Northeastern city. These authors suggested that more successful teachers set a different climate, including more use of student ideas, more praise and encouragement, verbal recognition of student feelings, more time on task, and more activities per period. In spite of the now commonly accepted notion that active responding and time on task are closely related to learning, Stanley and Greenwood (1983) found that relatively little time to respond was given to 93 elementary school students observed, with even less time given to Title I students, who were already well behind academically. In his review of a direct instruction model, Becker (1977) stressed that the small group situation for reading instruction increases verbal interaction with the teacher, provided that time is carefully structured, positive approaches are used to maintain student attention, and student progress is monitored regularly.

Language

Becker also discussed another area frequently addressed in the preschool literature—language development. After evaluating the progress of thousands of students in the first to third grade for Project Follow Through, he concluded, "Words are the building blocks of education. Teach the English language" (1977, p. 542).

Too often, however, we have looked at language development as an obvious need in the early years and abandoned it for individual specialty-area curricula in junior and senior high. Usova (1978) suggested techniques for motivating interest in reading with secondary disadvantaged students and included language-related methods, such as acting out reading material and reading aloud to students. The Upward Bound program to assist high school students in preparing for college emphasizes language-based skills such as reading, composition, ethnic literature, and creative writing (Koe, 1980).

Math and Science

As a group, disadvantaged minority students have not traditionally pursued advanced programming in math and science. Anick, Carpenter, and Smith (1981) noted that serious inequities exist in math education of black and Hispanic students; that their achievement levels were considerably lower than the national average; and that differences from the larger population increased for each consecutive age group. Their study also showed that although blacks appear to take less math than other groups, they report positive feelings about the subject. The authors concluded that motivation may not be a major problem and that general approaches used for all students would be appropriate for minorities. Lincoln (1980) suggested that disadvantaged students would learn best by the use of teaching tools in math and science and that those tools should be concrete objects known to the student outside of the school environment.

In a review of 24 studies done since 1975 on participation and performance of minorities in math, Mathews (1984) concluded that research is scanty. But her breakdown of the important factors of parent, student, and school influences is productive. Of special interest are indications that parents desire but often do not know how to help their children, that minority role models seem to have an effect on enrollment, and that lower SES youngsters may consider math to be lacking in utility.

Compensatory Education

Cooley (1981) and Stickney and Plunkett (1982) presented varying points of view on our national compensatory education program, Title I. Cooley faulted the program for being difficult to evaluate. He was equally concerned about the confusion that develops when children are removed from the classroom to receive services and then may be found alternately eligible and ineligible from year to year.

Stickney and Plunkett (1982) cited overall improvement in achievement for Title I students. Of special note are the features of the program that seem to reflect solid educational practices suggested in this review and elsewhere. The four major

61

components of programs that are successful in enhancing achievement among disadvantaged students are (1) to provide increased instruction time, (2) to evaluate student progress with pre- and posttesting, (3) to coordinate efforts among school personnel, and (4) to extensively involve parents.

Counseling

The role of counseling in the education of the disadvantaged has been somewhat controversial. Some have argued that affective programming takes time away from cognitive instruction and expands the role of the school to encompass issues that are better dealt with in the family. Yet, a strong case has been made for the preventive mental health benefits of counseling in the schools (Pedro-Carroll, Cowen, Hightower, & Guare, 1986; Weissberg, Cowen, & Lotyczewski, 1983). Responses to problem-solving and cognitive therapy techniques have been especially positive (Kendall & Braswell, 1985; Shure & Spivak, 1982).

Several authors have noted that counseling with disadvantaged minorities is enhanced by specific techniques addressed to that population. Griffith (1977) suggested that the counselor show respect for the minority culture by learning about it and that contact between minority youth and high-achieving minority adults be facilitated. Exum (1983) cautioned nonminority counselors to be aware of the various stages minority children may undergo in their adjustments to racism. Colangelo and Lafrenz (1981) suggested that the counselor be aware of possible peer pressure not to succeed. One of the ways in which minority children may differ greatly is in the degree to which they would like to identify with or differentiate from their culture (Colangelo & Exum, 1979). Successful counseling programs will allow for the exploration of this issue without making assumptions that one direction is preferable or "healthier."

Gifted Disadvantaged

In an interview with Draper (1980), Lopez and Payne emphasized that people are more alike than they are different. Therefore, much of what is already known about gifted education would apply to gifted minority groups. But they also cited research that suggested that disadvantaged minority students may have some specific strengths in spatial orientation, problem orientation, and artistic expression. At the same time, they also mentioned several cultural norms that *may* serve to hold back gifted disadvantaged. These include (1) the degree of importance placed on social acceptance, (2) a tendency to reject solitary activity, and (3) sanctions against questioning cultural values.

Colangelo and Exum (1979) postulated that culturally different students are likely to have different learning styles that can be better accommodated in an individualized open environment. Thus, creating hands-on experiences and a gradual movement from a more structured to a less structured environment in the classroom can facilitate these students more successfully. The use of mentors, community involvement, and early counseling to help broaden ideas on future career roles also have been recommended (Dunbaum & Russo, 1983).

The Ideal Program

Programs for disadvantaged gifted are certainly not places for fostering stereotypes. Frasier (1979) very aptly cautioned us not to assume that the disadvantaged are deprived of love or stimulation or that they are deficient in specific thought processes or language. Ideal programs would provide diverse opportunities for expression as well as for information gathering. They would allow for cultural differences in materials, curriculum, and, when possible, personnel (Clasen, 1979). They would address the whole child, including the development of basic building blocks for future life performance such as problem solving, decision making, seeking assistance, discriminating relevant from irrelevant information, and developing self-direction and control (Frasier, 1979). Such programs would involve parents in the educational process and provide them with the knowledge, skills, and attitudes necessary to nurture their talented children.

Table 5.1 summarizes the research findings on successful interventions with disadvantaged learners across several study areas. By synthesizing these findings across types of study, we gain a clearer picture of some generic interventions that appear to work well, given the nature of the population. These interventions include:

1. Early and systematic response to the needs of these children
2. Parental involvement in the educational program model
3. Effective schools' strategies (time on task, school leadership)
4. Use of experiential and hands-on learning approaches
5. Use of activities that allow for student self-expression
6. Use of mentors and role models
7. Involvement of the community
8. Counseling efforts that address the issue of cultural values in facilitating talent development

Based on these findings, some general directions clearly have been identified for intervention with the disadvantaged gifted learner. It remains for the field of gifted education to address these areas in systematic program development efforts.

TABLE 5.1
Topics and Successful Interventions for Disadvantaged Students

Research Topics	Successful Interventions
Early intervention	Preschool programs Small adult-child ratio Parent participation Service to families

School and classroom environment	Motivated leadership/principal expectations
	Supervision of teachers
	Teacher morale
	Emphasis on reading instruction
	Communication with parents/parental
	   involvement
	Instructional support
	Structured learning environments
	Staff development
	Matching of instruction to learning style/
	   diagnostic-prescriptive teaching

Effective teachers	Use of student ideas Praise and encouragement Verbal recognition of student feelings Time on task More activities per period
Language	Teaching of the English language Acting out of what is read Reading aloud Use of ethnic literature Creative writing
Math and science	Use of familiar concrete objects as teaching tools Use of minority role models Education of parents Focus on the *value* of math and science
Compensatory education	Increased instructional time Evaluation and monitoring of student progress (pre/post) Parental involvement Coordinated efforts by school personnel
Counseling	Teaching of problem-solving strategies Cognitive therapy techniques Mentors/role models Respect for minority culture and related issues Exploration of cultural identity issue

Focus on future career roles
Early intervention
Community involvement

Gifted disadvantaged

Use of mentors
Community involvement
Early counseling
Hands-on learning experiences

Key Issues in Addressing the Needs of Disadvantaged Gifted Students

Based on what we do know about the nature and needs of this population, we should be concerned about several issues if progress is to be made in providing for more disadvantaged gifted learners in gifted programs.

1. Because we have sufficient evidence to suggest that low socioeconomic status plays an important role in how even highly able students may score on tests (VanTassel-Baska & Willis, 1988), we must view the home environment as a critical piece of information in understanding and interpreting the phenomenon.

2. Another equally important issue concerns gifted programs themselves. Some evidence suggests that lowering entrance scores in a rigorous program with well defined expectations neither affects the student success rate appreciably nor affects the overall standards of the class (Olszewski, Kulieke, Willis, & Krasney, 1987). Consequently, we must carefully consider the "match" between identification and program in such a way that we are not excluding students who can succeed by arbitrarily establishing higher cutoff scores than necessary for the program intervention provided.

3. We also are forced to examine the purposes of existing gifted programs and what inferences can be made about levels or types of intellectual functioning required to participate. For example, if a given program requires students to engage in original production that requires rigorous high-level analytical and interpretive skills, only students with these "readiness" skills should be exposed to such a challenging intervention. If, however, the program only provides "mild" enrichment through a special unit on archaeology in which the expectations are open-ended, it is inappropriate to insist on high threshold scores for entry. Traditionally, as a field, we have not defined gifted programs well enough to justify the identification protocols used to determine the programs' student populations. This mismatch can make our identification process appear capricious or arbitrary.

65

4. We also must account for maintaining a logical consistency in our procedures regarding this issue. If we are willing to entertain a multiple criteria model of identification as well as a quota system, are we equally willing to entertain the idea of multiple program options based on aptitude and interest? If we accept the premise that disadvantaged gifted students have different characteristics and needs from other gifted students, we also must accept the premise that differential programming for these students will be required in order to meet differential needs.

This issue brings us to the point of asking the question, What program interventions do these students most need, and what are the implications of providing for the students differentially? Should the focus of gifted programs for such students be less academic, more creative, and more open-ended than for other groups of gifted learners? Or should all gifted students be immersed in a multifaceted set of program opportunities that allows for wide deviations among individual profiles? This is a central program issue that is much bigger than identification and is a critical area worth close scrutiny. To broaden identification criteria to include more disadvantaged students only to funnel them into a narrow conception of gifted program demands is to do the ultimate disservice—attach a label that conveys the opposite impression from the reality of the program experience.

These issues are central to gaining an appropriate perspective on the involvement of disadvantaged and minority students in gifted programs. We need to examine our fundamental purposes for running such programs, our capacities to manage individual differences and needs within them, and our willingness to operate multiple program options and to define reasonable student outcomes. Only then will we be in a position as a field to do justice to this special population of learners.

Summary

This chapter has presented a definitional structure for examining the issue of disadvantaged gifted learners and has reviewed various approaches to identifying these learners. Furthermore, it has presented an overview of what we know about effective interventions with the disadvantaged. The concluding section has focused on important issues and concerns in building effective programs and services. Through systematic efforts to identify and nurture these learners, society as a whole can accrue important benefits, and education can rightfully take credit for the progress.

References

Anick, C. M., Carpenter, T. P. & Smith, C. (1981). Minorities and mathematics: Results from the national assessment of educational progress. *Mathematics Teacher, 74*(7), 560–566.

Baska, L. (in press). Are current identification protocols unfair to the minority disadvantaged student? In J. Maker (Ed.), *Critical issues in gifted education*. Austin, TX: Pro-Ed.

Becker, W. C. (1977). Teaching reading and language to the disadvantaged: What we have learned from field research. *Harvard Educational Review, 47*(4), 518–543

Bernal, E. M. (1974). Gifted Mexican-American children: An ethno-scientific perspective. *California Journal of Educational Research, 25*(5), 261–273.

Bruch, C. B. (1975). Assessment of creativity in culturally different gifted children. *Gifted Child Quarterly, 19*(2), 164–174.

Bruch, C. B. (1978). Recent insights on the culturally different gifted. *Gifted Child Quarterly, 22*(3), 374–393.

Clasen, R. E. (1979). Models for the educational needs of gifted children in a multicultural context. *Journal of Negro Education, 48*, 357–363.

Colangelo, N., & Lafrenz, N. (1981). Counseling the culturally diverse gifted. *Gifted Child Quarterly, 25*, 27–30.

Colangelo, N., & Exum, H. A. (1979). Educating the culturally diverse gifted: Implications for teachers, counselors and parents. *Gifted Child Today, 6*, 23–24; 54–55.

Cooley, W. W. (1981). Effectiveness of compensatory education. *Educational Leadership, 38*, 298–301.

Draper, W. (1980). The creative and gifted minority student: Related research, developmental and teaching strategies: Part 2. Interviews with Ambrocio Lopez and Charles Payne. *Creative Child & Adult Quarterly, 5*(3), 171–179.

Dunbaum, G., & Russo, T. (1983). Career education for the disadvantaged gifted: Some thoughts for educators. *Roeper Review, 5*(3), 26–28.

Exum, H. H. (1983). Key issues in family counseling with gifted and talented black students. *Roeper Review, 5*(3), 28–31.

Frasier, M. M. (1979). Rethinking the issue regarding the culturally disadvantaged gifted. *Exceptional Children, 45*(7), 538–542.

Frasier, M. M. (1980). Programming for the culturally diverse. In J. Jordan & J. Grossi (Eds.), *An administrator's handbook on designing programs for the gifted and talented* (pp. 56–65). Reston, VA: Council for Exceptional Children.

Frasier, M. (in press). A perspective on identifying black students for gifted programs. In J. Maker (Ed.), *Critical issues in gifted education* (Vol. 2). Austin, TX: Pro-Ed.

Gay, J. (1978). A proposed plan for identifying black gifted children. *Gifted Child Quarterly, 22*(3), 353–360.

Griffith, A. R. (1977). A cultural perspective for counseling blacks. *Humanist Educator, 16*(2), 80–85.

Jencks, C. (1972). *Inequality*. New York: Basic Books.

Kagan, J. (1976). Resilience and continuity in psychological development. In A. M. Clarke & A. D. B. Clarke (Eds.), *Early experience: Myth and evidence* (pp. 97–121). New York: Free Press.

Kendall, P. C. & Braswell, L. (1985). *Cognitive behavior therapy with impulsive children*. New York: Guilford Press.

Koe, F. T. (1980). Supplementing the language instruction of the culturally different learner: Upward Bound program. *English Journal, 69*, 19–20.

Lazar, I. (1981). Early intervention is effective. *Education Leadership, 38*, 303–305.

Lezotte L. W., & Bancroft, B. A. (1985). School improvement based on effective schools research: A promising approach for economically disadvantaged and minority students. *Journal of Negro Education, 54*(3), 301–311.

Lincoln, E. (1980). Tools for teaching math and science students in the inner city. *School Science & Math, 80*, 3–7.

Mann, D. (1985). Effective schools for children of the poor. *Education Digest, 51*, 24–25.

Maskowitz, G., & Hayman, J. T. (1976). Success strategies of inner city teachers: A year long study. *Journal of Educational Research, 69*, 283–289.

Mathews, W. (1984). Influences on the learning and participation of minorities in math. *Journal for Research in Math Education, 15*(2), 84–95.

McClelland, D. C. (1978). Managing motivation to expand human freedom. *American Psychologist,*

67

33, 201–210.

Miller, L. (1974). *The testing of black students: A symposium.* Englewood Cliffs, NJ: Prentice-Hall.

Moore, B. (1978). Career education for disadvantaged gifted high school students. *Gifted Child Quarterly, 22*(3), 332–337.

Murphy, D. M. (1986). Educational disadvantagement. *Journal of Negro Education, 55*(4), 495–507.

Olszewski, P., Kulieke, M., Willis, G., & Krasney, N. (1987). *A study of the predictors of success in fast paced classes and the validity of entrance scores.* Evanston, IL: Northwestern University, Center for Talent Development.

Ornstein, A. C. (1983). Educating disadvantaged learners. *Educational Forum, 47*(2), 225–247.

Pedro-Carroll, J., Cowen, E. L., Hightower, D. A., & Guare, J. C. (1986). Preventive intervention with latency-aged children of divorce: A replication study. *American Journal of Community Psychology, 14*(3), 277–290.

Ramey, C. T., Yeates, K. O., & Short, E. J. (1984). The plasticity of intellectual development: Insights from preventive intervention. *Child Development, 55*, 1913–1925.

Royce, J., Lazar, I., & Darlington, R. B. (1983). Minority families, early education and later life chances. *American Journal of Orthopsychiatry, 53*(4), 706–720.

Samuda, R. J. (1975). *Psychological testing of American minorities: Issues and consequences.* New York: Dodd, Mead.

Sears, P., & Sears, R. (1980, February). 1528 little geniuses and how they grew. *Psychology Today*, pp. 28–43.

Seitz, V., Rosenbaum, L. K., & Apfel, N. H. (1985). Effects of family support intervention: A ten year follow-up. *Child Development, 56*, 376–391.

Sennett, R., & Cobb, J. (1972). *The hidden injuries of class.* New York: Random House.

Shure, M. B., & Spivak, G. (1982). Interpersonal problem solving in young children: A cognitive approach to prevention. *American Journal of Community Psychology, 10*, 341–356.

Stanley, S. O., & Greenwood, C. R. (1983). How much "opportunity to respond" does the minority disadvantaged student receive in school? *Exceptional Children, 49*, 370–373.

Stickney, B. D., & Plunkett, V. R. L. (1982). Has Title I done its job? *Educational Leadership, 39*(5), 378–383.

Torrance, E. P. (1969). Creative positives of disadvantaged children and youth. *Gifted Child Quarterly, 13*, 71–81.

Torrance, E. P. (1971). Are the Torrance Tests of Creative Thinking biased against or in favor of disadvantaged groups? *Gifted Child Quarterly, 15*, 75–80.

Torrance, E. P. (1977). *Discovery and nurturance of giftedness in the culturally different.* Reston, VA: Council for Exceptional Children.

Torrance, E. P. (1978). Dare we hope again? *Gifted Child Quarterly, 22*(3), 292–312.

U.S. Bureau of the Census. (1986). *Statistical abstract of the United States: 1987* (107th ed.). Washington, DC: U.S. Government Printing office.

Usova, G. (1978). Techniques for motivating interest in reading for the disadvantaged high school student. *Reading, 15*(1), 36–38.

VanTassel-Baska, J. (in press). The role of the family in the success of disadvantaged gifted learners. In J. VanTassel-Baska, & P. Olszewski (Eds.), *Patterns of influence: The home, the self, and the school.* New York: Teachers College Press.

VanTassel-Baska, J., & Chepko-Sade, D. (1986). *An incidence study of disadvantaged gifted students in the Midwest.* Evanston, IL: Northwestern University, Center for Talent Development.

VanTassel-Baska, J., & Willis, G. (1988). A three year study of the effects of low income on SAT scores among the academically able. *Gifted Child Quarterly, 31*(4), 169–173.

Weissberg, R. P., Cowen, E. L., & Lotyczewski, B. S. (1983). The primary mental health project: Seven consecutive years of program research. *Journal of Consulting & Clinical Psychology, 51*(1), 100–107.

Witty, E. P. (1978). Equal educational opportunity for gifted minority children. *Gifted Child Quarterly, 22*(3), 344–352.

Study Questions

1. Evaluate the proposition that gifted learners who are economically disadvantaged need programs/services different from those for advantaged gifted learners.

2. Factors that narrow, inhibit, or distort one's self-perception of capacity are likely to impede the talent development process. How does this statement apply to the concept of disadvantagement?

3. What definitional structure for disadvantaged gifted would have the most meaning in school districts? Why?

4. If you were to recommend an approach for identifying disadvantaged gifted students in a given context, what procedures would you follow and why?

5. How might schools approach developing a special program for the disadvantaged gifted learner? Where should they begin?

6. Many talented people have come from disadvantaged backgrounds—Barbara Jordan, Maya Angelou, Stephen Leacock, and others. What issues about poverty are important to consider in working with disadvantaged gifted learners?

6

The Highly Gifted

Linda Kreger Silverman

Who are the highly gifted, and why is it necessary to discuss special provisions for them in a textbook on the gifted? Simply stated, the highly gifted are those whose advancement is significantly beyond the norm of the gifted. Although it seems that these students are the ones most in need of gifted education, in a national study of identification procedures, exceptionally gifted and creative students were found to be a "disadvantaged" group at risk for being screened out of gifted programs (Richert, 1982).

Some students fail to qualify for programs that emphasize task commitment or evidence of creativity in their identification procedures. Others qualify but find the programs inadequate to meet their needs; this is a potential hazard in gifted programs that attempt to serve a large segment of the school population. Whatever the cutoff score may be, the vast majority of qualified students cluster at the borderline for admission. Teachers almost inevitably gear instruction to the majority of the students in the group; this situation may leave the highly gifted child academically and socially isolated from others in the program.

These problems are partially created by the rudimentary nature of our classification system. The field of mental retardation recognizes at least three degrees of retardation—mild, moderate, and profound—and prescribes interventions based on degree of severity (Grossman, 1977). But we have not yet reached that level of sophistication in the field of gifted education, as indicated by the omnipresent query, "Is this child gifted or not?" The question of *how* gifted is usually not taken into account in programming. This single classification system makes strange bedfellows. Two children labeled "gifted" may be as different from each other in ability as a severely handicapped child is from an average child.

Successful provisions take into account the strength of the children's abilities along with their various types of talent; otherwise, instruction will be aimed at the lowest common denominator and the highly gifted will be poorly served. This chapter provides guidelines for identifying, assessing, and serving students who vary from the majority of identified gifted children in terms of strength of their abilities.

Identifying the Highly Gifted

In keeping with the special education designations, it is possible to roughly categorize gifted children for school-based programs as mildly, moderately, and highly gifted. The various problems with IQ testing make it impossible to determine with any degree of certainty the full range of anyone's abilities. Multiple criteria have to be used, and any single test score that appears questionable to either parents or teachers should be cause for reevaluation on individual assessment instruments. Group IQ tests are only gross screening devices that tend to depress the scores of gifted students—especially highly gifted students—because of low ceilings (Pegnato & Birch, 1959). The following breakdown is based on individual IQ scores with the Wechsler Intelligence Scale for Children–Revised (WISC–R):

mildly gifted	115–129	(1 sd beyond the norm)
moderately gifted	130–144	(2 sd beyond the norm)
highly gifted	145 +	(3 sd beyond the norm)

Individual intelligence tests measure abstract reasoning abilities, and children whose measured abilities are 3 standard deviations beyond the norm are sufficiently advanced from their agemates to be considered highly gifted.

Another means of locating highly gifted children is through regional talent search programs, which enable high-achieving students to take the Scholastic Aptitude Test (SAT) in seventh or eighth grade (and as early as fifth or sixth grade in some communities). The average scores for college-bound seniors are approximately 430 on the verbal (V) section and 475 on the mathematics (M) section (this figure varies annually) (College Entrance Examination Board, 1986). High school seniors who attain scores in the high 600 range or greater on either V or M could be considered highly gifted.

The talent search programs usually select students who score 430 V or 500 M in seventh or eighth grade to participate in special programs, such as college-level courses. These students may be thought of as moderately gifted. Students who score significantly beyond this range could be considered highly gifted. VanTassel-Baska (1984) designated students in the 530 + range as significantly advanced from other talent search participants and in need of additional provisions. This score represents a composite of V and M scores, and is, therefore, a high estimate for verbal and a low estimate for mathematics scores. These figures would have to be adjusted for fifth and sixth graders because 80 to 90 point increases may occur from one year to the next in this age group. The original talent search cutoff scores have been found useful for selecting students for high powered content-based programs; extrapolations for differentiating highly gifted students from this group are yet to be tested by research.

If ability or aptitude testing is not available, a third way to select highly gifted children is to provide off-level achievement testing, which is at least one level beyond the student's current grade placement. Students can qualify for programs for the highly gifted if their scores are 1 sd greater than the mean of the gifted group in one or more areas on off-level testing.

These methods are likely to find academically precocious children but may miss children who are highly gifted in specific areas, such as the visual and performing arts, creative production, or ethical development. So as to include these children, teacher judgment should be used and observational data can be collected to locate children whose productivity, precocity, or advancement in any area is noticeably beyond the level demonstrated by others enrolled in the gifted program.

Problems in Assessing the Highly Gifted

The central problem in testing highly gifted children is the *ceiling effect*. Group tests and, today, even individual tests do not have items of sufficient difficulty for the highly gifted child. When the ceiling on a test is too low, it does not capture the full range of the child's abilities. There is no way of knowing how high the student's score might have been if there were harder items.

The talent search testing protocol helps us to understand more about ceiling effects and what happens when we remove them. The SAT has a much higher ceiling than grade-level achievement tests do because it was designed to assess the brightest high school seniors. Highly gifted students are clearly distinguishable from more modestly gifted students because of the range of the SAT (200–800), whereas both groups were indistinguishable from each other on grade-level tests because of ceiling effects.

None of the current intelligence tests was designed with the highly gifted in mind. Test constructors require an instrument to be functional for the vast majority of students and easy to administer within a reasonable time limit so that the child does not become fatigued. According to Hagen (Silverman, 1986), items are purposely omitted from IQ tests if they can be solved only by gifted students. Given the state of the art of measurement, it is nearly impossible to tell just how gifted those in the upper ranges might be.

Until 1986, the Stanford-Binet L-M was considered the test of choice for assessing gifted children because of its high range (Hagen, 1980; Martinson, 1974; Sattler, 1974). But in 1986, the Stanford-Binet Revision IV (Thorndike, Hagen, & Sattler, 1986) made the old version obsolete. Unfortunately, the new test is constructed in a completely different manner, which is less applicable than its predecessor to assessing the highly gifted. In addition, it eliminates the mental age that could be used to derive ratio IQs (mental age divided by chronological age × 100). The use of ratio IQs enabled us to estimate intelligence quotients for highly gifted students whose scores went beyond the norms in the manual.

The new Stanford-Binet has many improvements over the old, but it is unable to differentiate abilities at either end of the spectrum: profoundly retarded or highly gifted. Therefore, the older Stanford-Binet L-M should be used to supplement testing for children who come close to the ceilings of any standardized test or with those who are suspected for any reason of having depressed IQ scores.

Characteristics of the Highly Gifted

Highly gifted children may demonstrate developmental precocity early in life in ways such as early language development, the tendency to ask complex questions, rapid learning ability, extensive vocabulary, unusual attention span, advanced abilities with puzzles or numbers, or acquisition of reading while still toddlers. Complexity of thought and ability to understand abstract relationships may be manifested in startling ways.

The following example of developmental precocity comes from our case files at the Gifted Child Development Center in Denver. "A" turned pages in a book one by one at the age of 4 months. By 5 months, she had a four-word vocabulary. At 7 months, she stood alone, climbed into chairs unassisted, and went up and down stairs by herself all day long. Her mother says she "was never a baby." At 2, she ordered her own meal in a restaurant, composed a song, swam across the swimming pool, and began riding a horse. By age 5, she was a capable photographer, switching between three cameras with ease. She taught herself to play computer games and one day asked her mother to read her a high school physics book. By 6, she was learning geometry and logic at home.

Her mother writes, "I never taught 'A' anything. . . . I would put something out, and she would do it before I could teach her how." But school was an unending lesson in frustration for this child. In kindergarten, her teacher made fun of her precocity, saying things like, "What do you want to learn today . . . calculus?" She had trouble mixing with her classmates. She would come home from school crying, "I want to learn something. I want a challenge. I want school to be hard." Her first-grade teacher acknowledged that she was smart but said that she did not need more challenging material "because she doesn't finish her work early." The teacher discouraged A's mother from engaging a tutor for her to nurture her interests in geometry or advanced mathematics.

Hollingworth (1940) often spoke of exceptionally gifted children as "old heads on young shoulders" (p. 104). The boy in the following story aptly fits this description. Dr. Jerry Levy (1982) described a visit she made to some friends in which she attempted to strike up a conversation with their 4-year-old. The boy just stared at her curiously until she stopped and asked him what was the matter. The following dialogue occurred:

> The Boy: "Do you always talk in such a strange manner?"
> Dr. Levy: "What do you mean?"
> The Boy: "Well, your vocabulary is so limited. I thought you were on the faculty of the University of Pennsylvania."
> Dr. Levy: "I thought you were a 4-year-old boy!"
> The Boy: "I would prefer that you would talk to me as if I were a person."

Exceptionally bright children have the same characteristics as other gifted children, but they may appear earlier in the developmental sequence or in an intensified manner. A good sense of humor, for example, is a mark of giftedness, but the degree of sophistication of that humor increases with ability. While playing under his mother's bed, one child spontaneously knocked on the bedsprings and said, "Mommy, are you resting?" She replied, "Well, I'm trying to." He retorted, "Does that mean I'm under arrest?" This would have been amusing from a 9-year-old, but this boy was only 2 years old!

A major component of the learning style of this group is the ability to skip steps in learning and take giant intuitive leaps. Highly gifted children often surprise adults by arriving at insightful conclusions without being able to describe the steps they took to get there. ("I just figured it out!") The need to show their work in a precise, linear fashion is at cross purposes with their learning style. They may get a visual image of an intricate set of relationships and be unable to translate their thinking process in such a manner that others can follow it.

While their agemates are comfortable working with concrete material, highly gifted children are more at home with abstractions. They may have difficulty concentrating on isolated fragments of information, analyzing bits of learning such as phonics, or memorizing facts by rote. Yet they manipulate abstract symbol systems with ease and become animated when dealing with complex relations involving many variables. They are *systems thinkers*.

There are social ramifications to high levels of intelligence. The brighter the child, the more difficult it is to find true peers. True peers are mental equals

75

(Roedell, 1985), those who share common interests, understandings, and perspectives. A 5-year-old child who plays checkers, chess, Scrabble, and Monopoly will be unable to play those games with average or more modestly gifted 5-year-olds. Most 5-year-olds do not have a conception of rules. They make up the rules as they go along and then declare, "I win!" The highly gifted child is likely to say, "He cheats!" and refuse to play with agemates.

The highly gifted also deal with complex moral issues at a very tender age. A 5-year-old said to her mother, "Mommy, did you kill that chicken? If you did, I'm not going to eat it." One 9-year-old refused to eat any living thing that had to die for him, which left him very little to eat. More than one highly gifted child has become a vegetarian in a meat-eating family. They tend to ask difficult questions: "What is evil?" "Why is there violence?" "Is there a God?" "What happens when you die?" "How do we know we aren't part of someone else's dream?"

These philosophical questions and moral concerns may or may not translate into moral actions. Highly gifted children can generate excellent ideas about solving social conflicts in cooperative ways (Roedell, 1985) and then bite someone in the leg right after the discussion. Social concern must fuse with experience and maturity before it warms into consistent commitment to moral action. Yet, many highly gifted children are the protectors of handicapped children, the elderly, or the infirm.

Differential Problem Solving

The following two problems from different disciplines illustrate the manner in which highly gifted children's problem-solving techniques vary from those used by average and modestly gifted children. In the first example (Figure 6.1), second graders are asked to balance the equation by inserting two identical numbers into the squares.

An average second grader might not be ready to understand the concept of balance. He or she might insert two 9s in the squares on the left side to make all the numbers the same, just like they are on the right side, failing to see the connection between the two sides. The mildly gifted child tends to look for a formula to solve the problem. He or she adds all the numbers on the right, subtracts 9, and divides the answer by 2 to derive the solution.

But Justin, a highly gifted second grader, immediately apprehended the relationships among the numbers and was able to solve the problem in a unique way. Instead of writing down numbers, he just looked at the problem and then wrote 39 in each of the squares. When asked how he arrived at the answer so quickly, he explained that 29 was 20 more than 9, so he split the 20 in half and added 10 to the other 29s. Intuitive leaps and recognition of abstract relationships served him better than an algorithmic solution with concrete numbers.

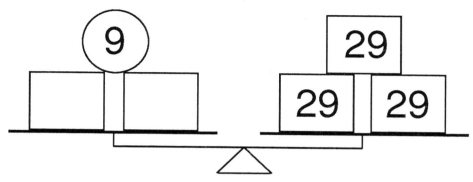

FIGURE 6.1
Sample Problem Differentiating Highly Gifted

Another example is drawn from the literature at the middle school level. In his poem on loneliness, e. e. cummings portrays a leaf falling through descending placement of the letters of the words "a leaf falls"—and then simply writes "loneliness." Average students notice the pattern of the words graphically representing the leaf falling from the tree, and they may associate the poem with seasons of the year or the death of the leaf. The mildly gifted student will look for a theme and begin to grasp the metaphor of life associated with the seasons. The highly gifted youngster interprets the poem on many levels and sees layers upon layers of meaning: The individual goes through life alone; death is an individual act; transitions in life are conducted alone; leaving the security of the known leads to loneliness; the fall from grace; and so on.

It is important to respond to the depth and intuitive insights of the highly gifted student rather than trying to get the child to adapt to the thought processes of others. When a spark of interest is ignited, it should be nourished through increasingly more in-depth experiences in that area.

Provisions

We can use the normal curve of distribution of intelligence as a metaphor to help us understand the need for special provisions for the highly gifted beyond those available for modestly gifted children in the school environment. The basic curriculum, textbooks, and teaching methods were designed for the average group of learners. Average students may need concrete experiences and several repetitions of material in order to grasp it. The amount of drill, repetition, and review incorporated into the curriculum was designed for the average student.

As we move down the intelligence continuum, more drill and repetition are needed to get across even the simplest concepts, and the degree of complexity and abstraction that can be understood markedly decreases with each standard deviation of ability. At 1 sd below the norm (approximately 85 IQ), the child is considered a slow learner within the regular classroom, and programs such as remedial reading and mathematics are made available. At 2 sd (approximately 70 IQ), the student qualifies by law for a complete individual diagnosis, staffing, and individualized education program (IEP). These children are mainstreamed whenever possible, but their academic needs usually are met in resource rooms with specially certified teachers. At 3 sd (approximately 55 IQ), students typically are in full-day placements with specially trained teachers and a curriculum specifically designed to meet their needs. At 4 sd or less (approximately 40 IQ), children are in special facilities.

As we realize how each standard deviation of ability is met with a different type of provision at the lower end of the intellectual spectrum, it becomes increasingly clear that each standard deviation at the upper end of the spectrum also requires unique consideration. As intelligence increases, so do abilities to deal with complexity, abstraction, and advanced concepts. The need for repetition dramatically decreases, and the pace of instruction increases accordingly. At 1 sd above the norm (approximately 115 IQ), children are the fast learners in the regular classroom and profit from general enrichment activities. At 2 sd (approximately 130 IQ), individual diagnosis, certified teachers, resource rooms, special classes, and individualized programs are needed. At 3 sd (approximately 145 IQ), full-day placements with specially trained teachers and a specially tailored curriculum actually provide the least restrictive environment for these children. At 4 sd or greater (approximately 160 IQ), special facilities or the flexibility to mobilize many provisions, dependent on the specific needs of the child, may be called for.

The following provisions, or combinations of provisions, are suitable for highly gifted children. Some are also appropriate for moderately gifted children. If certain numbers of students are needed to make the creation of a particular option financially feasible, there is no harm in grouping moderately and highly gifted students together, provided that the instruction is at a sufficient pace to keep the highly gifted children challenged. Highly gifted students often develop leadership abilities in classes with moderately gifted peers, whereas they may be isolated in the regular classroom (Hollingworth, 1926).

Individualized education programs	Mentors or tutors
Fast-paced, challenging courses	Special schools or programs
Self-contained classes	Community enrichment opportunities
Acceleration	Home teaching
University-based programs	Counseling

No matter which provisions are chosen, an individualized program is essential for highly gifted students. Lewis (1984) asserted:

> The higher the deviation above the mean, the greater the number of possible combinations and recombinations of abilities. No one highly gifted child can be expected to be like any other child with the same score. Therefore, no single-focus program, whether acceleration or any other design, can hope to adequately serve a population with such potentially complex profiles. (p. 134)

Individualized Education Programs (IEPs)

It would be wise to have an IEP for every highly gifted student in the district to assess the student's strengths and needs and to determine collaborative means of meeting those needs. If possible, the IEP should be preceded by a comprehensive individual assessment with a school psychologist in which not only intellectual capability, but academic strengths, self-concept, social development, and student interests are examined as well. An interview with the student also should precede development of the IEP because highly gifted students are often in the best position to tell us what they need for their optimal development. The IEP should represent the collaborative planning of administrators, parents, teachers, counselor, support personnel, and the student.

Acceleration

Acceleration is an appropriate response to a student's accelerated pace of learning. Until very recently, gifted children were automatically placed with children 1 or 2 years older, and the term *acceleration* was reserved for the type of advancement that we call "radical" today: 3 years or more of advancement. Research on the effects of acceleration supports it as a viable option, even in terms of social development (Daurio, 1979; Janos & Robinson et al. 1988). To determine if this is the proper option for a given student, ask the student. This is the critical factor. If the child wants to be accelerated, he or she will make a fine social adjustment, and vice versa.

University-Based Programs

The university is an excellent ally in the search for appropriate provisions for the highly gifted. The brightest students are often more at home and comfortable in a college setting than they are with agemates. It benefits the university to have these bright students on campus early because they often select a campus with which

79

they are familiar. Institutions of higher education have become involved in many creative ways in supplementing the education of the gifted: Saturday, summer, and after-school *enrichment courses* for gifted children of all ages, taught by faculty, graduate students, or skilled community members; *laboratory schools* for gifted students on campus; *summer residential programs* such as those that exist for talent search winners; *concurrent enrollment* programs in which high school students take college courses for both high school and college credit; *night or extension courses* to supplement offerings at the high school; *early entrance* programs that enable students to enroll as full-time students ahead of schedule; *advanced coursework at the high school; mentorships;* consolidated *high school/college programs*, such as the Program for Exceptionally Gifted girls at Mary Baldwin College, in which students complete high school and college simultaneously.

Mentors

Mentors or tutors who work with students individually in their areas of interest comprise an excellent alternative for the highly gifted. The mentor often has a powerful impact on the development of a talented young person. The brighter the child, the greater is the need for an individualized approach. Mentors can be drawn from the community, college faculties, college students, and older gifted students.

Community-Generated Opportunities

Parent groups can be encouraged to develop their own activities for these children to meet their social needs. Community agencies, such as museums, galleries, planetariums, zoos, community schools, parks, and camps, have special opportunities for gifted students. Private agencies also can be found that offer special programs for gifted students: computer camps, science schools, arts programs, archeological centers, music studios, centers for theater arts, and self-concept seminars.

Homeschooling

Homeschooling was once the only option available for extraordinarily gifted children—and one that yielded many eminent individuals, including Albert Einstein, Pearl Buck, John Stuart Mill, Franklin Delano Roosevelt, Andrew Wyeth (Kearney, 1989). In the 1980s, homeschooling is on the upswing, particularly in rural areas where services for gifted children are limited. Excellent guides to homeschooling with the highly gifted are available from Kearney (1984, 1989).

The more advanced the student, the more of these options should be considered. Determining which options to pursue at which points in the child's life can be a complex challenge. A counselor who is familiar with the student, the family, and the available options can be particularly helpful to the family in selecting appropriate provisions.

Counseling

Uneven developmental patterns in the highly gifted, as well as the degree of difference from age peers, creates a context in which counseling may be an important ongoing provision. It may be nearly impossible for highly gifted children to conform their thinking to the ways in which others think. Some do not "group" well. Some have difficulty developing relationships with others. Some argue continually because that is the way they learn. Some are intensely sensitive. Some have major discrepancies between their intellectual maturity and motor coordination and so appear "immature."

Those who are having difficulty with social relations may need systematic instruction in developing friendships and building others' self-esteem. Bibliotherapy is helpful; several books feature gifted children, and others teach children about making friends. Children and parents alike may need counseling to cope with the child's intensity, sensitivity, or perfectionism. Parents usually need some counseling to adjust to the idea of rearing a child who is so unique, as well as guidance in determining what to do. Within the school system there should be an advocate who appreciates the special needs and problems of highly gifted children. That person can become a trusted friend for the child and the family—someone who can help them deal with the myriad questions that plague them and help them sort out the truth from the fiction.

Summary

The best program for highly gifted children involves serious exploration of all existing possibilities with the assistance of an advocate who can help cut through the red tape. Cries of "she's too young," "you can't get credit for . . ." and "we don't allow . . ." have to be firmly met with "why don't we try?" Administrative support is essential to move a student into advanced experiences ahead of schedule. Parents and educators should work together to change rules, regulations, and laws that prohibit or penalize advancement.

Our society offers very little support—financial, emotional, or educational—for the highly gifted child. A knowledgeable, caring individual in the school setting can make a sizable difference in the quality of life of an exceptionally gifted student. Many exceptionally gifted children have endured their school years in perpetual misery, but with the kind of awareness and services available today, these students can thrive and develop their potential for themselves and for society.

References

College Entrance Examination Board. (1986). *National report college bound seniors*. Princeton, NJ: Educational Testing Service.

Daurio, S. P. (1979). Educational enrichment versus acceleration: A review of the literature. In W. C. George, S. J. Cohn, & J. C. Stanley (Eds.), *Educating the gifted: Acceleration and enrichment* (pp. 13–63). Baltimore, MD: Johns Hopkins University Press.

Grossman, H. J. (Ed.). (1977). *Manual on terminology and classification in mental retardation* (rev.). Washington, DC: American Association on Mental Deficiency.

Hagen, E. (1980). *Identification of the gifted*. New York: Teachers College Press.

Hollingworth, L. S. (1926). *Gifted children: Their nature and nurture*. New York: Macmillan.

Hollingworth, L. S. (1940). Old heads on young shoulders. In L. S. Hollingworth. *Public addresses* (pp. 104–110). Lancaster, PA: Science Press.

Janos, P. M., & Robinson, N. M. et al. (1988). A cross-sectional developmental study of the social relations of students who enter college early. *Gifted Child Quarterly, 32*, 210–215.

Kearney, K. (1984, May/June). At home in Maine: Gifted children and homeschooling. *G/C/T, 33*, 15–19.

Kearney, K. (1989). Gifted children and homeschooling. *Understanding Our Gifted, 1*(3), 1, 12, 13, 15-16.

Levy, J. (1982, November). *Brain research: Myths and realities of the gifted male and female*. Paper presented at the Illinois Gifted Education Conference, Chicago, IL.

Lewis, G. (1984). Alternatives to acceleration for the highly gifted child. *Roeper Review, 6*(3), 133–136.

Martinson, R. A. (1974). *The identification of the gifted and talented*. Ventura, CA: Office of the Ventura County Superintendent of Schools.

Pegnato, C. W., & Birch, J. W. (1959). Locating gifted children in junior high schools: A comparison of methods. *Exceptional Children, 25*, 300–304.

Richert, E. S., with J. J. Alvino & R. C. McDonnel. (1982). *National report on identification: Assessment and recommendations for comprehensive identification of gifted and talented youth*. Sewell, NJ: Educational Improvement Center—South.

Roedell, W. C. (1985). Developing social competence in gifted preschool children. *RASE, 6*(4), 6–11.

Sattler, J. M. (1974). *Assessment of children's intelligence*. Philadelphia: W.B. Saunders.

Silverman, L. K. (1986). An interview with Elizabeth Hagen: Giftedness, intelligence and the new Stanford-Binet. *Roeper Review, 8*(3), 168–171.

Thorndike, R. L., Hagen, E. P., & Sattler, J. M. (1986). *The Stanford-Binet intelligence scale (4th ed.). Technical manual*. New York: Riverside.

VanTassel-Baska, J. (1984). The talent search as an identification model. *Gifted Child Quarterly, 28*(4), 172–176.

Study Questions

1. Do you think that the highly gifted represent a special needs group within the gifted population? If so, why?

2. Have you ever worked with a highly gifted child? How was that child different from other gifted children?

3. How can the highly gifted be differentiated from more modestly gifted children in identification procedures?

4. What types of educational provisions are needed to serve the highly gifted?

5. How would you deal with the emotional and social ramifications of the highly gifted?

7

Identification and Assessment of the Gifted

John F. Feldhusen
Leland K. Baska

Identification of gifted and talented youth is a process through which we attempt to become aware of students whose abilities, motivational patterns, self-concepts, and creative capabilities are so far above average that differentiated educational services are needed if they are to make the full educational progress indicated by their potential (Brandwein, 1980). We assume that all youth have a right to educational services that will meet their needs, be adapted to their personal characteristics, and help them achieve to the highest possible level of their potential. Identification systems that merely enable us to label or categorize "gifted" youth are of no value and are potentially even harmful. The sole purpose of identification is to guide the educational process and serve youth (Hoover & Feldhusen, 1987).

The identification process has gone astray in many schools (Alvino, McDonnel, & Richert, 1981; Feldhusen, Asher, & Hoover, 1984), especially when identification becomes an end in itself. In other schools, educational services for the gifted are severely limited or nonexistent. Additionally, the identification process can exacerbate problems of elitism. We propose in this chapter to review some of the major issues and concerns related to identification and assessment, to suggest some methods of dealing with those issues, and to present a general set of guidelines for the identification and assessment processes.

Some Issues and Concerns

Validity and Appropriateness

A major issue related to identification is validity with respect to program goals and services. The identification process must be appropriate for selecting youth who need and will profit from a particular program service. The Future Problem Solving Program (Flack & Feldhusen, 1983) is one example of an excellent service offered in many gifted programs. Verbal skills and abilities, a high degree of motivation, creative capacity, and good independent study skills might be seen as appropriate abilities and characteristics of youth who need and would profit from that program. A valid identification process, then, would include assessment of the nominee's strengths in each of those areas. Assessment of math and science abilities as represented in standardized achievement test scores would be less relevant and could render the process invalid. The use of language achievement tests and creativity and study skill scores to identify youth for accelerated algebra classes might be equally questionable. In summary, the identification process should select youth whose needs, abilities, and characteristics fit the goals or nature of the program service to be offered.

We think that some programs at the early childhood level might identify generally gifted children who can profit from a general set of stimulating educational experiences. As children move through the elementary grades, however, their talents begin to crystallize in specific areas. Increasing attention must be paid to an individual's abilities and characteristics, matching them to appropriate and valid educational experiences (Bloom, 1982; Feldman, 1979, 1986; Keating, 1979).

Parent Input

Another issue of concern in identification of the gifted is parent input to the process. There is a myth that all parents think their children are gifted. In truth, few parents think their children are gifted or want to label their children as gifted, and few parents are willing to single out their children from age peers by labeling them gifted. Whether this comes about because of subcultural cautions against elevating oneself above the group or an unrealistic "child prodigy" image of giftedness, parents do not readily accept the label. They do begin to seek special remediation when they come to view the school's curriculum as substandard for their child or begin to hear rumblings of the child's negative attitudes toward peers and school. The label at that point seems a lesser evil even though it carries the stigma of hubris.

Nevertheless, parents do have a great amount of knowledge that is relevant to the identification process. They do not know the technical jargon of the gifted field, but they do know a great deal about the abilities, motivation, self-concept, and creative capacity of their children. Furthermore, they see their children in free behavior situations and less restrictive environments than the classroom. They often have information of which teachers are totally unaware that can be extremely valuable in the identification process.

Through rating scales, questionnaires, or open-ended instruments, parents can provide information concerning their children's reading habits, vocabulary, hobbies, interests, motivation, creative behavior, and self-views. All of this information can be valuable in the identification process. The ASSETS scale developed at Grand Rapids, Michigan, is one published example of an instrument to gain parent input in identification (ASSETS, 1979). Table 7.1 also shows an open-ended nomination scale that can be used to secure parent input for the identification process.

Combining Assessment Data

A major challenge in identification occurs when those who are carrying out the identification process wish to combine data from several sources for a unitary or synthesized evaluation of the child. Obviously, scores derived from different types of scales (for example, percentiles, IQs, stanines, and Z scores) cannot simply be added together. Must we settle simply for a subjective, intuitive combination?

TABLE 7.1
Parent Nomination Form

Child's Name _____ Grade _____

Parent's Name _____

Address _____ Zip _____

1. What are some things you have observed in your child's behavior that lead you to believe that he/she should be in the special program for high-ability children?

2. What problems, if any, is he/she having in school as a result of the high ability?

3. Describe briefly your child's reading habits, patterns, and levels at home.

4. Describe briefly your child's major interests, hobbies, art activities, and so on.

5. Describe any projects or studies your child has done (if not covered in Item 4).

6. Please give any other information about your child that you believe is relevant to his/her abilities or interests.

One answer, widely applied in the gifted field, is a simplified standardization process as represented in a matrix. All the scores are converted to a simple 5-level or 10-level scale without regard to the variance of individual measures, and then summed to derive a gross index of giftedness. Table 7.2 is an illustration of such a matrix. Each test score is converted to a 1-5 score, and then those numbers are added to get a total giftedness score (Baldwin, 1978).

Feldhusen, Baska, and Womble (1981) have detailed the serious weaknesses of such matrix approaches and argued that a standardized score approach be used instead. They advocate that all input variables be converted to T scores and then combined, as a more reliable way of synthesizing data. A standard score expresses the variability within the group's real scores that is consistent with the technical data presented for other tests.

Probably the best argument for the standard score is the ease of computation with a computer because this is now included as part of many software packages. The availability of personal computers and user-friendly software has become a major benefit for record keeping and assessment, not to mention part of the early home experiences of children. Teachers of the gifted must familiarize themselves with these tools if only to keep pace with the children in their classes.

One-Shot Versus Continuing Assessment

Identification often is viewed as a one-time process, particularly if it seeks simply to identify, label, and categorize youth as gifted or nongifted. Developmental psychology and the common sense of school personnel, however, indicate that children grow and children change. Most assuredly, their talents and abilities are undergoing processes of differentiation and specialization as they move through the elementary grades and into high school. Thus, the identification process demands periodic reassessment.

Reassessment should not be oriented to the question of whether the child is still gifted. Rather, it should seek to identify changing abilities or characteristics and the emergence of more specialized talent or ability. Furthermore, it should ask whether the student has special needs, related to the area(s) of talent or giftedness, for which new or different educational services are needed.

Reliability

Reliability means accuracy in measurement. The reliability of test scores, rating scales, observation data, and other measures used in assessing gifted youth varies tremendously. Some degree of imprecision is always present. Scores derived from intelligence and achievement tests are likely to be highly reliable. Other measures,

TABLE 7.2
Baldwin Identification Matrix

Assessment Items	Scores				
	5	4	3	2	1
1. Cognitive Abilities Test	140+	139–130	129–120	119–110	109–100
2. Metropolitan Achievement (percentile) – Reading	95%ile	94–90%	89–85%	84–80%	79–75%
3. Metropolitan Achievement – Math	sta. 9	8	7	6	5
4. Renzulli Leadership	40	39–35	34–30	29–25	24–20
5. Renzulli Creativity	40	39–35	34–30	29–25	24–20
6. In-school Psychomotor	5	4	3	2	1
7. Renzulli Motivation	36–34	33–30	29–26	25–22	21–18
8. Renzulli Learning	32	31–28	27–24	23–20	19–16
9. Teacher recommendation	5	4	3	2	1
Column Tally of Checks					
Weight	x5	x4	x3	x2	x1
Add Across	+	+	+	+	+
TOTAL SCORE					

Note. From "The Baldwin Identification Matrix," by A. Y. Baldwin (1978) in *Educational Planning for the Gifted,* Reston, VA: Council for Exceptional Children. Reprinted by permission.

such as nominating procedures, rating scales, creativity tests, and self-concept inventories, are likely to be low or very low in reliability. Thus, if the assessment is repeated or done by another examiner, the scores may differ substantially.

Technical manuals provided by test publishers and reviews such as are found in the *Mental Measurement Yearbook* (Mitchell, 1985) provide information on the reliability and validity of most of the widely used standardized tests. Although this information is not available for some tests, it is the ethical obligation of the author or publisher to provide accurate data about the test's psychometric properties and information about the norming process. Rating scales, self-concept inventories, and observation systems seldom provide technical information; yet they often are used as part of the selection process. Users of such informal measures have a similar obligation to secure their own reliability estimates through test-retest, split-half, or interrater-interscorer analyses. Knowing the reliability of tests or other assessment procedures allows for estimates of the accuracy of the identification process.

Ceiling Effect and Off-Grade Level Testing

When the form of test for a child's age level is too easy or does not give the child a chance to show the full range of his or her ability, the ceiling effect may be operating. A well known solution to this problem is the procedure called *off-grade level testing*. In this procedure a level of test higher than the child's age or grade level is selected; this is hoped to be sufficiently challenging so that the child will have an opportunity to display the highest level of his or her ability.

Thousands of children now participate in off-grade testing at the middle school or junior high level by taking the Scholastic Aptitude Test, an instrument not ordinarily administered until the junior or senior year of high school (VanTassel-Baska, 1986). Presumably the test will be at such a high level that these younger students will all be able to display their highest levels of ability. Even in this form of radical off-grade testing, however, a few youngsters score at the perfect (800) level. They seemingly need an even higher form of off-grade test to adequately assess their talents and abilities.

When students are given standardized achievement tests at their grade level, those who are very high achievers may score at the 95th percentile or greater and "ceiling effect" may be obscuring their true achievement. Because the child has missed very few test questions to arrive at this score, those errors could have been the result of careless mistakes, computer errors, or an imperfect test form rather than lack of knowledge. A more reliable picture of the child's achievement can be obtained through a sample of more difficult items. Ideally, a well written test in which the child obtains correct scores on only half the items would give a better picture of true achievement.

Current research has been directed at developing an interactive testing process (Nunnally, 1978) that utilizes large numbers of test-bank items. The procedure hinges on choosing items based on the student's performance so that as an item is passed, a more difficult one is presented. Similarly, as a problem is failed, the next easier one is selected for presentation. This results in a shorter test to arrive at the success/challenge level for the student but has the disadvantage of requiring interactive computer resources. Whereas the cost of this procedure once was prohibitive, the proliferation of sophisticated PC hardware and software indicates this will be feasible for all students in the not too distant future. The extremes of the school population represented in gifted and handicapped programs would be major benefactors of this kind of testing program.

Evaluation Procedures

Does the identification process select youth properly? Does it identify boys and girls who need special gifted program services? Will those who are selected do well in the special programs? Will those who are selected go on to high-level success in their life careers? Will they go on to college and to advanced degrees? These are questions we must answer through research, evaluation, and dissemination procedures. Often, the identification process is taken for granted, and educators assume that it is selecting the students who can benefit most from the program.

In reality, the identification process ought to undergo periodic validity evaluation. This should be done to determine if the process is bringing into the program the youth who have need for its services, especially those who will profit and grow as a result of receiving the services, and who will go on to use their potential to achieve at levels commensurate with their superior ability. These procedures involve gathering data concerning performance or achievement of youth in the program and data on students' achievements after they leave the program. Do they go on to college, to graduate training, to advanced degrees, to significant achievement in their fields?

Identification procedures also may fail to bring into the program youth who need its services, who would perform well, and who would achieve high-level success if given the opportunity. A variety of assessment supplements and experimentation can be used to get at this issue, but the problem is not easily dealt with by school personnel. Coordinators of programs, however, should be aware of the situation and attempt to minimize its dangers by vigilance in searching for and assessing potentially gifted youth. The safest error direction is false positive—that is, youth who are selected but really are not qualified. Most programs will not likely harm them. The greatest risk is to be left out when the program may be just the stimulus needed to motivate a student.

91

Performance or Potential?

The process of identifying gifted and talented youth is based primarily on current assessments of how well the youth are performing in tasks relevant to the areas of giftedness and talent. All test procedures are measures of performance; they are not measures of some hidden, innate, or basic capacity. All of the tasks included in intelligence and aptitude tests involve learned behaviors. Nevertheless, two kinds of inference are often made from the tests. First, intelligence test scores sometimes are used as an index to infer innate capacity. Second, test scores such as those yielded by the Scholastic Aptitude Test are considered by some as an indicator or prediction of how well a student will learn or perform some time in the future.

The point to be made is that *all assessments of ability or aptitude are measures of current performance levels* and that their major value is in identifying youth who might profit from special gifted program services and go on to higher-level success and achievement. Interpretation of test scores as representing innate abilities leads to misconceptions of giftedness as fixed and unchanging. Realistically, however, without nurture, abilities may decline, whereas with nurture they may increase. Identifiers of gifted and talented youth must develop an understanding of the nature and uses of ability and aptitude scores and use them properly in the identification process.

Tryout as Identification

The identification process cannot achieve perfect reliability, primarily because it cannot be more reliable than the tests, rating scales, and observation data on which it is based. To counteract the dangers of low reliability in identification procedures, program coordinators should view tryout in programs as an extension of the identification process and offer tryout opportunities to as many borderline youth as possible.

Observation of students' performance in programs can provide valuable supplementary information to assess potential giftedness. Performance or learning in programs is one of the major criteria for evaluating identification predictors. Youth who can perform well in a program are most directly demonstrating one desired criterion for gifted programs. The identification process is a special case of predictive validity that should be tested against the criterion of the program. To the extent that students succeed, we can be sure of good predictive validity.

Karnes (1987) also described a new approach to the identification of gifted youth that combines teacher training that will alert teachers to the characteristics of the gifted and training in how to structure classroom activities that optimize the opportunity for potentially gifted youth to demonstrate their talent or ability. The system is particularly effective in identifying gifted youth from culturally different backgrounds.

The Nature of Giftedness

Parents and teachers often erroneously believe that administration of tests and other measures will result in explicit identification of youth as gifted and talented, or not gifted. Gifted youth often are perceived as categorically different human beings, much like our classification of those who have diseases or handicaps. Thus, parents and teachers have been heard to ask if a particular child who seems to be precocious or bright is "really and truly gifted." The question seems to imply that some individuals are geniuses, others are pseudogifted, and if tested, rated, and observed properly, a gifted child will be clearly seen as gifted.

In truth, all types of giftedness and talent correspond to psychological characteristics and abilities that are continuous variables. The characteristics exist at some level in all human beings; they vary in intensity or level in each; and the abilities differ within each gifted individual. Thus, all living persons have some level of intelligence, as well as some adaptability, some ability in numerical or quantitative operations, and some ability for reasoning.

But some youth can reason rapidly and accurately with complex, abstract material, whereas others have limited reasoning capacity, can deal only with simple, concrete material, and are slow in reasoning. Furthermore, some youth have high mathematical reasoning ability but limited ability in verbal reasoning tasks, and vice versa. They differ in levels of different abilities within themselves. The identification process must take these conditions into account.

In a major national survey of identification procedures in the United States, Richert, Alvino, and McDonnel (1982), found widespread variability from city to city in the tests used, the cutting levels, and the general process of identification. Thus, definitions vary, and we should recognize that giftedness is a varying concept.

Proposed Identification Procedures

Procedures for identifying the gifted and talented must be closely linked to the nature of the program services, as discussed earlier in this chapter. Talents differ, assessment procedures differ, and different program services minister to different talents. In the broadest sense, elementary program services differ in their mathematical, verbal, and artistic orientation. Later, as youth move into junior high and high school, talents become quite specialized in science, mathematics, languages, literature, social studies, music, art, dance, and so on (Saunders, 1982). The identification process must increasingly recognize specialization of talent and fine-tune the identification process to fit the talent domain of a potentially gifted youth.

Here, for example, is the set of scores used to identify the gifted for an honors English class in a middle school:

1. The Purdue Academic Rating Scale for English
2. The Cognitive Abilities Test Verbal Score
3. A teacher recommendation
4. The total language score from the Iowa Test of Basic Skills
5. A grade average from previous language arts courses

But the set of selection tests for the honors mathematics class (algebra in seventh or eighth grade) is as follows:

1. The Purdue Academic Rating Scale for mathematics
2. A teacher recommendation
3. The Cognitive Abilities Test quantitative score
4. The total mathematics score for the Iowa Test of Basic Skills
5. A grade average from previous math courses

Nomination/Screening

The initial stage of identification may consist simply of a call for informal nominations. Parents, teachers, counselors, and gifted youth may be invited to submit the names of students they view as gifted or talented. Tables 7.1, 7.3, 7.4, and 7.5 present illustrative nomination forms to be completed by parents, the student him- or herself, peers, and teachers. Before requesting nominations, inservice workshops concerning the nature and characteristics of the gifted and talented are desirable for teachers, so that they will have an accurate understanding of the type of youth being sought (Borland, 1978). Rating scales also can provide guidance to nominators by focusing on salient characteristics of nominees. Rating scales, however, often are not used until a second stage, after initial nomination procedures have been completed and have generated a pool for further assessment.

Further screening can be carried out through examination of available test scores in school files. IQ, reading readiness, and standardized achievement tests are typically found in the files. An inspection of those files can serve to identify students in the top 5%–10%. These names, along with the file scores, can be added to the existing list of nominees.

The processes of securing nominations from relevant persons and from school files yield a list of nominees, many of whom are mentioned repeatedly. A particular child might be nominated by two teachers, the parents, and a counselor, as well as by high IQ and achievement test scores. The greater the number of nomination sources, the greater is our confidence that a youth is indeed talented and merits further consideration. If resources permit, however, all youth who have at least one nomination source should be assessed.

TABLE 7.3
Student Self-Nomination Form

Name _____ Date _____

Address _____ Grade _____

_____

Phone ( ) _____ Birthdate _____

1. In what areas do you have special talent or ability?

2. In which subjects or courses do you do superior work?

3. What are the areas, topics, or activities in which you have special or strong interests?

4. Describe a project, product, or performance that you have done or created in which you excelled.

5. How many hours per week do you spend in voluntary reading?

6. What are your areas of special interest in reading?

7. Why do you want to be in the special program?

Students in our special program are expected to strive for excellence in all their work and to work harder than they normally do in regular classes. If you agree with this expectation, sign your name below.

_____
Name

TABLE 7.4
Peer Nomination Form

1. Who are some kids who always seem to have a lot of good ideas?

2. Who are some kids who can write really good stories or scripts?

3. Who are some kids who seem to come up with far-out, crazy, or very unusual ideas?

4. Who are some kids who draw really well?

5. Who are some kids who are really good logical thinkers?

6. Who are some kids who are really good at solving problems?

7. Who are some kids who really do good work in science?

TABLE 7.5
Teacher Nomination Form

Student's Name _____ Grade _____

Teacher's Name _____ Date _____

1. What are some things you have observed in this student's behavior or school work that lead you to believe that he/she should be in a special program for high-ability children?

2. What problems, if any, is he/she having in school as a result of the high ability?

3. Describe briefly the student's reading habits, patterns, and levels.

4. Describe briefly the student's major interests, hobbies, art activities, and so on.

5. Describe any special projects or studies this student has done (if not covered in number 4).

6. Please give any other information about this student that you believe is relevant to his/her abilities or interests.

Assessment

The next stage in the identification process is to secure additional information that will aid in determining the youth's talents or giftedness and his or her fit with particular services. Tests, rating scales, and other observations should be selected to match the potential abilities of the youth and the nature of the program services.

For a pullout program in which students will receive instruction related to the language arts, creativity, research, and independent study, the following data might logically be secured:

1. Language arts standardized achievement test scores
2. Teacher ratings of the child's reading and writing skills
3. Motivation assessment using the motivation scale developed as part of the scales for Rating the Behavioral Characteristics of Superior Students (Renzulli, Smith, White, Callahan, & Hartman, 1976).
4. Creativity assessment, using the Torrance Tests of Creative Thinking (1974).

For a leadership and personal-social development program, the following data might be secured:

1. A self-concept scale
2. Leadership assessment using the leadership scale developed by Renzulli et al. (1976) as part of the Scales for Rating the Behavioral Characteristics of Superior Students
3. IQ from a group test
4. Sociogram information

For an accelerated mathematics program, the following three items might be particularly applicable:

1. Mathematics achievement test scores
2. Grade average in previous mathematics courses
3. Rating on the Purdue Academic Rating Scale for mathematics

The Purdue Academic Rating Scales (Feldhusen, Hoover, & Sayler, 1987)* are a series of five rating scales, each consisting of 15 items, focusing on signs of superior academic performance in mathematics, science, English, social studies, and foreign languages. The scales were designed for the identification of secondary students for honors, Advanced Placement, seminar, and accelerated classes.

Assessment should typically focus within two or more of the four domains of psychological functioning that relate to giftedness: (1) talents and abilities, (2) creative capacity, (3) self-concept, and (4) motivation. Test instruments are used to assess many talents and abilities, but some talents, especially in the arts, are typically assessed through expert judgment of students' performance or products. Creative capacity may be assessed using test instruments or rating scales. Self-concept usually is assessed using self-rating inventories such as the Piers-Harris (1969) Children's Self-Concept Scale or the ME scale (Feldhusen & Kolloff, 1981). Motivation can be rated with one of the Renzulli scales (Renzulli et al., 1976), or it can be inferred from achievements or products that the nominee has produced.

Assessment of intelligence is often carried out with children at the elementary school level with the Wechsler Intelligence Scale for Children–Revised (Wechsler, 1974) or the Stanford-Binet Intelligence Scale (Thorndike, Hagen, & Sattler, 1986). Assessment of general intelligence is the most appropriate with children at the early childhood, primary, and upper grade levels in cases in which the program is a broad, general instructional service. Intelligence tests also are used in making decisions concerning early admission or grade advancement.

Valuable assessment information also can be secured through interviews and from essays written by nominees. From essays, inferences can be drawn concerning writing skills, interests, and motivation. Essays were used in a career education

---

Available for use in schools without charge from the Purdue Gifted Education Resource Institute, Purdue University, SCC-G, West Lafayette, IN 47907.

97

project for the gifted (Moore, Feldhusen, & Owings, 1978) to assess the motivation and goals of nominees. They were asked to write a paper setting forth their own short- and long-range personal goals. In the same project, nominees were interviewed to assess their oral verbal abilities, social poise, and motivation/ enthusiasm.

One school uses the following interview questions to assess gifted students' readiness to participate profitably in elementary, full-time, self-contained gifted classes:

1. Tell me about your reading. How much time do you spend in voluntary reading each day? Do you like to read? What are your favorite books?
2. Do you like to work hard and study hard in school? Do you like to do homework? Have you got a lot of energy? Do you like to work on one project a long time?
3. Do you get a lot of good ideas? Do you get unusual or "far out" ideas? Do you like to write your ideas?
4. What hobbies do you have? Do you like to do projects? Do you have collections? Have you got a lot of interests?
5. Do you like to work with kids who have a lot of good ideas? Who are good thinkers? Who can solve problems easily and quickly?
6. What are your major goals in school? What do you want to accomplish? What do you want to do when you finish school?

Combining Data

All the data from tests, rating scales, product assessment, interviews, and the like should be drawn together into a folder for each nominee. Scores relevant to a particular program service for which a nominee is being considered should be standardized, preferably by conversion to T scores. They then can be added together, weighted (if there is a rationale for increasing or reducing the power of each score in the combination), and a total score derived. Feldhusen, Baska, and Womble (1981) have offered a detailed plan for combining standardized scores.

In some instances, program assignments might be made on the basis of a single test score. For example, children may be selected for an accelerated mathematics program on the basis of the mathematics score from the Scholastic Aptitude Test. In this case, the single score is highly relevant to the area of program service.

Diagnostic-Assessment Committee

Final decision making and selection of youth for program services should be a professional judgment. It should be dictated neither by a test score alone nor by some total or combination score. The cutoff level can be established, and for youth who score well above that level, the committee's decision may be perfunctory. For all the scores that are lower than the cutoff level, but within the standard error of measurement for these scales, committee judgment is necessary. In reaching a decision, the committee can take into account any other possibly relevant information. Although relatively subjective, the committee's decision nevertheless should be based on sound professional judgment with due regard to the potential errors or lack of reliability in all the assessment-identification procedures.

In some instances, the committee should be able to make a decision for tryout of a possibly gifted youth in a program service. This is often the case when youth are being selected for early admission or grade advancement. When doubt or uncertainty exists, the trial period should determine if the student can handle the demands of the new assignment and profit from the experience.

Continuing Student Evaluation as Identification

Students who have been placed in a program service (for example, a full-time self-contained class, a pullout program, an accelerated math class, an Advanced Placement [College Board, 1983] class, or a future problem-solving program) should be evaluated periodically to determine their progress and ascertain if the identification decision was sound. Are the students progressing well? Does the service meet some of their needs? The diagnostic-identification committee should receive this type of information periodically (for example, every 6 to 9 weeks), and the committee should make decisions concerning the desirability of a gifted youth's continuation in the program, withdrawal, or reassignment to another program service.

Repeated evaluation to determine if a child is gifted or not seems to be of little value. The critical issue is determining if the child has continuing special educational needs that cannot be served in a regular classroom and whether the special program service is meeting those needs.

Summary

The purpose of the identification process in gifted education is to identify youth whose abilities, motivation, self-concept, interests, and creative talents are so much greater than average that special education program services are needed to meet their needs. All youth have a right to educational programs that will help them achieve their highest potential. Program services for the gifted should be designed to fit each child's unique characteristics and needs. Because parents know their own children better than anyone else, their input should be a vital part of the identification process.

Identification is really a continuing effort. It should not be viewed as a one-time assessment. Children's performance in a program should be used to verify or contradict the results of tests and rating scales. Reliability and validity of the tests and rating scales are crucial to the process. Giftedness is not a unique diagnostic category; rather, it denotes children whose abilities are markedly higher but not fundamentally different from other children.

In practice, identification of the gifted begins with a nomination/screening process that seeks to find all possibly gifted youth. An assessment process should follow in which various measures are secured to determine the levels of a youth's special talents and abilities. After all the data have been gathered, a diagnostic-assessment committee should review the data, determine whether each nominee has special needs because of the superior talent or ability, and suggest appropriate educational service. Programs for gifted students should consist of a variety of services that can be used selectively to fit their special characteristics and needs.

At the secondary level, identification really becomes a selection process. Gifted youth may have been generally identified to become part of a talent pool, but with regard to assignment to specific program services such as an honors class or a seminar, specific selection criteria should be used to identify youth qualified for the class.

References

Alvino, J., McDonnel, R. C., & Richert, S. (1981). National survey of identification practices in gifted and talented education. *Exceptional Children, 48*, 124–132.

ASSETS. (1979). *User's guide to A.S.S.E.T.S.* Holmes Beach, FL: Learning Publications.

Baldwin, A. Y. (1978). The Baldwin identification matrix. In A. Baldwin, G. Gear, & L. Lucito (Eds.), *Educational planning for the gifted*. Reston, VA: Council for Exceptional Children.

Bloom, B. S. (1982). The role of gifts and markers in the development of talent. *Exceptional Children, 48*(6), 510–522.

Borland, J. (1978). Teacher identification of the gifted. *Journal for the Education of the Gifted, 2*, 22–32.

Brandwein, P. R. (1980). On the search for the gifted. *Roeper Review, 3*, 2–3.

College Board. (1983). *A guide to the advanced placement program*. New York: Author.

College Board. (no date). *10 SATs: Scholastic Aptitude Tests of the College Board*. New York: Author.

Feldhusen, J. F., Asher, J. W., & Hoover, S. M. (1984). Problems in the identification of giftedness, talent or ability. *Gifted Child Quarterly, 28*, 149—n-156.

Feldhusen, J. F., Baska, L. K., & Womble, S. R. (1981). Using standard scores to synthesize data in identifying the gifted. *Journal for the Education of the Gifted, 4*, 177–185.

Feldhusen, J. F., Hoover, S. M., & Sayler, M. B. (1987). *The Purdue Academic Rating Scales*. Paper presented at the annual convention of the National Association for Gifted Children, New Orleans.

Feldhusen, J. F., Asher, J. W., & Hoover, S. M. (1984). Problems in the identification of giftedness, talent or ability. *Gifted Child Quarterly, 28*, 149–156.

Feldman, D. H. (1979). The mysterious case of extreme giftedness. In A. H. Passow (Ed.), *The gifted and the talented: Their education and development* (78th yearbook of the National Society for the Study of Education)(pp. 335–351). Chicago: University of Chicago Press.

Feldman, D. H. (1986). *Nature's gambit*. New York: Basic Books.

Flack, J. D., & Feldhusen, J. F. (1983). Future studies in the curricular framework of the Purdue three-stage model. *G/C/T, 27*, 1–9.

Hoover, S. M., & Feldhusen, J. F. (1987). Integration, identification, school services, and student needs in secondary gifted programs. *Arkansas Gifted Educators' Magazine, 1*, 8–16.

Karnes, M. L. (1987). Bringing out Head Start talents: Findings from the field. *Gifted Child Quarterly, 31*(4), 174–179.

Keating, D. P. (1979). Secondary school programs. In A. H. Passow (Ed.), *The gifted and the talented: Their education and development* (78th yearbook of the National Society for the Study of Education, Part 1)(pp. 186–198). Chicago: University of Chicago Press.

Mitchell, J. V. (1985). *The ninth mental measurements yearbook*. Lincoln, NE: Buros Institute of Mental Measurements of the University of Nebraska–Lincoln.

Moore, B. A., Feldhusen, J. F., & Owings, J. (1978). *Professional career exploration program for minority and/or low income gifted and talented high school students*. West Lafayette, IN: Purdue University, Education Department.

Nunnally, J. C. (1978). *Psychometric theory* (p. 248). New York: McGraw-Hill.

Piers, E. V., & Harris, D. B. (1969). *The Piers-Harris children's self-concept scale*. Nashville, TN: Counselor Recordings & Tests.

Renzulli, J. S., Smith, L. H., White, A. J., Callahan, C. M., & Hartman, R. K. (1976). *Scales for rating the behavioral characteristics of superior students*. Wethersfield, CT: Creative Learning Press.

Richert, E. S., Alvino, J. J., & McDonnel, R. C. (1982). *National report on identification*. Sewell, NJ: Educational Improvement Center—South.

Saunders, R. J. (1982). Screening and identifying the talented in art. *Roeper Review, 4*, 7–10.

Sawyer, R. N. (1982). The Duke University program to identify and educate brilliant young students. *Journal for the Education of the Gifted, 5*, 185–189.

Terman, L., & Merrill, M. (1973). *Stanford-Binet intelligence scale*. Boston: Houghton Mifflin.

Thorndike, R. L., Hagen, E. P., & Sattler, J. M. (1986). *The Stanford-Binet intelligence scale (4th ed.). Technical manual*. New York: Riverside.

Torrance, E. P. (1974). *Torrance tests of creative thinking*. Bensenville, IL: Scholastic Testing Service.

VanTassel-Baska, J. (1986). The use of aptitude tests for identifying the gifted. *Roeper Review, 8*(3), 185–189.

Wechsler, D. (1974). *Wechsler intelligence scale for children—Revised*. New York: Psychological Corp.

Study Questions

1. What are major sources of information that should be tapped in identifying gifted and talented youth?

2. What is meant by reliability of test scores?

3. What is ceiling effect? Off-grade testing?

4. When we identify gifted youth, are we assessing accomplishment or potential?

5. What is giftedness?

6. What sources of information would you use to identify gifted and talented youth?

7. Why would interviews be useful in identifying the gifted and talented?

8. Is identification of the gifted and talented a one-time process? Why or why not?

Section Two

PROGRAM DEVELOPMENT

8

Program Models for Gifted Education

John F. Feldhusen

Programs are alternative administrative structures for bringing curriculum and instruction to gifted youth (J. F. Feldhusen, 1986b). These structures do not properly constitute a delivery system, for that implies the curriculum is simply a body of skills and knowledge imposed upon gifted youth. Rather, the curriculum might best be viewed as an organized set of skills and content that gifted youth can experience or interact with generatively to develop their own knowledge schemas, understandings, and skills (VanTassel-Baska, Feldhusen, Seeley, Wheatley, Silverman, & Foster, 1988). The program model is the system that facilitates interaction of gifted youth with curriculum to produce learning.

All learning occurs within planned or unplanned environments. If the environment is planned, it is a part of the program model (Maker, 1982). *All* learning yields products, at least in the sense that learning always implies a residual effect that enables a learner to behave (cognitively, verbally, socially, emotionally) in some new way. Of course, the concept of product advocated by Maker (1982) and Renzulli and Reis (1986) is a concrete entity that results from the research and project activity of gifted youth. Whatever the product residual, the learning activities that result in products are a part of the program model.

Programs for the gifted may be designed to speed up the delivery of content, to deliver more content, to examine content in greater depth, or to deal with more complex and higher levels of subject matter. All of these approaches are essentially *accelerative* in nature and are based on efforts to fit instruction to the precocity of the gifted student. Programs for the gifted also may seek to provide alternatives that will *enrich* the learning experiences of gifted youth and allow them to study topics that fit their interests. Enrichment programs often seek to keep gifted children in subject matter appropriate to their grade level but to allow study and investigation of supplementary content. Still other programs attempt to provide instruction that individually and explicitly fits the achievement levels, ability, interests, and learning style of the gifted student. This last approach is called "diagnostic prescriptive" by VanTassel-Baska et al. (1988) or an "individually prescribed" program model by Treffinger (1986). Perhaps the best overall approach to programming for the gifted will be a combination of these three approaches.

My concern in this chapter is to consider program arrangements and organized models to help gifted youth achieve the goals and objectives of the curriculum. I will begin the discussion at the elementary level.

Elementary Program Models

Enrichment

There are systematic program models such as the Enrichment Triad/Revolving Door Model advanced by Renzulli and Reis (1986), the Individualized Program Planning Model (IPPM) of Treffinger (1986), the Purdue Three-Stage Model advocated by Feldhusen and Kolloff (1979, 1986) and the Autonomous Learner Model presented by Betts (1986). All of these models provide relatively comprehensive plans for identification and program services for gifted children that are essentially enriching in nature. They were selected for description here because they are illustrative of a large number of models that seek to enrich learning experiences for gifted youth.

The Renzulli model is possibly the most comprehensive in its extensive treatment of identification, administration, staff training, and program delivery structure (Renzulli & Reis, 1986). There are three types of program experience.

1. Type I enrichment involves general exploratory experiences, which expose students to "new and exciting topics, ideas and fields of knowledge that are not covered in the regular curriculum" (p. 237). The actual activities include field trips, speakers, learning centers, readings, audiovisual materials, minicourses, museum programs, artistic performances, and so forth. Some Type I activities are offered to all children.

106

2. Type II enrichment, group training activities, consists of activities designed to develop cognitive and affective processes. The activities are offered to all children, not just the gifted.
3. Type III enrichment calls for individual and small-group investigations of real problems. Special identification procedures are used to select children for Type III enrichment—especially what is called "action information," or overt behavior of the child that reflects current interests, motivation, or behavior related to a specific topic or project. Type III enrichment activities usually are carried out in a special resource room and directed by a special resource teacher who is trained to work with gifted youth.

The Treffinger (1986) IPPM model stresses intensive use of information gathered during the identification process to plan individualized programs of study for the gifted based on their talents, strengths, and interests. The model also intends to develop independence and self-direction skills in the gifted. IPPM focuses attention on how to deal with or provide for the gifted in regular classrooms. Treffinger presented a wide variety of potential program services for the gifted. In this model, the entire staff receives intensive training to learn how best to provide for the diverse needs of the gifted.

The Purdue Three-Stage Model developed by Feldhusen and Kolloff (1979, 1986) is essentially an enrichment model, most often delivered as a pullout program. The three-stage model is implemented in many schools as the Program for Academic and Creative Enrichment (PACE) (Kolloff & Feldhusen, 1981). The model is implemented in resource rooms with small groups of 8 to 15 gifted children. At stage one, the children follow a curriculum focusing on thinking skills and basic subject matter content, meeting at least 2 periods a week and preferably 1 full day a week. The thinking skills and content should be taught at a high level and fast pace appropriate for the gifted.

At stage two, broader and more realistic strategies are taught. These include library skills, creative problem solving, future studies, and research skills, all of which pave the way to stage three activities, which are project-oriented applications in students' areas of personal interest. At stage three, students work on research projects and developmental tasks, and these efforts result in presentations, products, or performances. Stage three simulates real-life creative productivity.

The Antonomous Learner Model developed by Betts (1986) attempts to meet the academic, social, and emotional needs of the gifted while setting the goal of independence or autonomy so that the gifted will become responsible for their own learning. It probably is best characterized as an enrichment model. The model offers time for (1) orientation to the self as a gifted person and to program opportunities; (2) enrichment activities such as investigations, cultural activities, and field trips; (3) seminars on futurism, problems, and controversial issues; (4) individual development of learning skills, career knowledge, and interpersonal

107

abilities; and (5) in-depth study in individual and group projects and mentorships. This model is particularly strong in its focus on individual or personal development of gifted students.

Individualization

When pullout models are used, the danger is that the gifted child will languish and lose motivation in the regular classroom because all or most of the activities are too low-level or slow-paced. All children learn best when learning contains challenge and offers success. Thus, if the gifted are served in a regular classroom, instruction must be individualized and thereby adjusted to their skill levels (H. J. Feldhusen, 1986) or cluster grouping should be used to bring all the gifted together from several rooms at a grade level into one room with a teacher who is willing to differentiate instruction to fit the level and pace of the cluster while also dealing with all of the children at differing levels of ability in the classroom. A cluster usually consists of three to seven children in an otherwise heterogeneous classroom.

In the cluster group or individualized approaches, the use of individualized educational programs (IEPs) (Feldhusen, 1986a), developed cooperatively by the gifted coordinator and the regular classroom teacher, can be a useful mechanism to induce specific planning and teaching activities appropriate for the gifted. Regular classroom teachers need special inservice preparation to learn how to assess children's level of abilities in the different subjects, eliminate or reduce activities the gifted already know, and plan for higher level and faster paced instruction.

Acceleration

Some gifted children are so far advanced in their basic skills and knowledge that acceleration to a higher grade level is necessary (VanTassel-Baska, 1986). After reviewing the literature on early admission of precocious children to school, Proctor, Black, and Feldhusen (1986) concluded that early admission is desirable for many gifted children. Many gifted children have reading skills or numbers ability (or both) before they enter school. They should be admitted to kindergarten or first grade ahead of schedule. Research indicates that if they are carefully screened and evaluated, they will thrive on the accelerated school learning experience.

Feldhusen, Proctor, and Black (1986) also presented guidelines for grade advancement of precocious children. From a comprehensive review of the research on grade advancement, and personal experiences in consulting on grade advancement cases, the authors concluded that failure to advance children who are ready may be harmful to children's social-emotional-academic development. Those authors presented guidelines for decision making in grade advancement case studies, which include the following steps:

1. A comprehensive psychological evaluation of the child's intellectual functioning, academic skill levels, and social-emotional adjustment should be conducted by a psychologist.
2. Intellectually, the child should have an IQ of 125 or greater or have a level of mental development greater than the mean for the grade he or she desires to enter.
3. Academically, the child should demonstrate skill levels greater than the mean of the grade desired. If the child is high in several skill levels but low in only one, the child may be advanced to the appropriate grade if private tutoring is provided in the area of weakness.
4. Socially and emotionally, the child should be free of any serious adjustment problems. In specific cases, however, serious adjustment problems may result from inappropriately low grade placement. In such cases, the problem may be alleviated by grade advancement.
5. Physically, the child should be in good health. The child's size should be considered only to the extent that competitive sports may be viewed as important in later years.
6. The psychologist should determine that the child does *not* feel unduly pressured by the parents to advance. The parents must be in favor of grade advancement, but the child should express the desire to move ahead.
7. The receiving teacher or teachers must have positive attitudes toward the acceleration and be willing to help the child adjust to the new situation. If a receiving teacher is hostile or pessimistic, another receiving teacher should be located or the move should not be made.
8. Public school teachers are sometimes unduly pessimistic about children's social-emotional maturity. They might confuse a precocious child's misbehavior, which is caused by dissatisfaction with inappropriate instruction, with immaturity. Judgments about a precocious child's maturity therefore should include input from parents and the psychologist.
9. Midyear and year-end grade advancements appear to be equally successful. Midyear advancements may be more desirable because the teachers may more easily confer about how best to help the child make a smooth transition.
10. All cases of grade advancement should be arranged on a trial basis. A trial period of 6 weeks should be sufficient. The child should be aware that if it does not go well, he or she may ask to be returned to the original grade.
11. Care should be exercised not to build up excessive expectations from grade advancement. The child should not be made to feel he or she is a failure if it does not go well. Alternatively, some precocious children are so advanced in their intellectual and academic skills that one year of advancement may still leave them bored in school. For a very few precocious children, additional advancements may be necessary.

12. Grade advancement decisions should be made by a committee consisting of an administrator, a teacher, and a counselor or school psychologist. Examination of the research literature reveals that acceleration contributes to academic achievement. No negative effects on social or emotional development have been identified. If adjustment problems occur, they tend to be minor and temporary in nature. Conversely, failure to advance a precocious child may result in poor study habits, apathy, lack of motivation, and maladjustment.

Serving the Gifted in Regular Classrooms

Many gifted children will remain in the regular classroom and receive no special instruction of any kind. I believe that the model set forth by H. J. Feldhusen (1986) offers regular classroom teachers clear guidelines for differentiating instruction for gifted children while serving all children well. The model emphasizes the following:

1. Frequent evaluation of performance levels in basic skills areas
2. Extensive use of a variety of individualized instructional materials that permit individual progress
3. Daily planning by children of their appropriate learning activities
4. Instructional units and learning centers in which students can access materials by themselves
5. Effective record keeping that permits a teacher to monitor each student's progress
6. Instructional emphasis on teaching children to be independent and self-directing
7. Cluster seating to encourage cooperative learning among children

H. J. Feldhusen (1981) evaluated her model while it was being developed and found it to be effective in producing higher levels of achievement, favorable attitudes, and good motivation in gifted children.

Special, Full-Time, Self-Contained Classes for the Gifted

The gifted thrive best, learn best, in special classes where they are together on a daily basis for all or most of the school day. In many schools that do offer special classes for the gifted, these children are mixed for art, music, physical education, and playground (recess) to facilitate social interaction among children of all ability levels. Feldhusen and Treffinger (1985) noted a growing interest in special classes

110

for the gifted because pullout models often fail to meet their academic needs. Special classes are also more cost-effective. Pullout classes always involve added cost, but special classes simply involve regrouping a gifted group into a class of typical size for the school, and one teacher serves them just as one teacher would serve a mixed group of the same number of students.

After surveying programs for the gifted in U.S. schools, Cox, Daniel, and Boston (1985) concluded that pullout classes are often weak and ineffective. They called for stronger offerings such as special classes, especially for the highly gifted. Belcastro (1987) also presented a substantial argument concerning the weaknesses of enrichment and pullout program models by asserting that they often fail to meet the basic needs of the gifted, which is instruction at an appropriate pace and level.

Other Options

A variety of other options such as the following are offered at the elementary level as special services for gifted and talented children:

- Special computer classes
- Junior Great Books
- Future problem solving
- Foreign languages
- Mentors
- After school, Saturday, and summer enrichment classes
- Special classes in art, music, and dance

All of these options can be of value to gifted and talented students if the options are taught at a sufficiently high level and pace to constitute a real challenge. If the gifted return to regular classes taught at the normative level and pace for all students, however, they will languish, learn how to get by without effort, or become systematically demotivated toward school learning. Thus, the crucial problem is how to provide appropriate, challenging learning experiences for the gifted at the elementary level on a daily basis in basic subjects matter as well as in the supplementary learning experiences.

Secondary Program Models

By the time gifted youth reach middle school, junior high, or high school, many have found their areas of special talent or strength (Keating, 1979) in addition to their general levels of giftedness or intelligence. Thus, programming at the secondary level must provide for special talents and aptitudes as well as for the general

111

precocity of gifted youth. Furthermore, because their social and emotional development differs from the norm for youth of average or low ability, special types of counseling service may be needed. Table 8.1 presents a variety of options for middle school and high school programs, and Figure 8.1 enumerates the basic components that should be considered for all gifted programs (Feldhusen & Reilly, 1983; Feldhusen & Robinson, 1986). This is an eclectic program model recognizing that among gifted youth at the secondary level a variety of needs, talents, characteristics, and levels of ability calls for differing programs services.

Eclectic Program Model

Counseling Services

The eclectic model presented in Figure 8.1 begins in box 1 by focusing on the role of the counselor, whose assistance is needed in identifying the special talents or

TABLE 8.1
Gifted Program Services

Junior High or Middle School Services	High School Services
Counseling	Counseling
Group	Group
Individual	Individual
Honors classes	Honors classes
Future problem solving	Advanced Placement classes
Junior Great Books	Foreign languages
Odyssey of The Mind	Seminars
Career education	Mentorships
Seminars	Internships
Mentors	Concurrent college enrollment
AP or college classes	College classes in high school
Acceleration	Special opportunities in
Math	Art
Science	Music
English	Drama
Special Opportunities	Dance
Art	Special projects for the
Music	vocationally talented
Drama	Debate
Dance	Correspondence study
Special projects for	Independent study
vocationally talented	
Foreign language	
Correspondence study	
Independent study	

112

aptitudes of gifted youth and in playing several counseling roles. Galbraith (1984) suggested that the gifted and talented have special areas of social-emotional concern, such as understanding their own giftedness and talents, dealing with parents' and friends' expectations, coping with feelings of being different, clarifying attitudes and values, and developing peer social relationships that accommodate giftedness. A major role proposed for counselors is to conduct small-group sessions to help gifted youth understand their abilities and deal with special problems of being gifted (VanTassel-Baska, 1983). Counselors also can play roles in career education and mentoring services (box 5) for the gifted. They also may assist in selecting gifted youth for special Advanced Placement (AP) or honors classes.

Advanced Placement and Honors Classes

Boxes 2 and 3 point to Advanced Placement (Colleg Board, 1983) and honors classes as desirable program services for gifted youth. Ideally, such classes are taught by teachers who know the discipline well at advanced levels and who know how to differentiate for the gifted. In practice, however, these classes often are taught by teachers who vary instruction only to the extent of increasing the amount of homework and imposing a more severe grading standard than would be used in regular classes. Thus, in such schools gifted youth often avoid these special classes or are persuaded to enroll only because a grade weighting system is in use. Ideally, AP and honors classes should do the following:

1. Focus on the issues, problems, major concepts, or themes that characterize the discipline
2. Involve much discussion, debate, small group work, and active involvement of students with the content
3. Operate at an accelerated level and pace
4. Help students learn to think more effectively at advanced levels
5. Develop a deep intrinsic motivation for learning
6. Help students develop well-organized structures or knowledge bases in the discipline

Most secondary teachers need special training through inservice or courses to learn how to teach AP or honors classes well.

Seminars

Seminars for the gifted (box 4) are conducted in many high schools. Kolloff and Feldhusen (1986) described a number of seminar programs operating in schools in the Midwest and listed the following as characteristics of the seminar:

113

FIGURE 8.1
An Eclectic Program Model for Secondary Level Gifted

1. Counseling Services

   1. Talent identification
   2. Education counseling
   3. Career counseling
   4. Personal counseling

2. Advanced Placement Classes

   1. Open to students in top 10%
   2. Grades 9-12

3. Honors classes

   1. English
   2. Social studies
   3. Biology

4. Seminars

   1. In-depth study
   2. Self-selected topics
   3. Career education
   4. Affective activities
   5. Thinking, research, and library skills
   6. Presentations

5. Career Education

   1. Mentors
   2. Seminar experience
      A. Study of careers
      B. Study of self
      C. Educational plans

6. Acceleration

1. Begin algebra grade 7
2. Enroll in English and social studies courses early
3. Open science courses to early admission

7. The Arts

1. Art
2. Drama
3. Music
4. Dance

8. Extraschool Learning Experiences

1. Saturday school
2. Summer classes
3. Correspondence study

9. Extraschool Cultural Experiences

1. Concerts, plays, exhibits
2. Field trips
3. Museum programs

10. Foreign Languages

1. Latin or Greek
2. French or Spanish
3. German or Oriental

11. Vocational Programs

1. Home economics
2. Agriculture
3. Business
4. Industrial arts

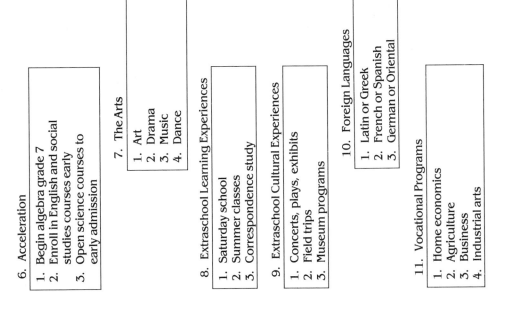

1. An organized, regularly scheduled class
2. Much time for discussion, small group work, and student presentations
3. A focus on a theme or concept, when relevant
4. A goal of teaching thinking skills, library skills, research skills
5. A focus, when relevant, on personal-social development and understanding of giftedness
6. In-depth projects
7. Incorporation of career education, when appropriate
8. Incorporation of art and cultural experiences

Career Education

Career education (box 5) for the gifted helps them come to understand their own career potentials, talents, abilities, and limitations; to know better the nature and demands of higher level occupations; and to know the educational routes to and requirements for selected occupations (Feldhusen & Kolloff, 1979; Hoyt & Hebeler, 1974; Moore, Feldhusen, & Owings, 1978). Career education for the gifted may consist of classroom experiences exploring self, occupational specifications, and educational programs leading to the occupations. It also may offer mentoring experiences (Ellingson, Haeger, & Feldhusen, 1986), which provide more explicit and intimate experiences related to target occupations.

By way of example, one gifted student is working with an attorney mentor at a law firm, another spends time with a professional in a welfare agency, and a third works with a university professor of astronomy. These students get a close look at the professional life as well as the related lifestyle of the mentor and thereby have a better information base on which to make career goal and educational decisions.

Acceleration

Special acceleration opportunities (box 6) to higher level courses in mathematics and science are especially important for precocious youth, but similar acceleration to advanced classes in English and social studies also may be desirable to provide appropriate challenges (Feldhusen, 1983; Stanley, 1979; VanTassel-Baska, 1986). Thus, a seventh grader might be taking algebra, a ninth grader taking English literature, a tenth grader enrolled in the chemistry course, and an eighth grader taking world history. I wish, of course, that the classes to which a gifted youth is accelerated would be taught following the foregoing guidelines for differentiation, which might be possible in larger high schools where special accelerated groups can be organized. But in most schools the gifted student simply moves into a normal class taught in no special way and is mixed with students of average ability (albeit at a higher developmental level). Thus, seventh-grade Ronald is taking algebra with ninth graders who are of average and high ability. Nevertheless, this acceleration can provide greater challenge and a learning experience closer to the gifted youth's readiness level (Benbow & Stanley, 1983).

The Arts

Box 7 calls for special opportunities for gifted and talented youth in the arts and for intellectually gifted youth who are not destined for high-level careers in the arts but who wish to pursue competence in an art form avocationally. Several different models are being developed in connection with gifted programs to assure advanced art experiences for the gifted and talented (Clark & Zimmerman, 1984, 1987). Larger cities such as New Orleans offer special schools for the artistically talented; others offer school-within-a-school approaches in which artistic experiences are offered on a part-time basis. The major goal is to assure that art opportunities are not relegated to a secondary or nonexistent status while academic and intellectual program services predominate.

Extraschool Learning

Box 8 suggests that programming for the gifted should include extraschool or beyond-school learning experiences. Counselors or program coordinators should lead in the effort to guide gifted youth to these experiences. Saturday programs are widely available (Feldhusen & Sokol, 1982), as are summer programs (Feldhusen & Clinkenbeard, 1982). For secondary gifted youth, the Saturday and summer programs at Purdue University offer opportunities to take advanced high school and college-level courses. These experiences give gifted youth special opportunities to get into challenging learning experiences and areas of special interest and to associate with other precocious youth.

Extraschool Culture

The next area, extraschool cultural experience (box 9), also calls for guidance from school counselors or gifted program coordinators. Eisner (1985) argued that through aesthetic and cultural experiences we do more than simply enjoy or re-create; we come to know or understand the world around us better. Early introduction to aesthetic and cultural experience establishes receptivity to and enthusiasm for them in gifted youth. These extracurricular activities include going to concerts, plays, art exhibits, historical restorations, museum programs, and then having an opportunity to discuss them. A group of gifted youth who had attended a play had

117

an opportunity to discuss the drama with the cast following the performance. Other gifted programs provide the discussion experience before and after the cultural experience in a seminar-like setting.

Foreign Languages

Foreign language learning (box 10) also provides invaluable experiences for gifted youth (Garfinkel & Prentice, 1985; VanTassel-Baska, 1982). Such experience should begin in the elementary grades and lead to early enrollment in foreign language classes in high school. Learning a foreign language enhances gifted students' grasp of their own native language, provides an extended perspective on the function of language in our lives, readies gifted youth for a multicultural future, and provides insights about differences among cultures.

Vocational Programs

The last element (box 11) suggests that special program services should be provided for vocationally talented youth. Feldhusen (1986) argued that vocational talent, along with academic, intellectual, and artistic talents, should be viewed as a major domain of gifted education. Milne (1982) argued the case for giftedness in the vocational domains of home economics, agriculture, business, and industrial arts. Youth who exhibit unusual talent and potential in these areas clearly should have special opportunities to develop those talents as part of the school's total program for the gifted.

Secondary Triad Model

At least two other secondary models are now well recognized as viable program models. The first is Reis and Renzulli's Secondary Triad Model (1986). As at the elementary level, the Secondary Triad Model is implemented after a comprehensive orientation of all students who have been selected for a "talent pool." Implementation is carried out in special sections of regular courses; extra courses, seminars, and electives; and off-campus experiences. Compacting the regular course curriculum is advocated by Reis and Renzulli, and the triad enrichment experiences are delivered in regular classes.

Betts Autonomous Learner Model

The second widely recognized secondary model is the Betts Autonomous Learner Model (1986). The model was described earlier in this chapter as an elementary school model, but it originally was developed as a secondary-level model whose functions are typically delivered through a special "autonomous learner" class offered each year in the secondary program. This model also includes program orientation activity, such as understanding giftedness, group dynamics, understanding self, and developing personal growth and career plans. The Betts model stresses personal-social development of the gifted while offering a wide variety of alternative activities.

Other Secondary Models

A number of other excellent secondary program reviews and models are available to guide development of instruction for the gifted. Silverman (1980) based her insights on a review of previous research and development of programs for secondary gifted students. Much of VanTassel-Baska's work (1986) focused on the secondary level. Keating (1979) reviewed secondary models and programs in the 78th yearbook of the National Society for the Study of Education; and Stanley (1980) and Benbow and Stanley (1983) have devoted considerable attention to the nature and structure of programs for the gifted at the secondary level. A great deal of guidance is available to program developers.

Some larger cities can organize magnet schools for the gifted or schools-within-a-school to offer more intensive activities for the gifted and to provide more accelerated and in-depth experiences in the several disciplines. I believe the gifted need opportunities to discover their own talents or academic strengths in accelerated curricula and through intensive experiences at advanced levels in interaction with the key concepts of the disciplines. High school level gifted students need to discover their special talent areas early (Gagne, 1985) and have opportunities for accelerated growth in those areas with other gifted youth.

Summary

Various program models are available to provide sound curriculum experiences for gifted and talented youth (VanTassel-Baska et al. 1988). The best models provide accelerated, enriched, and challenging learning experiences that help gifted youth clarify their talent strengths and potential and give them opportunities to move ahead in learning to higher levels and at a pace that fits their abilities.

119

References

Belcastro, F. P. (1987). Elementary pullout program for the intellectually gifted—boon or bane? *Roeper Review, 9*(4).

Benbow, C. P., & Stanley, J. C. (1983). *Academic precocity: Aspects of its development*. Baltimore, MD: Johns Hopkins University Press.

Betts, G. T. (1986) The antonomous learner model for the gifted and talented. In J. S. Renzulli (Ed.), *Systems and models for developing programs for the gifted and talented* (pp. 27–56). Mansfield Center, CT: Creative Learning Press.

Clark, G. A., & Zimmerman, E. D. (1984). *Educating artistically talented students*. Syracuse, NY: Syracuse University Press.

Clark, G. A., & Zimmerman, E D. (1987). *Resources for educating artistically talented students*. Syracuse, NY: Syracuse University Press.

College Board. (1983). *A guide to the advanced placement program*. Princeton, NJ: College Board Publications.

Cox, J., Daniel, N., & Boston, B. O. (1985). *Educating able learners, programs and promising practices*. Austin: University of Texas Press.

Eisner, E. (1985). Aesthetic modes of knowing. In E. Eisner (Ed.), *Learning and teaching the ways of knowing* (84th yearbook of the National Society for the Study of Education, Part 2) (pp. 23–26). Chicago: University of Chicago Press.

Ellingson, M. K., Haeger, W. W., & Feldhusen, J. F. (1986). The Purdue mentor program: A university based mentorship experience for gifted children. *Gifted Child Today, 9*(2), 2–5.

Feldhusen, H. J. (1981). Teaching gifted, creative, and talented students in an individualized classroom. *Gifted Child Quarterly, 25*(3), 108–111.

Feldhusen, H. J. (1986). *Individualized teaching of gifted children in regular classrooms*. Buffalo, NY: DOK.

Feldhusen, J. F. (1983). Eclecticism: A comprehensive approach to education of the gifted. In C. P. Benbow & J. C. Stanley (Eds.), *Academic precocity: Aspects of its development*. Baltimore: Johns Hopkins University Press.

Feldhusen, J. F. (1986a). A new conception of giftedness and programming for the gifted. *Illinois Council for the Gifted Journal, 5*, 2–6.

Feldhusen, J. F. (1986b). Policies and procedures for the development of defensible programs for the gifted. In C. J. Maker (Ed.), *Critical issues in gifted education, defensible programs for the gifted* (pp. 235–255). Rockville, MD: Aspen Systems.

Feldhusen, J. F., & Clinkenbeard, P. R. (1982). Summer programs for the gifted: Purdue's residential programs for high achievers. *Journal for the Education of the Gifted, 5*(3), 178–184.

Feldhusen, J. F., & Kolloff, P. B. (1979). An approach to career education for the gifted. *Roeper Review, 2*(2), 13–17.

Feldhusen, J. F., & Kolloff, P. B. (1986). The Purdue three-stage model for gifted education at the elementary level. In J. S. Renzulli (Ed.), *Systems and models for developing programs for the gifted and talented* (pp. 126–152). Mansfield Center, CT: Creative Learning Press.

Feldhusen, J. F., Proctor, T. B., & Black, K. N. (1986). Guidelines for grade advancement of precocious children. *Roeper Review, 9*(1), 25–27.

Feldhusen, J. F., & Reilly, P. (1983). The Purdue secondary model for gifted education: A multi-service program. *Journal for the Education of the Gifted, 4*(4), 230–244.

Feldhusen, J. F., & Robinson, A. W. (1986). The Purdue secondary model for gifted and talented youth. In J. S. Renzulli (Ed.), *Systems and models for developing programs for the gifted and talented* (pp. 153–179). Mansfield Center, CT: Creative Learning Press.

Feldhusen, J. F., & Sokol, L. (1982). Extra-school programming to meet the needs of gifted youth: Super Saturday. *Gifted Child Quarterly, 26*(2), 51–56.

Feldhusen, J. F., & Treffinger, D. J. (1985). *Creative thinking and problem solving in gifted education*. Dubuque, IA: Kendall-Hunt.

Gagne, F. (1985). Giftedness and talent. *Gifted Child Quarterly, 29*(3), 103–112.

Galbraith, J. (1984). The eight great gripes of gifted kids. *Roeper Review, 7*(1), 15–18.

Garfinkel, A., & Prentice, M. (1985). Foreign language for the gifted: Extending cognitive dimensions. In P. B. Westphal (Ed.), *Meeting the call for excellence in the foreign language classroom* (pp. 43–49). Lincolnwood, IL: National Textbook.

Hoyt, K. B., & Hebeler, J. R. (1974). *Career education for gifted and talented students*. Salt Lake City: Olympus.

Keating, D. P. (1979). Secondary-school programs. In A. H. Passow (Ed.), *The gifted and talented: Their education and development* (78th yearbook of the National Society for the Study of Education)(pp.186–198). Chicago: University of Chicago Press.

Kolloff, P. B., & Feldhusen, J. F. (1981). PACE (Program for Academic and Creative Enrichment): An application of the three-stage model. *G/C/T, 18*, 47–50.

Kolloff, P. B., & Feldhusen, J. F. (1986). Seminar: An instructional approach for gifted students. *Gifted Child Today, 9*, 2–7.

Maker, C. J. (1982). *Curriculum development for the gifted*. Rockville, MD: Aspen Systems.

Milne, B. G. (1982). *Vocational education for gifted and talented students*. Columbus, OH: National Center for Research in Vocational Education.

Moore, B. A., Feldhusen, J. F., & Owings, J. (1978). *The professional career exploration program for minority and/or low income gifted and talented high school students*. Washington, DC: U.S. Department of Health, Education, and Welfare, Office of Education.

Proctor, T. B., Black, K. N., & Feldhusen, J. F. (1986). Early admission of selected children to elementary school: A review of the research literature. *Journal of Educational Research, 80*, 70–76.

Reis, S. M., & Renzulli, J. S. (1986). The secondary triad model. In J. S. Renzulli (Ed.), *Systems and models for developing programs for the gifted and talented* (pp. 267–305). Mansfield Center, CT: Creative Learning Press.

Renzulli, J. S., & Reis, S. M. (1986) The enrichment triad/revolving door model: A schoolwide plan for the development of creative productivity. In J. S. Renzulli (Ed.), *Systems and models for developing programs for the gifted and talented* (pp. 216–266). Mansfield Center, CT: Creative Learning Press.

Silverman, L. K. (1980). Secondary programs for the gifted. *Journal for the Education of the Gifted, 4*(1), 30–42.

Stanley, J. C. (1979). The case for extreme educational acceleration of intellectually brilliant youths. In J. C. Gowan, J. Khatena, & E. P. Torrance (Eds.), *Educating the ablest, a book of readings* (pp. 93–102). Itasca, IL: Peacock.

Stanley, J. C. (1980). On educating the gifted. *Educational Researcher, 9*, 8–12.

Treffinger, D. J. (1986). Fostering effective, independent learning through individualized programming. In J. S. Renzulli (Ed.), *Systems and models for developing programs for the gifted and talented* (pp. 429–460). Mansfield Center, CT: Creative Learning Press.

VanTassel-Baska, J. (1982). Results of a Latin-based experimental study of the verbally precocious. *Roeper Review, 4*(4), 35–37.

VanTassel-Baska, J. (1983). *A practical guide to counseling the gifted in a school setting*. Reston, VA: Council for Exceptional Children.

VanTassel-Baska, J. C. (1986). Acceleration. In C. J. Maker (Ed.), *Critical issues in gifted education, defensible programs for the gifted* (pp. 179–196). Rockville, MD: Aspen Systems.

VanTassel-Baska, J., Feldhusen, J., Seeley, K., Wheatley, G., Silverman, L., & Foster, W. (1988). *Comprehensive curriculum for gifted learners: An integrative approach*. Boston: Allyn & Bacon.

121

Study Questions

1. What all would you include in a good elementary program model for the gifted and talented?

2. Contrast any two elementary models.

3. Should we accelerate gifted and talented students? Why or why not?

4. How can the gifted be served in regular classrooms?

5. What should be done for the gifted and talented at the middle school and high school levels?

6. Why should the focus of secondary programs be on specific talents or abilities?

7. How can we serve the gifted in the arts?

8. Why is foreign language study important in educating the gifted and talented?

9

A Comprehensive Model of Gifted Program Development

Joyce VanTassel-Baska

Program development efforts for the gifted require careful planning and implementation. Recent work (Cox, Daniel, & Boston, 1985) on local program efforts documents the need for systematic comprehensive program development to ensure adequate services to gifted learners. The Pyramid Project advocates multilevel service delivery, which would differentiate the nature of the population to be served through multiple options. Other program development resources also support the need for organizing and planning the gifted program in a systematic manner (Jordan & Grossi, 1980; VanTassel-Baska, 1982).

School districts also have to consider many factors in developing programs for the gifted. One such factor is the *community.* How will it respond to such a program initiative? A second factor is the *institution of school* itself. How will the institution respond to the change process being undertaken? A third factor is the *students* to be served. What programs and services will best match their current and future needs? Another factor is *school personnel.* Who can best implement school programs, and how will they gain staff acceptance? Clearly, there are other factors as well, but the issue is that various publics and social contexts must be understood before meaningful program development in gifted education can occur.

To gain insight into those client groups and social contexts, let us consider specific steps that might be taken in the program development process, many of which reflect the aforementioned factors. These steps are a whole piece, and are related to the overall processes of program development. The ordering of the steps represents a deliberate attempt to illustrate the relative importance of some tasks early in the process rather than later. Many of the steps can be and should be worked on simultaneously.

Step 1:
Set Up a Steering Committee and Establish a Basic Philosophy Toward Programming

To discuss philosophical attitudes and possible barriers to establishing programs for the gifted, it is essential to have a representative testing ground. A steering committee made up of members from key groups is one way of determining the "threshold of tolerance" for gifted programs and of providing help in actual program planning. At a minimum, members should represent these areas within the district structure:

- Administration (central and building)
- Teacher(s)
- Parent(s)
- Student(s) identified as gifted (junior high school age and older)
- Pupil personnel services (counselor, social worker, preferably psychologist)

It would also be desirable to have representation from the business, arts, and professional communities.

The steering committee might address the following questions and thus agree on a general programmatic thrust:

1. What group of gifted students is most in need of special programming within our district: intellectual, creative, artistic?
2. What are their needs from a programmatic point of view: more in-depth work in academic areas, more creative projects, more independent work?
3. What organizational approaches to a program would be appropriate: a separate center or magnet school, part-time grouping in individual buildings, grouping within the regular classroom?
4. At what grade level(s) should the program begin, and how great a span should it encompass initially?

The work of the steering committee should be used to conduct the second step in planning—a formal needs assessment. In a sense, the steering committee will have brought data forward in an informal manner that would document the need for such a program. But a formal assessment of needs is also important.

Step 2: Conduct a Needs Assessment

An understanding of student and program needs and then of the interaction of student data and program data will lead to informed decisions about a planned gifted program. Table 9.1 illustrates one form that has been used in school district gifted programs. The aggregation of data from such a form usually provides a good source of people's thinking about gifted education. The extent to which planners can rely on the data to guide program development likely will depend on the extent to which responding to perceived needs is important in the context of the district. Even if a program coordinator does not develop programs in the areas suggested, the instrument still provides important information for baseline purposes.

Student needs can be determined by surveying students, teachers, and perhaps parents. It usually is easier to provide a list of "typical" gifted student needs, such as the following (VanTassel, 1979), and ask respondents to rank those needs they think are most important:

1. To be challenged by activities that enable them to operate cognitively and affectively at complex levels of thought and feeling
2. To be challenged through opportunities for divergent production
3. To be challenged through group and individual work that demonstrates process/product outcomes
4. To be challenged by discussions among intellectual peers
5. To be challenged by experiences that promote understanding of human value systems
6. To be challenged by the opportunity to see interrelationships in all bodies of knowledge
7. To be challenged by special courses in their area of strength and interest that accelerate the pace and depth of content
8. To be challenged by greater exposure to new areas of learning within and without the school structure
9. To be challenged by the opportunity of applying their abilities to real problems in the world of production
10. To be taught the following process skills in the context of meaningful content:
    a. critical thinking

125

TABLE 9.1
Needs of Gifted Students

Please rate the following according to the extent they are incorporated into your current program for gifted learners.

	To a great extent			Not at all		
	5	4	3	2	1	

	5	4	3	2	1	Cannot Judge
Basic cognitive skills						
Critical thinking	5	4	3	2	1	0
Creative thinking	5	4	3	2	1	0
Problem solving	5	4	3	2	1	0
Research	5	4	3	2	1	0
Decision making	5	4	3	2	1	0
Basic affective skills						
Tolerance of self and others	5	4	3	2	1	0
Constructive use of humor	5	4	3	2	1	0
Coping with being different	5	4	3	2	1	0
Discriminating between the real and the ideal	5	4	3	2	1	0
Use of high-level sensitivity	5	4	3	2	1	0
To be challenged by mastery-level work in areas of strength and interest	5	4	3	2	1	0
To be challenged by exposure to new areas	5	4	3	2	1	0
To be challenged by the opportunity to see interrelationships	5	4	3	2	1	0
To be challenged by experiences that promote understanding of human value systems	5	4	3	2	1	0
To be challenged through discussions with intellectual peers	5	4	3	2	1	0
To be challenged by activities at complex levels of thought	5	4	3	2	1	0
To be challenged through opportunities for divergent production	5	4	3	2	1	0
To be challenged by the opportunity for real-world problem solving	5	4	3	2	1	0

126

b. creative thinking
c. research
d. problem solving
e. coping with exceptionality
f. leadership

The needs most frequently identified from this list can be clustered for purposes of establishing goals and objectives for student programs.

One also can identify a sampling of students who are considered gifted or talented and then examine their current classroom experiences to determine the extent of the gap between what these youngsters are capable of doing and what they are actually doing. For example, what kinds of assignment are they being given? What is the overall cognitive level of the discussions in which they are taking part? To what extent are these students given opportunities to work independently? To what extent are they grouped with other students within the classroom who have similar abilities and interests? To answer these questions, one person or a team probably will have to talk to the teachers and make classroom observations. Interviewing the students, or, in the case of young children, their parents, may be a good technique. Written survey forms also may be used.

To save time, it might be wise to call together a group of teachers and administrators interested in gifted education to determine the following kinds of issues:

1. What should be the goals of a program?
2. What should be the overall program model?
3. How should the program be organized?
4. What should be the content focus of the program: academic areas (if so, which one(s), interdisciplinary areas (if so, which content cluster)?
5. Who should be involved in the program: teachers, administrators, parents, psychologists, counselors?
6. To what extent should they be involved and for what specific purpose (for example, psychologists for testing only)?

Another important approach to needs assessment is to ascertain what the district currently is doing that addresses the needs of these learners, how extensively it is being done, and where the gaps are. One starts from the premise that any given school district is providing some important aspects of gifted program services already. The needs assessment function is then to determine the discrepancy between what is happening now that is appropriate and what more should be happening. The discrepancy "gap," as it is called, can be seen as the core area for proposed program development activities. The following program options might be viewed as categories to be explored:

127

1. Academic courses-classes (for example, honors, Advanced Placement)
2. Independent study-mentoring-seminars
3. Accelerative options
4. Extracurricular services (for example, Future Problem-Solving, Odyssey of the Mind, Junior Great Books, debate, science club, astronomy club)
5. Counseling services (for example, meetings with gifted/talented students individually or in small groups, individualized education programs, career education, vocational, or anything especially designed for GT)
6. Community services (for example, college classes, museum programs, Saturday classes, cultural opportunities, library programs)
7. By-mail options (correspondence, Duke program, Northwestern program, and so on)
8. Foreign language classes
9. Summer program options

Once this step has been completed, a coordinator can be appointed.

Step 3: Appoint a Coordinator for the Program Development Effort

Even in a small district, having one person in charge of planning a program will save considerable time in implementing it. At an initial stage of program development, the coordinator might focus on the following tasks:

- Assembling the needs assessment data and using them to develop a program plan, including goals, objectives, and types of appropriate activity for students
- Developing a plan for technical assistance (what are the training needs?)
- Developing and implementing an identification process

Several months will be necessary for completing these tasks, which are so critical to a successful program. These tasks should be an ongoing part of the coordinator's duties, which also include conducting meetings with relevant groups about the program, working on curriculum development, developing and implementing the evaluation component, and acting as a gifted resource conduit within and without the district. The coordinator also should be responsible for all relevant reports and public relations work conducted about the program.

A local coordinator has to have enough authority to carry out these responsibilities. For this reason, selection of a coordinator is important, for ongoing duties require a certain finesse in working with people, in understanding how to set up programs, and in acquiring a working knowledge of gifted education.

In addition to these qualities, the coordinator should possess the following:

128

- Coursework in gifted education (depending on the state, anywhere from 6 to 24 hours may be considered necessary)
- Experience in working with gifted children directly, either in a small group in a regular classroom or in a special program
- Administrative experience or coursework (or both) that reflects an understanding of how schools operate and how innovation occurs

Step 4: Delineate Program Model and Service Alternatives

Given the needs assessment information, the coordinator and steering committee should develop concept papers that present alternative program models. An outline for such a concept paper might include:

1. Summary of assessment data
2. Nature of population to be served
3. Overall program philosophy and approach
4. Major goals and objectives
5. Curricular areas to be explored
6. Grouping approach to be used
7. Program organization and schedule
8. Staff involvement
9. Evaluation approach
10. Budget considerations

With budgetary restraints being a reality in most local school districts, it is advisable to work out alternative budgets based on alternative approaches to programming so that the superintendent and the board of education can easily see the effects of reduced funding.

Current resources are available that aid in the process of comparing general program models (Renzulli, 1986), teaching models (Maker, 1985), and curriculum models (VanTassel-Baska et al., 1988). Yet the task of tailoring such models for a given school district must rest with the steering committee and the coordinator of the program.

Step 5: Initiate a Staff Development Plan

For a gifted program to be implemented successfully, all people in the district must be aware of its existence and purpose. In addition, individuals working closely with the program need more in-depth information on the nature and needs of gifted children. Also, because gifted programming is still somewhat embryonic, provi-

129

sion for sharing among gifted programs can be extremely profitable.

Thus, a staff development plan should address at least three levels:

- Level One: Awareness

    This level may best be accomplished through brochures, newsletters, and workshops. The information should be available to all educational personnel and parents as well as to key community leaders. Content should focus on the who, what, and why of the district gifted program as well as provide information on the general characteristics and needs of gifted children.

- Level Two: Developmental

    This level of technical assistance may be accomplished through extended workshops and group consultations. It should be available primarily to individuals working directly with the gifted program. Content should focus on specific developmental issues, such as assessing individual student needs; specific project models for working with students who are gifted in language arts; or how to teach critical thinking to the gifted.

- Level Three: Reflective

    This level of technical assistance may be accomplished through a seminar approach. Seminars should be available to educators integrally involved with the program for at least 1 year and should attempt to involve several districts for purposes of exchange. The seminars should focus primarily on strengths and weaknesses in gifted programming and should be conducted as problem-solving workshops by a consultant with group process skills.

Ideally, the technical assistance plan should also have minimum expectations for participants at each level. For example, at the awareness level, participants should gain information about the gifted program that can be documented. At level two, participants should be able to demonstrate competency in specific content and process areas on which the training has focused. At level three, participants should be able to analyze the program and make recommendations for modification based on seminar discussions. An excellent resource for program planners at this stage is the special issue of *Gifted Child Quarterly* (Summer 1986, *30* (3)), devoted entirely to articles on staff development.

Step 6: Develop and Implement an Identification Process

Some experts in the field might argue that identification should occur earlier in the process of starting a program. Nevertheless, the program and the selected population must match in a defensible fashion. Unfortunately, it is easy to identify a population you cannot serve if the nature of the program and the resources available to carry it out aie not in place first. Therefore, it may be appropriate in some instances not to identify students until a program plan has been worked out.

Given that chapter 7 has discussed identification in depth, only an outline of key issues is discussed here. The following factors should be carefully considered by local program developers:

- Use objective and subjective data. Recommendations should be balanced by tests that document performance or potential or both.
- Use multiple criteria in the process. Developmental levels of the student population should guide which criteria are most appropriate. For example, use of parent nomination and inventory procedures for young children have proved very effective (Roedell, Jackson, & Robinson, 1980; Ehrlich, 1984). At later stages of development, self-nomination and special aptitude measures are useful (VanTassel-Baska & Strykowski, 1987). According to Gallagher (1985), the three most frequently used criteria for programs for the intellectually gifted are teacher recommendations, achievement tests, and intelligence instruments.
- Develop an identification process. Once you have determined the criteria for consideration, you must create a system for determining that selection. Will all criteria weigh equally? Will a point value be assigned to each? Will the selection be made on points or by a person or committee examining other factors?
- Include at least some criteria at the scoring level that are easily accessible, such as scores on annual achievement tests, IQ tests on file, and so on.
- Ensure the cooperation of classroom teachers; it is critical to the program's success. Teacher recommendations may be time-consuming, but they are an important part of the process.
- Be sure the instruments used for selection of students are appropriate to the nature of the program and defensible in terms of identifying giftedness. For example, if you are going to initiate an advanced math program for sixth graders, math scores on achievement and aptitude tests are more important to consider than is an IQ test score. Research evidence (Stanley, 1981), as well as common sense, suggests the feasibility of such an approach.

The selection process should allow for discussion among educators and the "trying out" of various ways of thinking about the data collected. Identification is human process, not a numbers game. Consequently, having a selection committee review and talk out procedures as well as individual cases seem appropriate. Although some school districts might argue that this "messing around" is not a clean process, it is an honest one that takes seriously the issue of cutting arbitrarily on the continuum of human abilities.

Once students have been selected, meetings should be scheduled with them and their parents to discuss the nature of the program. "Permission to participate" cards should be collected from parents, and "commitment" cards from students. This approach is a good way to gain early acceptance and responsibility for the program from those who will be most affected by it.

Step 7:
Decide on a Curriculum Development Plan

Curriculum development for the gifted means integrating the following components in a way that fits the goals and objectives of a particular program design:

- Content, process, product, and concept dimensions
- Instructional strategies
- Selected materials and resources

Some program coordinators would see one of these components as more important than others. For example, accelerated content would place a great emphasis on content organization, whereas districts using an enrichment triad approach might focus more on classroom management and instructional strategies. Work with the structure of the intellect (SOI) model implies heavy concentration on the model as the primary vehicle for planning and generating curriculum. Thus, the focus of a curriculum plan may depend on the general direction selected for the program model. No one model has been judged superior, and several offer interesting, productive approaches for working with gifted students. In fact, many programs attempt a synthesis approach and cull the best from each model to develop a curriculum plan. (For a complete treatment of curriculum content issues, see chapters 12–17.) Other models employed by gifted programs include Bloom's taxonomy; Frank Williams' model for implementing cognitive and affective behaviors; and the Purdue Three-Stage Enrichment Model.

All gifted program curricula should employ good teaching strategies, some of which are more conducive to certain kinds of program. For example, inquiry teaching is a wonderful technique in social studies and English—courses in which discussion is a key component—whereas it may not be as helpful in foreign language or mathematics, in which application of skills is the overriding concern. In the final analysis, strategies for working with the gifted are more heavily predicated on understanding individual and group needs than on demonstrating special techniques. But at a minimum, a teacher of the gifted should have in his or her arsenal the ability to do inquiry teaching, ask good discussion questions, organize small groups and independent work, and lecture effectively.

Another important aspect of curriculum development is choice of selected materials and resources. Because there are no such things as "gifted materials," it is useful to examine criteria for selecting materials appropriate for use with gifted learners:

132

- Materials should be geared to an appropriate reading level, slightly above the gifted students' tested level.
- Materials should stimulate discussion opportunities in small groups through including good higher-level questions.
- Materials should be varied, offering diverse points of view and representing multiple media.
- Materials should be geared to complex thought processes, especially the development of analytical skills.
- Materials should be organized around key issues, themes, and ideas within or across domains of inquiry *or* represent the underlying structure of a given discipline.
- Materials should be supplementary, not the substance of the program.

Step 8: Select Teachers

Teacher selection is an extremely important step in program development, because the teacher has been found to be the single most important factor in whether a program benefits gifted students (Renzulli, 1977). Consequently, the school district should have its selection committee establish a protocol for deciding who will teach the gifted program. Such a committee also may be used to interview candidates if this procedure becomes part of the selection model. Generally teachers tend to nominate themselves for consideration in such programs. This is a desirable part of the process, but other factors also should be considered. Certain qualities are essential to a teacher of the gifted:

- Good academic record. The prospective teacher of the gifted need not be as gifted as many of the students, but he or she cannot be borderline average either.
- Keen interest in at least one academic or creative area.
- The ability to be flexible in terms of time, pace, materials, instructional patterns, and so forth.
- A good sense of humor.
- A strong individual who is not easily intimidated or threatened by able learners.

To shape a new program, these teachers also must be energetic and creative. More complete lists of teacher characteristics are available from several studies (Gallagher, 1985; Maker, 1982).

A process for teacher selection could incorporate the following steps:

1. Accept self-nomination through an application form.
2. Study the records of those who apply, keeping in mind key characteristics.
3. Observe candidates in the classroom, using a list of instructional behaviors deemed appropriate to classrooms for the gifted (see Table 9.2).

133

TABLE 9.2
Instructional Process Goals

*During the program the teacher will:
1. Conduct group discussions.
2. Select questions that stimulate higher-level thinking.
3. Use varied teaching strategies effectively.
4. Utilize critical thinking skills in appropriate contexts.
5. Encourage independent thinking and open inquiry.
6. Understand and encourage student ideas and student-directed work.
7. Demonstrate understanding of the educational implications of giftedness.
8. Utilize creative thinking techniques.
9. Utilize problem-solving techniques.
10. Synthesize student assessment data and curriculum content effectively.

*The Martinson-Weiner scale has been adapted to link these goals to an assessment tool.

4. Interview top candidates individually or by committee.
5. Select according to criteria developed within the parameters of district policy.

Step 9: Implement the Program

Start-up times for gifted program vary, but allowing 12 months is advisable—6 months to plan the program and another 6 months to implement a pilot effort. Planning is essential in making the program work, but too long a time expended for this effort can dampen enthusiasm and support. Moving into the program is important. Curriculum can be developed during the program as long as the overall conceptual ideas are in place and teachers feel comfortable working with the students. Ideally, spring and summer planning with fall implementation is best, but winter implementation also can work after first-semester planning.

The first 6 weeks of implementation yield much information crucial to program continuance. The following problems are apt to occur or will surface, if they are going to, at this time:

- Selection of students who do not fit the program
  Possible solution: Have in place a policy to facilitate moving students in and out of programs. Such a policy should be in place when the program is set up; let parents and students know about it at the orientation session. Also have an alternative to suggest for these students, such as meetings with counselor or special projects.
- Disenchantment of teachers who "lose" students to the program
  Possible solution: Keep these teachers carefully informed of what is happening in the program, how their students are progressing, and how the teachers can help.

134

- Students' feelings of being overwhelmed/overworked

  Possible solution: Delineate student expectations of the orientation meeting, complete with estimates of extra time involvement. Listen to concerns and try to help. Sometimes the gifted program represents the first time a student has been challenged, and therefore he or she does not know how to cope. Let some time pass.

- Teachers' feelings of being overwhelmed/overworked

  Possible solution: More planning is a good remedy for this problem. New programs are energy-draining, but they should not make excessive demands. Another approach might be to allow some additional time off for planning and for attending sharing sessions with other educators in gifted programs.

Step 10: Evaluate the Program

For an administrator, evaluation is important because it aids in improving programs and in making decisions about program worth and desirability on an ongoing basis. It is especially important to evaluate gifted program efforts carefully because of the tenuousness of long-term financial commitment to such programs by school boards. Good data alone will not necessarily maintain a program, but they are facilitative.

Two kinds of data should be collected: *student data* and *program data*. In designing a gifted evaluation, structure questions that you want answered about the program, such as:

- How have students benefited from this program?
- Are students operating more independently now than before?
- How well does the identification process work?
- How effective is the staff development component?

Incorporate such questions into a format that allows for appropriate instrumentation selection, timetables for data collection, and data collection procedures. The format also should allow for involvement by key persons in the process. A balanced concern for student growth data and program process data is an important consideration. (See chapter 10 for an in-depth discussion of the evaluation topic.)

Step 11: Use Community Resources

Although many local educators may not view the community as an essential component of successful gifted program development, it is a tremendous resource that can be used to enhance any gifted program. A key to community involvement is to identify key contacts and develop a resource directory. Key contacts can come from civic and professional organizations, many of which are highly predisposed toward helping gifted education.

Other important contacts come through universities. University personnel tend to be approachable about helping with gifted programs without a fee because of their natural interest in gifted students. They are a good source for establishing mentorships. School district personnel also can be tapped for program development. Curriculum specialists and pupil personnel workers are often willing to work on some aspect of the gifted program.

Step 12: Structure a Counseling Component

The need for gifted students to receive counseling help already has been cited (also see chapter 19). Too many gifted students currently receive incidental counseling at best, which ill prepares them to make decisions about their school program or focus on career options. It also fails to prepare them to cope with being gifted.

Involve school counselors with the gifted program and encourage them to meet with these students in small groups on a regular basis. Some of the issues of coping that a counselor can explore with identified gifted students include discussing questions such as the following, which capitalize on affective aspects of being gifted:

- How do you feel different from others? Knowing that each person is unique, how can you cope with the ways in which you differ?
- What do you perceive to be your strengths and weaknesses? How can you capitalize on and minimize them, respectively?
- Why do you like to work alone? When do you prefer not to, and why?
- How do you handle criticism? Do you feel "picked on" when suggestions are made to you?
- Do you feel confident about your ability? How do you "practice" it with others?
- Do you criticize yourself for mistakes? How do you feel when you make mistakes?
- Do you like to lead others? In what kind of enterprise?
- How do you make decisions?

The school counselor or other designated person can work with identified gifted students at least twice a month in a group setting to explore these kinds of issues. Counselors also should provide special programs, perhaps once a month, in school and career opportunities based on the perceived needs of the groups.

Sometimes teachers or program coordinators would like to be involved with this aspect of the gifted program. They should be encouraged to participate, for much can be learned about gifted children from informal sessions.

Step 13: Develop Gifted Program Policy

New programs represent change in a school district. Consequently, no program development effort will be successful unless the change process is accounted for and addressed in a deliberate way. Not only are we, as gifted educators, interested in individuals "changing"; but we also are interested in the school system changing. Consequently, there is a need to develop policies at the local level that will facilitate the ongoing growth of the gifted program. A sample list of policies developed by a 10-state region in gifted education can be seen in Table 9.3 (VanTassel-Baska, 1986). Such a list is highly applicable at the local level.

Additionally, reviewing the basic elements involved in the process of change is helpful. Key aspects of the process include:

1. Change generally must be viewed as desirable by relevant constituencies.
2. At least a few people must be committed to change.
3. Change must be planned for and implemented systematically.
4. Change must be monitored.
5. Change requires skilled leadership at each stage of the process.
6. Change is slow but steady.
7. Positive change represents growth in individuals and systems.
8. The critical unit for implementing change is the individual school.

The goal of local policy development is to ensure that the gifted program becomes integrated with the regular education programs at the appropriate levels of decision making. In this way it comes to be viewed as a part of the school system program, not as a "frill" or "extra." Boards of education must understand gifted education programs as a part of the total fabric of quality education for all. Policy development and enactment provide the mechanisms to create such an understanding.

Activating the Model

These thirteen steps of program development are important interactive pieces in institutionalizing a model program effort for gifted learners (see Figure 9.1). Neglect or deletion of any of these steps can have a deleterious effect on the program in its formative stages. Furthermore, as local programs grow and expand, more opportunities for using this program development cycle, albeit in tailored form, will emerge. Sound program development practices are essential in building defensible programs for the gifted and in keeping them going. Yet this is not meant as a linear model. Rather, it is a simultaneity model in which individual steps constitute clusters of ongoing activities and individual program developers make decisions on an appropriate plan of action for proceeding. Formats for such plans may vary, but typically they include the following components:

137

FIGURE 9.1
A Model of Program Development Steps in Building Gifted Education Programs
at the Local Level

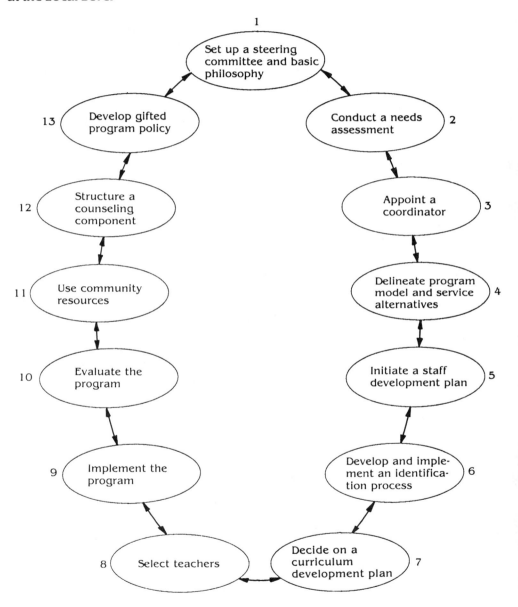

TABLE 9.3
Midwest Policy Initiatives in Gifted Education:
Outcomes from the Richardson Study

Policy Issue #1   "Casting a wider net" in identification procedures

Statement of Policy
   There are students with exceptional levels of ability whose needs are not being met
by existing regular educational programs or special services for the gifted.
Identification practices should address these unserved and underserved populations.

Policy Issue #2   Comprehensive Program Development (CPD)

Statement of Policy
1. School districts should develop a comprehensive philosophy that articulates goals,
    programs, and services for able learners. This statement should be formally
    adopted by the appropriate governing group, and communicated.
2. CPD should be "infused" into a multiyear implementation schedule with areas of
    responsibility carefully delineated.
3. CPD implies defining the school role at several levels: direct service providers,
    facilitators, and linkers to nonschool resources.
4. CPD should be developed to appropriately match definition/assessment/program/
    service provisions.
5. CPD implies developing a broad-based, comprehensive, talent-find mechanism
    that embraces recognized concepts of talent.

Policy Issue #3   Teacher Training and Staff Development

Statement of Policy
   To provide the best possible educational experiences for gifted children, persons
involved with them should be engaged in training programs at the awareness through
skill development levels based on their rates and levels of expertise. This would include
providing information on gifted students to all preservice candidates. Training, which
should reflect research on effective models and practices, can be conducted through
collaborative efforts.

Policy Issue #4   Utilization of Outside Resources

Statement of Policy
   Able learners exhibit a wide range of special and specific educational needs. The
assumption that the local school can adequately meet all the needs of its student
constituency, especially in light of declining tax revenues, is inherently limited.
Therefore, infusion of external resources is a vital and necessary adjunct to the
educational experiences the local school provides for its able learners.

139

Policy Issue #5   Funding

Statement of Policy
    The local district must assume the responsibility for a free and appropriate education of high quality for students of all abilities. Providing well managed, comprehensive programs for able learners requires priority and continuity of funding by those responsible parties. Excess costs related to the special needs of gifted students should be provided as an ongoing function of state and federal agencies. Special initiatives can be supported by short-term grants from foundations, corporations, government agencies, and community resources.

Policy Issue #6   Curriculum Flexibility

Statement of Policy
    All students should be placed in the curriculum according to demonstrated competence. For able and slow learners, special attention should be given to out-of-grade placements.

1. Area to be addressed (for example, counseling, policy, identification)
2. Tasks to be undertaken
3. Responsibility
4. Timeline for completion
5. Documentation of progress (agendas, minutes of meetings held, products such as brochures, and so on)

Table 9.4 provides a sample plan of action format. Only when such an action plan is developed will progress be made in the program development process. Knowing what to do and how to do it is still only part of program development. Activating a plan of action that involves others is a key to a successful venture in this area.

TABLE 9.4
"Plan of Action" Form

What problems or issues have to be addressed? (What?)	What solution options should be considered? (What?)	Option feasibility (Costs/ Benefits?)	Processes for change (How?)	Responsibility (Who?)	Timeline (When?)	Documentation of progress

Summary

Developing and activating programs and services for gifted learners are important enterprises that are ongoing and dynamic in nature. One gifted program will not meet the needs of all gifted learners in a given school district, nor will activation of all the program development steps described here guarantee a sufficient effort. Only as we continue to work at the individual and collective aspects of the program development cycle are we likely to build the quality programs we envision. The building process also takes time. Years of effort usually are required to establish and fine-tune a program of quality. Gifted program developers should view the task of program development as a major undertaking, full of challenges and frustrations on the way to creating a "willed future" for gifted learners.

References

Cox, J., Daniel, N., & Boston, B. (1985). *Educating able learners*. Austin, TX: University of Texas Press.

Ehrlich, V. (1984). *The Astor program for young gifted children: 10 years later*. Unpublished report.

Gallagher, J. (1985). *Teaching gifted children*. Boston: Allyn & Bacon.

Jordan, J., & Grossi, J. (1980). *An administrator's handbook on designing programs for the gifted and talented*. Reston, VA: Council for Exceptional Children.

Maker, J. (1982). *Curriculum development for the gifted*. Rockville, MD: Aspen Systems.

Maker, J. (1985). *Teaching models in gifted education*. Rockville, MD: Aspen Systems.

Renzulli, J. (Ed.). (1986). *Systems and models for developing programs for the gifted and talented*. Mansfield Center, CT: Creative Learning Press.

Renzulli, J. (1987). *The enrichment triad model: A guide for developing defensible programs for the gifted and talented*. Wethersfield, CT: Mansfield Center, CT: Creative Learning Press.

Roedell, W., Jackson, N., & Robinson, H. (1980). *Gifted young children*. New York: Teachers College Press.

Stanley, J. (1981). Using the SAT to find intellectually talented seventh graders. *College Board Review, 122*, 3–7.

VanTassel, J. (1979). A needs assessment model for gifted education. *Journal for the Education of the Gifted, 2*(3), 141–148.

VanTassel-Baska, J. (1982). *An administrator's guide to gifted program development*. Washington, DC: National Association of State Boards of Education.

VanTassel-Baska, J. (Ed.). (1986). *The Richardson study: A catalyst for policy change in gifted education*. Evanston, IL: Center for Talent Development.

VanTassel-Baska, J., Feldhusen, J., Seeley, K., Wheatley, G., Silverman, L., & Foster, W. (1988). *Comprehensive curriculum for gifted learners*. Boston: Allyn & Bacon.

VanTassel-Baska, J., & Strykowski, B. (1987). *An identification resource guide on the gifted and talented*. Evanston, IL: Center for Talent Development.

Study Questions

1. How might various aspects of the program development process be organized effectively in a school district?

2. What variables about a school district and community must you take into account as you conduct gifted program development?

3. What are the types of barriers that inhibit gifted program development in school districts? How might they be overcome?

4. If you were a school superintendent, how would you proceed with gifted program development? What would be your major concerns?

5. Evaluate the advantages and disadvantages of competing program models, identification models, and curriculum models. What direction appears most feasible?

6. What other programs in a school district might be useful in studying and understanding gifted program development?

10

Evaluating Programs for the Gifted

Ken Seeley

"The general purpose of evaluation is to gather, analyze and disseminate information that can be used to make decisions about educational programs" (Renzulli, 1975, p. 2). In any discussion of evaluation, we must examine the area of decision making, given that we rarely encounter situations in which only one simple decision is to be made. In fact, evaluation provides information for a series of interactive decisions that are typically directed toward program improvement. The decisions themselves also should be subject to evaluation such that evaluation and decision making continue to intertwine in the evolution of a program. Evaluation is the "bottom line" for creating defensible programs.

Who Should Do Evaluations?

Many think that evaluation is the province of administrators and that teachers should not be involved. Nevertheless, because evaluation affects the future of the gifted program (and sometimes its continued existence), teachers now are taking a leadership role in carrying out effective evaluation. At certain times in the evolution of programs, it may also be helpful to have someone from outside help the

143

gifted staff and administration with the evaluation. These times usually occur at the early stages of a program, or when critical decisions have to be made relative to some areas that are difficult to evaluate. The program staff should request help from an outside consultant in transferring the expertise into the existing system so that future outside services will be unnecessary. In this way, the consultant functions in a "teaching" capacity, and the gifted program avoids creating a dependency for outside services.

The appropriate person(s) to do the evaluation depend upon many factors, such as audience, level of sophistication needed, and scope. But teacher input is vital. As those closest to the program and its students, teachers bring the best understandings of what is going well and what should be improved.

How Does a Needs Assessment Relate to Evaluation?

Scriven and Roth (1978) stated that "needs assessment is absolutely fundamental to evaluation: There is no way to do a complete evaluation without knowing (or at least making a reasonable guess) about what clients or consumers need" (p. 1). A needs assessment is the logical first step in program development and program evaluation. Even if a gifted program has been in place for a number of years, a periodic needs assessment is important. Needs change, as do programs and services within schools.

Developing and maintaining a special program depend on demonstrating that gifted student needs are not being met in the existing program. We also must show how these needs are being met in the gifted program and at what level. Thus, needs form the base and rationale for the efficacy of the program. As such, the needs typically underlie the evaluated goals and objectives.

VanTassel-Baska (1981) provided a representative list of student needs that are commonly addressed in programs for the gifted:

1. To be challenged by activities that enable them to operate cognitively and affectively at complex levels of thought and feeling
2. To be challenged through opportunities for divergent production
3. To be challenged through group and individual work which demonstrates process/product outcomes
4. To be challenged by discussions among intellectual peers
5. To be challenged by experiences which promote understanding of human value systems
6. To be challenged by the opportunity to see interrelationships in all bodies of knowledge
7. To be challenged by special courses in their area of strength and interest which accelerate the pace and depth of content
8. To be challenged by greater exposure to new areas of learning within and without the school structure

9. To be challenged by the opportunity of applying their abilities to real problems in the world of production
10. To be taught the following units:
    a. critical thinking
    b. creative thinking
    c. research
    d. problem-solving
    e. coping with exceptionality
    f. leadership. (pp. 6–9)

Table 10.1 presents an outline of the steps to follow in carrying out an effective needs assessment. Educators often need information about gifted education before rating their attitudes toward certain approaches to it. I strongly recommend that any needs assessment be preceded by some staff development activity so that the assessment reflects informed choices about preferences. For example, there are prevailing negative attitudes toward acceleration, so educators must be informed about the positive aspects, particularly as they are supported by research and practice.

What Is the Difference Between Research and Evaluation?

The implicit basis of research is comparison. Research requires approaches different from evaluation approaches. Research designs are required to make comparisons in order to control variables. Statistical analysis is also required to account for variance or relationships that may exist in comparing groups or approaches. Certainly research is needed, and it can be included as part of an evaluation design. But different standards must be used in designing research than in designing evaluation. If decision makers want a comparative study, research is required with all its attendant standards and procedures. Research usually is more time-consuming and costly to carry out than is evaluation.

An evaluation design should be conceptualized as an integral part of program development so that each facet of evaluation relates to program objectives or anticipated outcomes. Evaluation provides decision-making information regarding how close a program comes to its predetermined standards. The resulting discrepancies allow decision makers to address program improvement needs.

The critical issue in differentiating research from evaluation appears when evaluators attempt to answer research questions with evaluation designs not intended to provide research data. Decisions are then based on designs that did not adequately control variables or adequately analyze comparative data. The classic example of a research question that uses evaluation designs, with unsuccessful answers, is, "Is enrichment better than acceleration for gifted students?" A comparative study must be done to answer this question.

145

TABLE 10.1

Outline for a Needs Assessment

   I.   Current status of gifted programs

         A. Pilot programs?
         B. Administrative commitment?
         C. Any staff development?

  II.   Approach

         A. Questionnaires for all administrators
            1. Central office instructional administrators
            2. Building principals

         B. Structured interviews
            1. All curriculum coordinators
            2. Assistant superintendents for instruction
            3. At least 50% of principals

 III.   Content of needs assessment

         A. Essential elements of a definition

         B. Philosophy and attitudes
            1. Toward acceleration
            2. Toward enrichment
            3. Regular teacher role
            4. Toward giftedness
            5. Toward IQ testing and identification

         C. Prioritizing major identification models and elements

         D. Program prototype preferences
            1. Rating of major options
            2. Amount of time for special instruction
            3. Amount of hard money staff time commitment
            4. Space commitment for program
            5. Materials budget support
            6. Parent involvement

         E. Staff development
            1. Released time for teachers
            2. Administrator involvement in training

         F. Community resources already developed
            1. School partnerships (for example, Adopt-a-School)
            2. Community volunteer program

         G. Leadership role for principal
            1. Organizing building-level planning
            2. Initiating parent education activities

146   3. Demonstrating commitment to past educational innovations

What Instrumentation Is Needed for Evaluation?

Instruments are needed to gather data for evaluation. Instruments have a broad definition for purposes of this discussion. They can range from a structured interview with parents to a test such as the Wechsler Intelligence Scale for Children–Revised. The purpose of instruments is to measure and describe a condition or level of performance. Instruments also include a means to record data in some systematic manner.

Critical issues for evaluation reside in two areas of instrumentation and measurement. The first issue is the *appropriateness* of the instrument to provide pertinent and meaningful information for the evaluation. The second issue is the *interpretation and presentation of data* gathered by the instrument.

The field of gifted education is replete with teacher-made evaluation instruments. These typically survey students, parents, teachers, mentors, and administrators to gain their perceptions of the gifted program. These data are aggregated into a report upon which decisions are made concerning program modification and maintenance. Often these "soft" data are supplemented with "hard" data from standardized tests of achievement, intelligence, and creativity.

Although this framework for evaluation is sound conceptually, it is too often done with instruments that are subject to a good deal of measurement error. The soft data from teacher-made surveys can provide excellent descriptive information for program administrators, but these data are global and too often are interpreted as specific. Groups of respondents are compared to each other using different instruments, which results in measurement error. For instance, a student may respond to the survey item, "How did you like the unit on computer-based retrieval systems (Rate 1–5)." The parents might be asked to respond to, "Rate your child's attitudes toward computer usage (Rate 1–5)." Although these items are similar in some ways and provide some descriptive data, they are different enough that comparisons should not be made. Yet we find mean scores extrapolated from such samples of the population and decisions made on the basis of these scores. Unfortunately, measurement errors persist and affect evaluation.

Even hard data from standardized measures are subject to misuse and misinterpretation. In gifted education we continue to wrestle with balancing hard data against soft data. Hard data comprise test scores and quantifiable measures. Soft data usually consist of observations, rating scales, and professional judgments. The ceiling effects of achievement tests and the variations and biases of intelligence tests and creativity tests confound decision making.

This discussion is not intended to dissuade anyone from using both soft and hard data in evaluating programs. Rather, we must attend to the measurement problems inherent in using any kind of instrument and guard against sweeping generalizations upon which important decisions are to be made. We must use all the data we can gather to create defensible programs for gifted children. But the measure-

147

ment and interpretation must be done well with good instruments that attend to the focus of the evaluation and to the audience for the evaluation. Principles of *validity* and *reliability* should be addressed in all instruments. Local norms that attend to these principles can be established for frequently used instruments.

What Constitutes Excellence in Evaluation?

The model guidelines in Table 10.2 represent a synthesis of ideas and concepts from these major authors in education evaluation: Gage (1970), Stake and Denny (1969), and Stufflebeam (1971). The primary areas to be addressed in planning comprehensive education evaluation are (1) context of the evaluation, (2) audience for the evaluation, (3) classes of decisions to be made, (4) usefulness of evaluation information, and (5) ethical considerations. These areas should guide the formulation of evaluation objectives, design, instrumentation, data gathering, and dissemination of results.

Context

Context of the evaluation refers to the setting, including people and program. Front-end analysis by the evaluator is necessary to determine attitudes of the audience toward the evaluation process. These attitudes can determine the accuracy of data sources and the level of openness to evaluation information. The context also attends to variations within and between programs. Rarely is a program not impacted by other programs. The interactive effects of programs should be part of the context description. Finally, the roles and goals of the evaluator and audience have to be made explicit during the course of the evaluation. The audience may expect a summative evaluation when a formative evaluation would be appropriate.

Audience

Audience for the evaluation greatly affects formulation of the evaluation design. If the audience is homogeneous, with similar information needs, gathering and reporting data are easier and more focused. If there are a number of different audiences, the design should differentiate objectives, methods, and reporting procedures.

TABLE 10.2
Model Guidelines for Evaluation

Major Areas	Subcomponents	Comments
1. Context of the evaluation	1.1 *Attitudes* toward evaluation	1.1 Evaluation raises anxiety and often negative attitudes.
	1.2 *Variations* within and between programs	1.2 Programs being evaluated are rarely homogeneous within themselves.
	1.3 *Roles and goals* of evaluator and audience	1.3 There must be a good match between evaluator and audience.
2. Audience for the evaluation	2.1 *Single-channel reporting* to a person or group with the same information needs.	2.1 A homogeneous audience is helpful in identifying decisions, sources of information, and appropriate reporting procedures.
	2.2 *Multichannel reporting* to several audiences	2.2 Several audiences require separate considerations based on information needs for decisions.
3. Classes of decisions	3.1 *Intervention* information for decisions	3.1 This is information for dichotomous decisions. Is intervention needed?
	3.2 *Reaction* information for decisions	3.2 Information from evaluation data must allow for easy retrieval and reaction to a decision request.
	3.3 *Planning* information for decisions	3.3 Planning decisions require a broad information base for viable alternatives.
	3.4 *Adoption* information for decisions	3.4 Adoption decisions are based on known, effective alternatives to be applied to local conditions.

149

	3.5 *Individual vs. group decisions* requiring different evaluation data	3.5 Individual decision information is attained with some certainty. Group decisions require attention to various levels and types of information for members of the group.
4. Usefulness of evaluation information	4.1 *Scientific nature* of data to assist credibility	4.1 The validity and reliability of the data should be made clear.
	4.2 *Relevance* of data to make it useful	4.2 To be relevant, the data must apply to contingencies in meeting program objectives.
	4.3 *Significant* data important in making decisions	4.3 Data must be weighted in its importance to specific conditions
	4.4 *Scope* of data to cover evaluation problems	4.4 Scope of the evaluation must key on its major elements related to necessary decisions.
	4.5 *Credibility* as perceived by the audience from the information	4.5 The evaluator must consider the audience's cognitive and affective response to the evaluation data.
	4.6 *Timeliness* as a major factor in usefulness of data	4.6 Time has three dimensions in evaluation: lag time (time between information need and information availability), time points (specific times when data are needed), and readiness (when the audience is most open to receive information).

150

	4.7 *Efficiency* of evaluation data (financial value of information related to its usefulness)	4.7 The value of data to be gathered must be weighted based on cost of obtaining it. Priorities must be set by evaluator working with audience.
5. Ethical considerations	5.1 *Candor* to ensure accuracy and completeness of information	5.1 The evaluator should avoid unsupported judgments and biases and be candid with the audience.
	5.2 *Confidentiality*	5.2 The evaluator must be sensitive to when confidentiality can be and should be guaranteed in sharing evaluation data.
	5.3 *Scientific caution* to guide interpretation or inferences from data reported	5.3 Limitations on inferences from the evaluation must be a part of the final evaluation report.

Classes of Decisions

Classes of decisions to be made from the evaluation are important determiners of methodology. Some decision makers may need to know only if intervention in a program is needed or not needed. Other decision makers may want the evaluation to produce a pool of data that can be drawn on for a specific reaction to a decision request. Such a data pool is important for planning decisions that require a number of alternatives. Adoption decisions that are based on data from other successful programs elsewhere and could be transported for adoption locally are often necessary. Data for individual decision makers can be directed to the decision maker's needs, but when decisions are to be made by groups, the evaluator must attend to various levels and types of information required by group members.

Usefulness of Information

The usefulness of evaluation information is perhaps the hallmark of good evaluation practice. Too often evaluation is an "add-on" activity to meet minimal accountability demands. In these situations, decisions are based on limited information from selective sources that do not represent relevant constituencies.

151

To be useful, evaluation data must be valid and reliable. The scientific nature of the data gathering and analysis lends credibility to the results. This information should be relevant to the audiences in its application to program decisions. The most precise evaluation data are useless if they do not translate into effective decisions significant to program management. The evaluator must assist the audience in weighing the significance of data when applied to specific conditions. Audiences tend to infer significance to specific situations from data that are not directly applicable. These types of inference error result in poor decisions. The scope of the evaluation must be sufficiently broad to address the evaluation problems. Credibility of the data must be considered from both cognitive and affective dimensions. Evaluation information can be well founded, but sensitivity to its impact on people should guide its format for reporting. Timeliness is another important component of how useful evaluation data are viewed. The information should be available when needed for decision making but also reported when the audience is most open to receive it.

The final dimension of usefulness of the evaluation is efficiency. Often evaluation demands exceed resources. The evaluator must assist the audience in setting priorities with attendant costs, so that the most useful information can be gathered for the best financial value.

Ethics

Ethical considerations must overlay all aspects of program evaluation. To this end, three areas should be considered: candor, confidentiality, and scientific caution. *Candor* requires openness and accuracy in gathering and reporting data. *Confidentiality* may have to be assured when providing certain information to different audiences. *Scientific caution* has to be a part of the interpretation in order to limit inferences. Even the best instruments and statistical designs have limitations. Cautions must be clearly stated in reporting data.

Table 10.2 synthesizes these major dimensions of evaluation into guidelines for reference. They constitute a comprehensive model for excellence in evaluation of educational programs.

How Do We Get Started?

To get started in program evaluation, an overall view of an evaluation system might be helpful. Table 10.3 presents an overview of an evaluation system and outlines what is done to get started and how to follow through. Figure 10.1 presents a flow chart of evaluation activities that graphically represents this process.

152

TABLE 10.3
Overview of an Evaluation System

Before You Start	When You Get Started	After You Get Started	Down the Road
Justify the need for this type of program.	Start small and add on later.	Have faith in your decisions and choices.	Use a variety of instruments to check on your perceptions of how the program is going: rating scales checklists observation systems questionnaires logs interview schedules anecdotal records inventories
Review District procedures for starting pilot programs.	Allow enough lead time to bring all those involved along with you as you go.	Keep thorough, accurate records of the process used and the students' progress.	
Gather input from *all* publics who will be affected by this program. (What are their concerns and interests?)	Continually check your perceptions with one or more of the easy feedback techniques.	Document with lots of pictures, graphs, diaries, and so on.	Using a "buddy system"— exchange visits with another program and see if you can verify their perceptions of that program.
Write an evaluation plan with readily observable activities that anyone can follow.	Identify those things that should be changed, and make appropriate recommendations.	Get a good idea of the costs in terms of time, money, people involvement, and so on.	
	Be on guard for little problems that can grow into bigger problems a little later.	Make some judgments about the program as implemented in comparison to the intended program.	Change those things that need to be changed to make the program effective and efficient.
		Change according to pupil needs and building-level priorities.	Prepare appropriate information to support the continuation of your program and allow others to adopt some or all of your model.

Note. Adapted from evaluation materials prepared for the Jefferson County Schools, Lakewood, CO, 1979.

153

FIGURE 10.1
A Model for Evaluation of Gifted/Talented Program

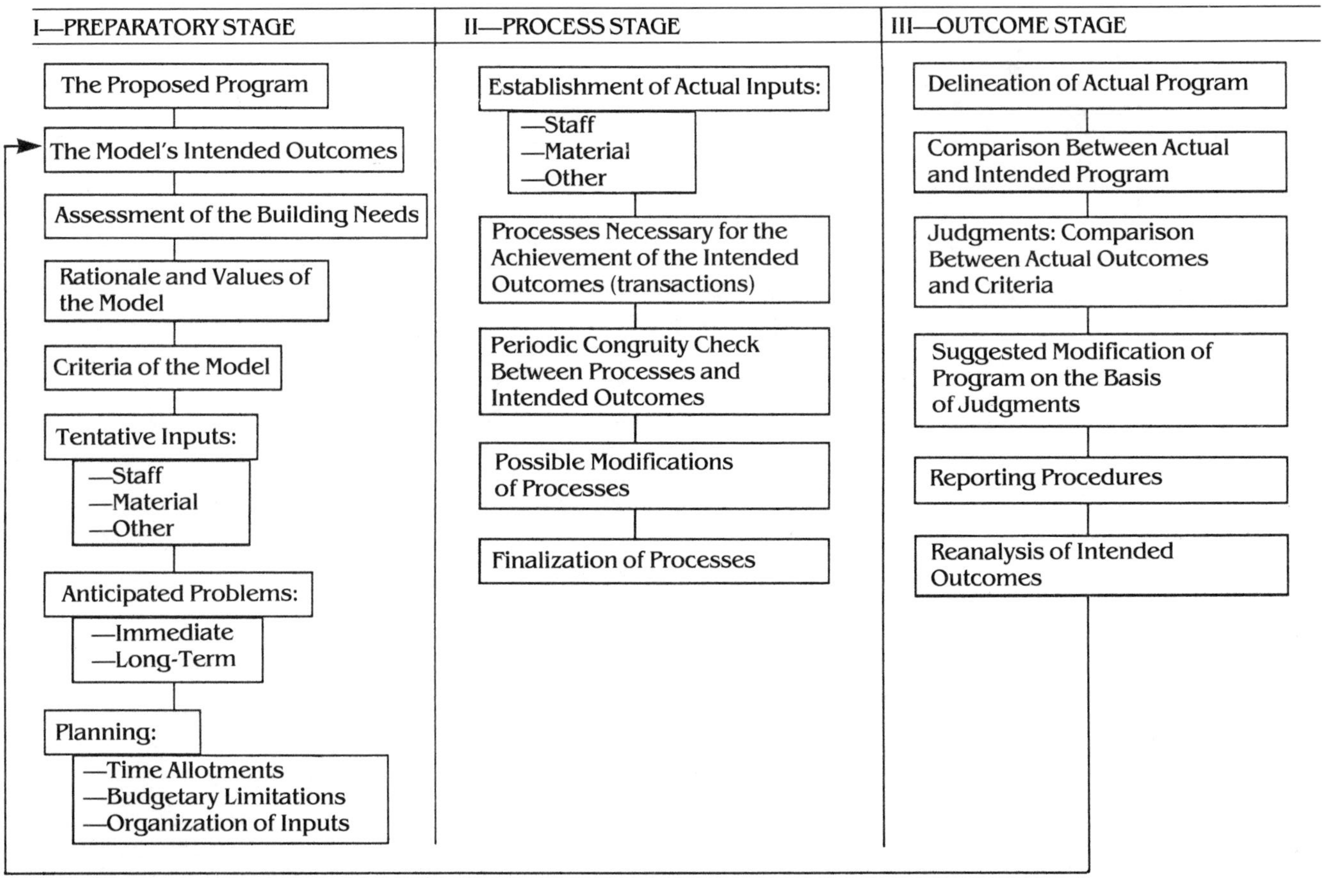

I—PREPARATORY STAGE	II—PROCESS STAGE	III—OUTCOME STAGE
The Proposed Program	Establishment of Actual Inputs: —Staff —Material —Other	Delineation of Actual Program
The Model's Intended Outcomes	Processes Necessary for the Achievement of the Intended Outcomes (transactions)	Comparison Between Actual and Intended Program
Assessment of the Building Needs	Periodic Congruity Check Between Processes and Intended Outcomes	Judgments: Comparison Between Actual Outcomes and Criteria
Rationale and Values of the Model	Possible Modifications of Processes	Suggested Modification of Program on the Basis of Judgments
Criteria of the Model	Finalization of Processes	Reporting Procedures
Tentative Inputs: —Staff —Material —Other		Reanalysis of Intended Outcomes
Anticipated Problems: —Immediate —Long-Term		
Planning: —Time Allotments —Budgetary Limitations —Organization of Inputs		

Note. Adapted from materials prepared for the Jefferson County Schools, Lakewood, CO, 1979.

Summary

An evaluation of programs for the gifted begins with a needs assessment and continues through development of the program. Evaluation monitors program development in order to inform decisions along the way. Sometimes consultants from outside the program are needed to assist in evaluation, but teachers of the gifted always should be intimately involved in the process.

The model guidelines for evaluation should help practitioners view the major considerations in design and implementation. These also can be used as a means of structuring an evaluation when using outside resources.

References

Gage, G. (1970). Distribution of information. In C. F. Paulson (Ed.), *A strategy for evaluation design.* Salem: Oregon State System of Higher Education.

Renzulli, J. (1975). *A guidebook for evaluating programs for the gifted and talented.* Ventura, CA: Office of the County Superintendent of Schools.

Scriven, M., & Roth, J. (1978, Spring). Needs assessment, concept and practice. *New Directions for Program Evaluation, 1,* 1–11.

Stake, R. E., & Denny, T. (1969). Needed concepts and techniques for utilizing more fully the potential of evaluation. In R. W. Tyler (Ed.), *Educational evaluation: New roles, new means* (68th yearbook of the National Society for the Study of Education, Part 2). Chicago: University of Chicago Press.

Stufflebeam, D. L. (1971). *Educational evaluation and decision-making* (pp. 49–105). Itasca, IL: F.E. Peacock.

VanTassel-Baska, J. (1981). *An administrator's guide to the education of gifted and talented children.* Washington, DC: National Association of State Boards of Education.

Study Questions

1. Why should teachers of the gifted be involved in evaluating programs?

2. What kind of research could be done to help answer questions as part of an evaluation design?

3. What kind of program decisions might be made as the result of a good evaluation?

4. What could be some common problems in attempting to evaluate too much, too soon?

5. How can program evaluation make programs for the gifted more defensible during times of budget cuts?

11

Key Administrative Concepts in Gifted Program Development

Joyce VanTassel-Baska

In many respects, administrative arrangements such as grouping, articulation, and cost-effectiveness are superficial issues in the education of the gifted. Yet, when those arrangements have little or no flexibility, they begin to account for substantive problems that gifted students may encounter. In examining administrative arrangements, then, it may be helpful to think of them as being either facilitative or impedimentive as they impinge on the lives of gifted students.

Key Concept #1: Grouping

The importance of finding an appropriate peer group or at least one significant other for the emotional development of the gifted is well documented (Colangelo & Zaffrann, 1979; Gowan, 1964; Gowan & Bruch, 1971; Silverman, 1983). Also, high-level and extensive cognitive functioning is facilitated by a core group of intellectual peers with similar goals (Hall, 1956; Hollingworth, 1942; Keating, 1976; Terman, 1921). Thus, it is understandable that grouping of the gifted has always been advocated in some form by educators of the gifted.

157

Certainly in terms of the historical context of gifted programs since the early 1900s, those that have been the most effective and the longest running clearly have been the programs with full-time grouping as the underlying strategy. These programs include the Hollingworth schools in New York City, the Terman classes in St. Louis, San Diego, and other cities, and the Cleveland Major Work Program. At the secondary level, the Bronx High School of Science in New York City and the Walnut Hills High School in Cincinnati are examples of the success of this approach.

Not only is the cognitive development of these students enhanced by grouping arrangements, but so is affective development. Numerous case studies point up that students who have been in a full-time grouping arrangement believe that they have benefited greatly. One example is Bob Sharpe, president of Bell and Howell, who testified that his involvement in the Major Work Program gave him the confidence and perceptiveness to be able to rise to the presidency of the corporation (Hauck & Freehill, 1972). Another argument for the full-time grouping approach is that it represents tremendous benefits to the organization of the school because it is an integrative program run at no additional cost to the system.

Yet, little empirical evidence specifies the exact beneficial effects of grouping versus nongrouping among populations of gifted students. The lack of evidence derives partly from the difficulty of controlling variables and isolating the treatment of grouping as a single variable in any chosen design. The lack of evidence also proceeds from the logistical difficulty of organizing such a research effort in a school setting where the dictates of the study involve withholding treatment that is perceived as important to the development of all children identified as gifted.

General Research on Ability Grouping

Ability grouping is defined differentially from study to study, school to school, district to district. Procedurally, groups are often divided within the classroom, and sometimes more broadly within the institution. Groups are sometimes categorized by specific subject area and other times not.

Methodology for Group Selection

Methodologically, aptitude is determined in different ways. Sometimes it is determined on the basis of selective test scores or prior achievement in a given academic area, other times on the basis of overall standardized achievement tests, and often on the basis of teacher recommendations.

Outcome Variables

Measured outcomes differ from study to study. Some are concerned with self-concept; others with friendship patterns, attitude toward subject matter and school; and still others with achievement results.

The literature on ability grouping also is characterized by methodological flaws. Internal validity is not always controlled for.

> In cases where homogeneous or heterogeneous ability grouping is related to improved scholastic performance, the curriculum is subject to substantial modification of teaching methods, materials and other variables which are intrinsic to the teaching-learning process, and which, therefore, may well be the causative factors related to academic development wholly apart from ability grouping per se. (Findley & Bryan, 1970, p. 16)

Pros and Cons of Ability Grouping

Arguments do exist in the literature to support ability grouping in general. Homogeneous grouping (1) allows students to advance at their own rate with others of similar ability, (2) offers students methods and materials geared to their level, (3) provides a challenge for students to excel or to be promoted to the next level within a realistic range of competition, and (4) makes teaching easier by restricting the range (Esposito, 1971; Morrison, 1976).

The cons of ability grouping include the usual arguments that (1) ability grouping is undemocratic and affects the self-concept of all children adversely by placing a stigma on those in lower groups while giving higher-group children an inflated sense of their self-worth; (2) most adult life experiences do not occur in homogeneous settings and students must learn to work with a wide range of people; (3) students of lesser ability may profit from learning with those of greater ability; (4) ability grouping tends to segregate children along ethnic, socio-economic lines as well as ability lines; and (5) achievement of truly homogeneous grouping even along a single achievement variable is impossible because test data represent only one type of distinction among varying patterns of individual differences (Findley & Bryan, 1970).

American education has found more comfort in assuming responsibility for socializing children than for meeting their unique educational needs. The issue of grouping conflicts with this overarching socialization goal, for its rationale is educational, based on the psychological differences inherent among children with respect to learning at any given stage of their development. Thus, social role behavior has become embedded in the dilemma of whether to group children according to their ability and in the last 20 years has taken precedence over the educational issues involved. Thus, when we compare the rationale for and against ability grouping and note the lack of definitive research, it is reasonable to concur with

159

Morrison's (1976) sense that "grouping practices have been determined by social and political rather than by purely educational considerations" (p. 67).

Research on Positive Effects of Grouping Gifted Students

One study suggested that the heterogeneity of students' entering achievement levels in a given class limits the teacher's successful adaptation of instruction to individual students' academic needs (Evertson, Sanford, & Emmer, 1981). More heterogeneity also was associated with a lesser degree of student task engagement and cooperation. The researchers also cautioned that heterogeneous grouping places unusual demands on teachers, particularly in the area of classroom management skills.

The Findley and Bryan research review (1970) noted that grouping within a classroom for instruction in particular subjects was an accepted and commended practice and that achievement grouping by individual subjects may be used to advantage. Several studies point to somewhat positive results or effects of ability grouping within specific subjects. In a controlled study of 360 seventh and eighth graders, a computation test revealed better performance by those who were assigned to one of three ability levels on the basis of academic achievement and teachers' recommendations than those who were not (Adamson, 1971).

On the basis of a review of the empirical literature on ability grouping for math instruction, Begle (1975) recommended that school systems should be encouraged to experiment with grouping students within the classroom and that research on team teaching should be done. He mentioned that in math there is "little evidence to indicate that students at one ability level benefit from the presence of students at other ability levels" (p. 9). The Study for Mathematically Precocious Youth Project, in operation since 1971, continues to report positive results from highly selective grouping strategies (Keating, 1976; Stanley, Keating, & Fox, 1974).

With regard to achievement, positive results were obtained from grouping in the Illinois Gifted Experimental Study (Bent, 1969). According to Justman (1954), "The segregation of intellectually gifted pupils in a special class is generally accompanied by academic achievement superior to that normally attained by equally gifted pupils who remain in normal progress groups" (p. 150).

Kulik and Kulik (1982) recently employed meta-analysis to review the empirical literature on ability grouping. They found that students gained somewhat more from grouped classes than from ungrouped ones. The benefits were slight but existent in the area of achievement, with an average increase of 1 sd on achievement exams. The special honors programs often had beneficial effects on the performance of gifted and talented students (p. 426).

Research also tends to support the positive attitudinal effects of grouping gifted students, noting that high-ability students benefited from the stimulation of other high-ability students and from the special curricula (Kulik & Kulik, 1982, p. 426). Wilcox (1963) studied 1,157 eighth grade students to determine the multiple effects of grouping upon their growth and behavior. He found that for the total group, self-concept and attitude toward school were unrelated to grouping, but low-ability groups had a more positive self-concept and attitude toward school with a homogeneous grouping.

A more recent synthesis approach to the review of ability grouping studies was conducted by Slavin (1987). He cited the positive effects of in-class grouping according to ability in order to carry out instruction in key areas of the curriculum, such as reading and math at the elementary level. Nevertheless, he was generally disparaging about homogeneous grouping.

It seems safe to conclude that research data on the positive effects of grouping gifted students are sufficiently favorable to recommend grouping strategies based on the academic needs of gifted students as such needs can be diagnosed for follow-up educational intervention.

Why Group the Gifted?

Being caught in the crossfire of conflicting educational philosophies on grouping can be a major detriment to the academic development of gifted students. Even when a classroom has been purposely devised as heterogeneous, in reality teachers either group within such a schema to deliver instruction appropriately to different learning levels or they lower the overall instructional level to ensure total group understanding. In both cases, grouping has occurred.

The real question seems to center on the purpose for which grouping is done. If it is done to segregate students by income, race, or gender, it should not be tolerated in a public school context. But if it is done to facilitate instruction at appropriate levels, it is indeed meritorious and merely formalizes at a different level (the classroom) what individual teachers have done within heterogeneous classrooms in the name of individualized instruction.

Table 11.1 presents four grouping strategies: heterogeneous classroom, pull-out, semi-separation, and homogeneous classroom. Each grouping arrangement has possible effects, both positive and negative, that educational planners must consider. The key to decision making on this issue must rest with the overall educational purpose of the school as perceived by its administration, board, and community. Are efficient institutional approaches too costly in other dimensions? What is the school's primary purpose? Can both academic concerns and social concerns be accommodated through a choice of grouping models?

TABLE 11.1
Range of Grouping Strategies

Heterogeneous Classroom (no formal grouping of the gifted)	Pullout Grouping Arrangement (3 hours or less per week)	Semi-Separation (5–15 hours per week)	Full-Time Grouping (homogeneous classroom)
Possible Positive Effects	*Possible Positive Effects*	*Possible Positive Effects*	*Possible Positive Effects*
potential for social interaction with all ability ranges development of tutorials to help "slower" students development of independent work habits	some access to appropriate curriculum some contact with intellectual peers more group work with intellectual peers	opportunity to address academic strengths potential for social adaptation in both settings rewarding peer contacts	maximum opportunity to develop intellectual peer group potential for appropriate and integrated curriculum opportunities for classroom work in small groups that share abilities and interests
Possible Negative Effects	*Possible Negative Effects*	*Possible Negative Effects*	*Possible Negative Effects*
no organized ability peer group less challenging curriculum student *always* working independently to achieve appropriate level	fragmentation of curriculum heightened awareness of being labeled "gifted"	lack of group identification difficulty in integrating the curriculum problems associated with being labeled "gifted"	development of insensitivity to nongifted students development of self-concept based on perceptions of ability rather than total person

162

If one examines the possible effects of a given grouping strategy on gifted students, it becomes clear that the more they are grouped in terms of contact time, the more their unique educational needs are met; and conversely, the less they are grouped, the more likely those needs will not be met in any organized and systematic way. Thus, full-time grouping for the gifted should be strongly considered by any school whose primary purpose is perceived to be the development of individual potential.

Strategies for Accomplishing Full-Time Grouping

Full-time grouping of the gifted for academic purposes within the context of a school or district can be handled in various ways. A separate classroom within a school building is perhaps the most common approach at the elementary level. In schools in which this strategy is employed, gifted students participate with all other agemates for physical education, lunch, and art and music periods. Another strategy used successfully is cross-age/cross-grade grouping, especially in small schools in which each grade level does not have enough gifted students to establish a class. In that arrangement, a primary classroom for the gifted might contain children from age 4 to age 7 or 8, working at fifth and sixth grade levels in basic skill areas.

Still another strategy is to establish academic periods, already commonly found in middle schools and high schools, during which students of similar ability study the various content fields offered. Usually the academic period approach carries with it some disadvantages such as (1) fragmentation of learning into visibly separate content fields, (2) the use of several teachers to deliver instruction, thereby limiting opportunities for curriculum integration and knowing individual students well, and (3) a certain regimentation of scheduling.

Nevertheless, any or all of these strategies can be used effectively to bring about an instructional delivery system that will facilitate the education of gifted students. Developing a delivery system for grouping the gifted is crucial to good program development practice and also to the individual student, for each individual needs a sufficiently challenging context in which to experience growth.

Key Concept #2: Program Articulation

Any discussion of the issue of program articulation at a time when many programs are just beginning and others are working to maintain themselves seems rather presumptuous, but the issue of program articulation is central to meaningful program development practices (Tyler, 1958). The term *program articulation* refers to development of appropriate offerings for gifted students on a K–12 basis, with planned curriculum experiences that allow for progressive development of both content and process skills. To examine the issue intelligently, however, we must look at necessary components in the educational enterprise that affect schools' ability to carry out such efforts.

Components of Articulation

One of the assumptions that underlie the ability to carry out program articulation is that schools are willing to accept a primary role for developing individual academic potential. To implement an articulation plan effectively, schools must modify their basic educational program to meet the academic needs of gifted students. In so doing, schools must be willing to abandon a chronological age basis for determining curriculum skill levels and examine instead a *competency-based model* for progress. (Although many educators purport to employ a continuous progress model, in reality it is usually related to steps taken for slower students only.)

A second ingredient of good program articulation is that identification of gifted children occurs when they enter the school district, usually at kindergarten level. The argument frequently given for not identifying at this age is that the tests available to measure giftedness are not reliable or valid for such young children. Several recent studies (Roedell, Jackson, & Robinson, 1980; VanTassel-Baska, Schuler, & Lipschutz, 1982) have indicated, however, that several effective tools can be used in combination for successful identification of young children. Obviously, no identification system at entry will identify all gifted children who could profit from later programming, so provision for an ongoing identification procedure is essential. But from the articulation perspective, *early programming* is critical for ensuring appropriate skill development and commensurate excitation for learning.

A third component underlying articulation is that schools must have some provision for *grouping* gifted children together in the academic areas. Carrying out an articulated program with gifted students who are not seen frequently or for reasonable periods of time is almost impossible. Thus, effective grouping must be employed to make an articulation plan workable.

Another aspect of program articulation is the need for *self-pacing* of the gifted in the core content areas in which the program is offered. A euphemism for self-pacing in the field of education of the gifted is content acceleration and modification, in which scope and sequence in reading, mathematics, science, and social studies for gifted students is programmed from kindergarten through the secondary level. Especially important, given the learning rate differences and intellectual power of gifted students, is the use of (1) a diagnostic/prescriptive approach over

164

time to assure that the learning is progressive; (2) a conceptually organized curriculum that compresses content into major schemas, systems, and matrices for ease in mastering important knowledge areas; and (3) a teacher who facilitates and monitors progress in relationship to student mastery.

An articulation plan also has to address the *integration of process skills, special projects, mentorships, internships, and other modifications* of the overall curriculum for these students into the traditional subject matter provided within the context of the school. Working on the process skills within the traditional domains of knowledge to ensure that gifted students both master them and are able to transfer that mastery to applicable areas makes the most sense.

Assumptions About Teachers and Teaching

Program articulation carries certain assumptions about the selection and training procedures for teachers who work with gifted students. To facilitate conceptual learning in the gifted, the teacher must understand a given domain of knowledge well enough to organize it effectively for able learners and be able to develop advanced-level work for which they may be ready early. Even elementary teachers of the gifted need good content mastery so they can work effectively with the gifted in these areas. Selecting a teacher to work with the mathematically gifted, then, would require high-level ability and training in mathematics, as well as demonstrated effectiveness with gifted students at a given age level. A differentiated staffing pattern within the traditional elementary school could be an effective strategy for obtaining appropriate staff for such programs.

Finally, program articulation implies a sustained confluent approach to meeting the needs of the gifted population. The strategies of acceleration, enrichment, and counseling all have their part in the delivery of an appropriate program effort. A carefully conceived long-range plan that incorporates all of these issues can be effected in any school district that is willing to expend the effort on behalf of gifted students.

Key Concept #3: Cost-Effectiveness

Programs for the gifted may be entering a new cycle in regard to how educators perceive their benefits. More than ever before, cost-effectiveness is an issue in educational programming. Because of general cuts in educational funding at federal, state, and local levels, special programs, including those for the gifted, are being examined more critically.

First, what constitutes an effective gifted program? There are perhaps two ways to respond to that question. One is to cite limited research available on the evaluation of gifted programs (Gallagher, Weiss, Oglesby, & Thomas, 1982).

165

Another is to cite the standards used to judge exemplary programs on a statewide basis (*Illinois Exemplary Program Handbook*, 1979). To be judged effective by the first approach, a program must demonstrate specific benefits to students in the areas of cognitive and/or affective growth. Few programs have found their way into the literature through such an evaluative perspective. The one sustained evaluation effort in this area in the last 20 years is the work of the Study for Mathematically Precocious Youth at Johns Hopkins University, where student growth gains have been impressive.

Standards for what constitutes an effective program for the gifted are more general, yet taken as a whole may be helpful in determining the issue of effectiveness. The standards used for identifying exemplary programs in the Illinois study were:

1. That identification of gifted students (a) focus on the top 5%–8% of a school population; (b) use appropriate instrumentation based on the nature of the program planned; (c) utilize a balance between objective criteria, such as tests, and subjective criteria, such as teacher recommendations and peer inventories; and (d) provide an ongoing process for inclusion of eligible students
2. That the program have appropriate objectives and activities for the nature and needs of the population selected
3. That teaching strategies stress the use of higher-level thinking processes, problem-solving techniques, discussions, and high-quality students products
4. That appropriate measures be taken to select and train the best teachers available for the specific program to be implemented and that community resources be utilized
5. That programs provide comprehensive articulation for students across grade levels and subject areas as need indicates
6. That materials be selected and used in accordance with program objectives
7. That the school and community demonstrate involvement with the program through regular interaction in activities such as parent education seminars, board meetings, and special workshops
8. That the program evaluation be comprehensive, utilizing appropriate instrumentation to document student growth, attitudes of significant publics, and efficacy of program processes

Classroom observation, interview, and review of pertinent documents (*Illinois Exemplary Program Handbook*, 1979) constituted the strategies used by the teams to ascertain if self-nominated school districts were operating exemplary gifted programs.

If these are reasonable standards to consider in finding a gifted program effective, what are the criteria to be used in assessing cost-effectiveness? Given that 80% of any program budget is usually allocated for personnel costs, a gifted program should have a plan for flexible use of existing human resources in order to keep costs under control. Several strategies can be employed to heighten this possibility:

- Grouping and scheduling
- Differentiated staffing
- Planned use of community volunteers
- Extended school day and year

The examples of low-cost gifted programs given in Table 11.2 employ these strategies to varying degrees.

Summary

The administrative issues of grouping, program articulation, and cost-effectiveness have been highlighted in this chapter because of their importance in structuring an effective program for gifted students within the context of current educational practice. No doubt, grouping decisions will continue to be made on philosophical and political bases, but an understanding of the educational implications of such decisions for gifted students is crucial. Programs that offer short-term services will continue to run, but an understanding of long-term linkages may shortcircuit the proliferation of these models. Although some gifted programs may be able to ignore the trend for educational cost accountability, the majority will feel obligated to consider the cost-effective measures that enhance rather than reduce program services.

Based on the discussion in this chapter, effective administrative strategies in implementing gifted programs are critical to the success and longevity of these programs. Full-time grouping of gifted students is recommended to provide maximum benefits in both cognitive and affective areas. A plan for K–12 articulation of programs and services is suggested to enhance individual student development. Cost-effective strategies for sustaining educationally effective programs are strongly advocated.

References

Adamson, D. (1971). *Differentiated multi-track grouping vs. uni-track educational grouping in mathematics*. Unpublished doctoral dissertation, Brigham Young University.

Begle, E. J. (1975). *Ability grouping for math instruction—A review of the empirical literature* (SMEG Working Paper No. 17). Stanford, CA: Stanford University.

Bent, L. (1969). *Grouping of the gifted—An experimental approach*. Peoria, IL: Bradley University.

Colangelo, N., & Zaffrann, R. (1979). *New voices in counseling the gifted*. Dubuque, IA: Kendall-Hunt.

167

TABLE 11.2
Some Examples of Low-Cost Gifted Programs

	Example Program A	Example Program B	Example Program C	Example Program D	Example Program E
Grouping Procedures	Shared instruction periods coordinated through individual education plans made by regular teachers	Cluster grouping of primary-level gifted students to a class; other students also assigned	Part-time class of gifted children from a mixed grade grouping for grades 3–5	Separate course/class for gifted middle school students or cluster in class with other students	Individual mentorships or internships set up with community resource persons
Frequency of contact	150 minutes per week for shared instruction; ongoing differentiated education in regular classroom	All day	1 hour per day or portion of 1 day per week (about 300 minutes total per week)	One class period or more per day depending upon student's needs	2 hours or more per week
Site	Each school: grades 4–6	Each school: grades 2–3	Each school: resource room, media center, and so on.	Each school	Home studio or work site of mentor

Teaching Arrangement	All 4th–6th grade teachers plan together once a week for gifted students and arrange for a group contact time under leadership of teacher or other person	One regular primary teacher works with cluster of gifted and with other assigned students	Itinerant teacher or regular teachers freed for 1 hour per day to work with students	Junior high teacher conducts advanced instruction in subject as part of regular load	Students are given release time to pursue independent research generated by mentor or internship; school coordinator meets regularly with students and mentors to discuss progress
Resources Needed	Training of all teachers involved, plus materials	Aide, resource teacher, and/or volunteers to assist, plus training for teacher, plus materials	Training for teacher, plus a room or area to conduct class, plus materials	Training for teachers, plus some materials	Volunteer mentors, plus transportation to off-school sites, plus a coordinator to find mentors, match students, and monitor progress

Note. From *An Administrator's Guide to the Education of the Gifted and Talented* (p. 81) by J. VanTassel-Baska, 1981, Washington, DC: National Association of State Boards of Education. Used by permission.

169

Esposito, D. (1971). *Homogeneous and heterogeneous grouping: Principal findings and implications of a re-search of the literature.* Bloomington, IN: Phi Delta Kappa Educational Foundation.

Evertson, C., Sanford, J., & Emmer, E. (1981). Effects of class heterogeneity in junior high school. *American Educational Research Journal, 18*(2), 219–232.

Findley, W., & Bryan, M. (1970). *Ability grouping 1970: Status, impact and alternatives.* Atlanta: Center for Educational Improvement.

Gallagher, J., Weiss, P., Oglesby, K., & Thomas, T. (1982). *Report on education of gifted, II: Surveys of education of gifted students.* Chapel Hill: University of North Carolina, Frank Porter Child Development Center.

Gowan, J. C. (1964). Twenty-five suggestions for parents of able children. *Gifted Child Quarterly, 8,* 192–193.

Gowan, J., & Bruch, C. B. (1971). *The academically talented student and guidance.* Boston: Houghton Mifflin.

Hall, T. (1956). *Gifted children, the Cleveland story.* Cleveland: World.

Hauck, B.B., & Freehill, M. F. (1972). *Gifted case studies.* Dubuque, IA: Wm. C. Brown.

Hollingworth, L. (1942). *Children above 180 I.Q.* New York: World Book.

Illinois Exemplary Program Handbook. (1979). Springfield: Illinois Office of Education.

Justman, J. (1954). Academic achievement of intellectually gifted accelerants and non-accelerants in junior high school. *School Review, 62,* 142–150.

Keating, D. P. (Ed.) (1976). *Intellectual talent: Research and development.* Baltimore, MD: Johns Hopkins University Press.

Kulik, C. L., & Kulik, J. (1982). Effects of ability grouping on secondary school students: A meta-analysis of evaluation findings. *American Educational Research Journal, 19*(3), 415–428.

Morrison, C. M. (1976). Ability grouping and mixed ability grouping in secondary schools. *Educational Issues Review 1.* Glasgow: Scottish Council for Research in Education.

Roedell, W., Jackson, N., & Robinson, H. (1980). *Gifted young children.* New York: Teachers College Press.

Silverman, L. (1983). The affective needs of gifted children. In J. VanTassel-Baska (Ed.), *A practical guide to counseling the gifted in a school setting.* Reston, VA: Council for Exceptional Children.

Slavin, R. (1987). *A synthesis of research in group therapy.* Baltimore, MD: Johns Hopkins University, Center for Research on Policy.

Stanley, J. C., Keating, D. P., & Fox, L. H. (Eds.). (1974). *Mathematical talent: Discovery, description, and development.* Baltimore, MD: Johns Hopkins University Press.

Terman, L. (Ed.). (1921). *Genetic studies of genius* (Vol. 1). Stanford, CA: Stanford University Press.

Tyler, R. (1958). *Principles of curriculum and instruction.* Chicago: University of Chicago Press.

VanTassel-Baska, J. (1981). *An administrator's guide to the education of the gifted and talented.* Washington, DC: National Association of State Boards of Education.

VanTassel-Baska, J., Schuler, A., & Lipschutz, J. (1982). An experimental program for gifted four-year-olds. *Journal for the Education of the Gifted, 5*(1), 45–55.

Wilcox, J. (1963). *A search for the multiple effects of grouping upon the growth and behavior of junior high school pupils.* Unpublished doctoral dissertation, Cornell University.

170

Study Questions

1. Why has grouping gifted learners become a major issue in public schools?

2. We have difficulty articulating gifted programs from elementary to middle school and from middle school to high school. What are some ways to enhance these transition points?

3. What arguments would you put forth to have local schools provide funding for gifted programs?

4. How might differentiated staffing support the administrative feasibility of a gifted program?

5. What potential problems might be encountered in building an exemplary gifted program?

CURRICULUM AND INSTRUCTION

12

Appropriate Curriculum for the Gifted

Joyce VanTassel-Baska

As one examines the issue of appropriate curriculum for the gifted, several questions deserve to be asked and considered before moving into curriculum development.

1. What should be the *content* of curriculum for the gifted? Should it be different in substance from the curriculum of other learners or merely reorganized more efficiently?
2. How do we treat the cognitive processes of critical and creative thinking, problem solving, and decision making—as content in themselves or as overlays to existing content areas? Do we treat the processes as appropriate *only* for the gifted or as a part of a curriculum for all?
3. Can we define with precision and integrity what we mean by "differentiating" the curriculum for the gifted?
4. For what group of learners are we planning curricular experiences—only the high achievers or a broader base of students who may vary in their profiles to the extent that a planned set of experiences may not be responsive to their needs?

175

5. How can we sequence curriculum experiences in such a way as to provide maximum learning for the gifted?
6. How can we best effect curriculum change for the gifted in schools—by selecting certain grouping patterns, by training, or by monitoring curriculum implementation?

These questions continue to haunt us as a field partly because so little emphasis has been placed on curriculum matters in general during the last 20 years in our schools and partly because we have not successfully been able to settle on workable answers to these questions. As we begin to educate the gifted for the year 2000, it is clearly time to tackle some of these issues with renewed vigor.

Research on Curriculum for the Gifted

Research into appropriate curriculum for gifted children is fairly recent. Until the *Sputnik* era of the late 1950s—which resulted in programs that addressed specific content areas—few ideas about differentiated curriculum for the gifted had been systematically studied. Even though special classes had been in operation since 1919 in selected locations such as New York and Cleveland, the actual differences in instructional strategies, content, or materials were not examined. Grouping based on intelligence and achievement was the predominant strategy employed, and curriculum outlines and, sometimes, units were prepared for use with identified gifted students (Hall, 1956; Hollingworth, 1926).

More recently, however, educators in the field of the gifted have conceptualized some general principles about appropriate curriculum for gifted children. Ward (1961) developed a theory of differential education for the gifted that established specific principles around which an appropriate curriculum for the gifted could be developed. Meeker (1969) used the Guilford structure of intellect to arrive at student profiles highlighting areas of strength and weakness so that curriculum planners could build a gifted program to improve weak areas. Curriculum workbooks were structured specifically to address this need in the areas of memory, cognition, convergent thinking, divergent thinking, and evaluation. Renzulli (1975) focused on a differentiated curriculum model that moved the gifted child from enrichment exposure activities through training in thinking and research skills into a project-oriented program that dealt with real problems to be solved. Gallagher (1975) stressed content modification in the core subject areas of language arts, social studies, mathematics, and science. Stanley, Keating, and Fox (1974) concentrated on a content acceleration model to differentiate programs for the gifted.

Recent writings, including Feldhusen and Kolloff (1978), Kaplan (1979), and Maker (1982) have stressed a confluent approach to differentiation of curriculum for the gifted that includes both acceleration and enrichment strategies. Passow

(1982) and his colleagues formulated seven cardinal curriculum principles that reflect content, process, product, behavioral, and evaluative considerations. VanTassel-Baska et al. (1988) developed an outline of 20 aspects of good curriculum for the gifted.

State of the Art

In examining the state of the art with respect to curriculum, one is struck by the abstract broadness of the principles compared to the one-dimensionality of the practice. To implement appropriate curriculum for gifted students, there must be concern for the translation of theoretical principles into good practice in a holistic manner so that education of the gifted is complete, not fragmented. This can be accomplished if we focus on the core elements to be addressed:

1. Gifted children learn at a different rate from other groups of children, and accommodating that rate is crucial to their development (Keating, 1976). Furthermore, differences in rate or pace can be so great that these necessitate differences in *kind*, not merely degree, of instruction (Ward, 1961).

2. Gifted children crave *depth* in key areas of learning. Educators have addressed this need through "enrichment," which tends to become a superficial add-on to the curriculum. The issue of depth cannot be addressed by this type of approach.

   It can be addressed by examining key areas of learning in terms of their essence, core, and inherent concepts and exploring with gifted children through Socratic means what these key concepts are and how they relate to all areas of learning. Appropriate learning materials for such work include *Ascent of Man*, by Jacob Bronowski (1973); *Connections*, by James Burke (1978); and *Civilization*, by Kenneth Clark (1969).

3. Gifted children need the challenge and stimulation of being together for at least part of every school day, with expectation levels set high enough to stretch their potential ability to realize them. Setting high expectation levels does not imply more work at low levels of difficulty but, rather, unending work at complex levels of operation. In that sense, meaningful work for the gifted is that which creates more questions that require exploration and leads to continued study on an individual or small-group basis. These expectations can be set and worked on only in a climate in which children have similar levels of ability and understanding. Therefore, grouping of gifted children becomes essential.

4. Gifted children need programs and services across the span of years that they are in school. Their giftedness frequently manifests itself by age 3 and requires nurturance on a regular basis from that time forward. Thus, K–12 articulated planning and programming for all gifted students is essential.

177

Once these basic elements have been understood, we can begin to examine the areas of content learning that are most facilitative for gifted students.

Traditional Content Learning

The myth persists that some semblance of a program is better than no program at all. Once students are in a gifted program, they tend to respond favorably to it, regardless of its structure or its focus. Consequently, we sometimes are hard-pressed to show that the *nature* of a particular treatment has made a difference, as opposed to the mere fact that some treatment occurred. Even positive evaluations overall may be more a manifestation of the Hawthorne effect* than of "significant difference." Many gifted programs, just by their existence, offer emotional and motivational support for many gifted children, who then "take off" on their own.

By the same token, as we become more knowledgeable about identifying talent at early ages, we must plan for programmatic intervention much more carefully and consistently. Solid research shows that mathematical talent and foreign language ability can be most economically developed through an accelerative mode (Keating, 1976; Stanley et al., 1974; VanTassel-Baska, 1981). Only descriptive studies imply that enrichment is useful to a student's fuller understanding of the world (Gallagher, 1985). We have teachers who are trained to teach content. We may have teachers who can teach creative processes. We know that schools are organized to handle gifted children best within content areas (especially at grades 7–12). Based on these observations, it seems prudent to build a foundational program for gifted students within the basic domains of knowledge—the sciences, mathematics, the humanities, the social sciences, and the behavioral sciences.

Why should curriculum for the gifted be conceptualized within the framework of the basic domains of knowledge? To satisfy gifted students' need for depth, exposure to these traditional areas of learning is essential, not only to develop and refine proficiency skills in verbal and quantitative areas, but also to allow for expanded growth into related disciplines and interdisciplinary studies. A firm understanding of a field of inquiry must precede "creative dabbling." Gifted writers have thoroughly mastered techniques of writing and have refined their skills through repeated practice. The "creative" aspect of writing demands a high level of proficiency in the skill and repeated use of both ends of the writing implement before a product could be perceived as art. By the same token, gifted students benefit greatly from curriculum experiences that go beyond and across the traditional content areas in order to acquire an integrated understanding of knowledge. Cur-

---

The Hawthorne effect refers to the positive effect brought about by the act of experimentation itself, based on a set of studies and conducted at the Hawthorne plant of the Western Electric Company by researcher Elton Mayo from 1923 to 1932.

riculum for the gifted should connote the literal meaning of the Latin root for the term *education*—a "leading out" from one point in experience to view the larger perspective.

A curriculum that does not have a strong content base or focus has little richness. In reality, identifying aptitude that corresponds to a content area such as mathematics and the verbal arts is far easier than conceptualizing programming in another fashion. Specific content areas provide the appropriate match for specific aptitudes. We would not think of providing a child with high musical aptitude a program in futuristics or an independent study in building an electrical car. Yet, these practices frequently are applied to students who have readily identifiable aptitudes in specific academic areas. Students with high mathematical aptitude should receive a strong program in mathematics concepts and systems. Students with high verbal abilities should be provided programs in foreign language, rich literature, and writing.

By this rather obvious connection, we do not intend to imply that serving the gifted appropriately requires only a direct match to a specific identified aptitude area. In the minds of most educators of gifted students, much more is needed. The research base on the positive effects of this approach with precocious students, however, is impressive (Durden, 1979; Stanley et al., 1974). Yet, this deceptively simple approach of matching aptitudes to curriculum offerings rarely occurs in the average elementary school in this country and is subverted at the middle school and high school levels by inflexible scheduling and programming.

Misconceptions in Teaching Traditional Content

Perhaps traditional content domains have been passed over for curricular work in the education of the gifted because of several misconceptions. One of these is that the gifted "get" these content areas in their regular school program and, therefore, the gifted should have a "special" curriculum. Unfortunately, the content that the gifted receive is minimal compared to what they are capable of learning. If content were rearranged and restructured around a conceptual framework, the gifted could master whole content areas in half the time currently spent.

This compression of content facilitates proficiency and the learning of conceptual wholes. It also allows more time for gifted learners to pursue related areas of interest. For example, the gifted can master all the principles of English grammar and syntax in less than 4 weeks of instruction in any given year. By demonstrating this proficiency on a criterion-referenced test, they then can begin to apply that knowledge to their specific areas of language interest: a course in Latin, a workshop in composition writing, a debate team. Instead, we tend to introduce grammar in minute sections, drag it out over 12 years of English instruction, and never present it so that the gifted have the opportunity to grasp the total linguistic picture or to learn new language systems.

179

Another misconception is that content acceleration merely means moving through the same material faster. In reality, good content acceleration allows for faster pacing of well organized, compressed, and appropriate learning experiences for the gifted. Real enrichment for the gifted in the content areas can occur *only* if a fast-paced compressed model is utilized. Otherwise, content is trivialized or disconnected to what is happening in the general program. We can focus on teaching logic as an enrichment topic for the gifted in math but must be prepared to accelerate and compress it to accommodate the gifted learner. Thus, enrichment topics only define a content focus, not an appropriate treatment.

A third misconception concerning the use of content areas with gifted students is that there are more important areas of learning for them to explore for purposes of developing their potential creativity. Yet, creativity without subject matter competency has no meaning (Stanley, 1980). Creative mathematicians in real life must be proficient in mathematics before they can apply math principles and concepts in new and diverse ways. Even in applied areas of endeavor such as engineering, medicine, and education, conceptual proficiency in core content domains of knowledge is critical.

Values Education

Most would agree that high-level ability that is not directed in socially constructive ways may be socially dangerous. Thus, curriculum for the gifted should include components of values education through which students can learn to examine their own values as well as the values of others. Some research tends to suggest that gifted students often are concerned about the moral and ethical dimensions of questions (Gallagher, 1985). Therefore, the study of competing value systems would serve to enhance the understanding of an area of identified interest. Assuming that gifted students often become the leaders of tomorrow, the moral, social, and ethical dimensions of topics seem particularly relevant as an area for study.

Thinking Skills Learning

If accelerative and in-depth experiences are provided to the gifted as a framework, the development of skills in critical or creative thinking and research can become an overlay to programs, even though they have been conceptualized in a content modality. By their nature, good critical and creative thinking experiences are adaptable with respect to content, age level, and the experience of participants. These experiences tend to be presented through teaching strategies that create diverse and motivated responses. Their purpose is primarily to provide a prelude to analytical and creative endeavors, regardless of type, and to open up children to

180

fuller expression of their potential (Feldhusen & Kolloff, 1978). Because this is the case, restructuring and infusing a program with these aspects of the curriculum is easier than sacrificing traditional content areas or treating them as an add-on to the curriculum.

Development of process skills in students should be viewed as basic to their curriculum and should begin as soon as they enter school. These "basics for the gifted" would reflect practice in the following skill areas:

Critical thinking
Creative thinking
Problem solving
Research
Decision making

Each of these skills should be linked directly to a content domain. Thus, gifted students would learn problem solving in mathematics, critical thinking in literature, and decision making in history. Skill development in all five areas is stressed on a hierarchical K–12 basis. This approach appears to be promising in light of the lack of research on process programs that demonstrate transfer of these skills to content dimensions after the skills have been mastered in isolation.

Learning the Arts

Certainly gifted children need the rigor of a program in a content area in which they excel, coupled with the overlay of the process skills of critical and creative thinking, and research. In addition to these components, gifted children need the arts for development of high intellectual potential, and they need them as early as kindergarten. A good gifted program should incorporate the arts, both in terms of developing performance skills and developing aesthetic judgment throughout the education continuum. For students with special abilities in these areas, intensive training may be most appropriate.

Why the arts? Real enrichment, it can be argued, consists of offering new awareness about the world that has a deep relevance to the individual. Surely the arts can offer this in a way that other fields cannot, for the arts tap into the emotional center of human beings (Eisner, 1984). We are responsive to art and music and the performing arts because we are human, and they touch us as human beings. The immense difference one senses in live performance versus the electronically filtered reproduction of a recording makes the point eloquently.

What we know about the nature of the gifted child would lead us to include a strong component in the arts. Differential characteristics such as high-level sensitivity, keenness of perception, and the ability to understand interrelationships and

181

grasp meanings (Clark, 1980) all reflect a need for exposure to aesthetic experiences that allow for further development of these traits. In addition, research studies on eminence point to the passion for and importance of the arts displayed by individuals who were exceptional in fields other than artistic endeavor (Cox, 1926; Goertzel & Goertzel, 1962).

Teaching the arts to the gifted is also particularly critical in developing an understanding of self and others, based on the interrelationship of thoughts and feelings. All of the arts offer a medium for understanding the congruence of ideas and emotions. The arts provide direct access to emotional response, but through a rational process and presentation. The arts can be a vehicle for developing aesthetic judgment, thus offering many opportunities for the acquisition of evaluation skills. Setting criteria to measure the value of art objects, a piece of music, or a performance enables gifted students to act as "critics" and to develop the intellectual framework for this kind of effort.

Offering an arts component in a curriculum for the gifted can be a good stimulus for some students to begin the formal study of a particular area. For example, a student may wish to pursue musicology as a result of early music experiences. Another may wish to intern in a museum to learn the job of curator. Thus, career exploration can be merged with serious study in a specific area of interest.

The arts also lend themselves well to development of meaningful projects, not only in terms of conceptualization but also in terms of the actual mode of presentation. Children who have experienced theater are more apt to try to create it than those who have not. Similarly, children exposed to the visual arts are more apt to employ them in a creative product. Consequently, product development can be enhanced greatly by systematic work in the arts.

Relating the arts in some manner also offers to gifted children an excellent opportunity to analyze and synthesize information in the aesthetic domain. It builds on their strong ability to grasp interrelationships and comprehend meaning at high levels. Deliberately planned experiences that use "forced association" as a technique work well in the arts and begin to move children toward free association among other arts experiences. At junior high and high school levels, the interrelationships can take the form of a humanities program in which the arts are seen as an avenue to other fields, such as philosophy, history, and literature.

Additional Services and Programs

I have argued strongly for traditional content, process skills, and the arts as key components in an ideal curriculum for the gifted. Other special services and programs uniquely appropriate for this population are needed as well. Areas such as counseling, career education, and mentorships should be considered.

182

Counseling

Counseling is not usually considered a part of curriculum; yet, it is a service that provides the key framework for the curriculum delivery system to work for gifted students. Therefore, counseling services become a curricular concern. Particularly at middle school and high school levels, counseling (or lack of it) determines what courses the students take and what level of course. For gifted students to receive appropriate curriculum, they must be informed about specific courses that address their area(s) of strength. In addition, gifted students should have the opportunity to understand and cope with their exceptionality in small group sharing sessions, receive training in decision-making skills, and be provided alternative choices involving course taking, colleges, and careers (VanTassel-Baska, 1983).

Counseling for the gifted should occur during the span of school years. Although coping skills may be most critical at the elementary level, academic counseling becomes important by junior high school, as decisions often have to be made four years in advance. Choices of what college to attend and what career to pursue become important counseling issues by ninth grade and should be reflected in a specific structured program provided by the school. Parent involvement in all aspects of the counseling program is essential, as is the use of teachers to perform the counseling function. Utilization of counseling specialists may be necessary in the case of gifted youths who experience unusual difficulty in adjustment, achievement, and other school-related issues.

Career Education

Concern for career education for gifted individuals stems from their natural profusion of riches in regard to life's alternatives. Because many of these students are good at so many kinds of task, to focus attention and energy on one line of endeavor is sometimes difficult and even painful for them. Career education can enhance their powers of decision making by enabling informed choices based on assessments of strength, interest, and values (Hoyt & Hebeler, 1974). Furthermore, the gifted can learn to appreciate the uniqueness of their potential through recognizing life themes as a basis for career choice (Silverman, in press).

By the same token, some gifted students are very sure at an early age about the career avenue they wish to pursue. Career education can supplement these students' avid interest in a field by providing internship experiences in the desired career area as early as junior high school. In addition, it can help both student and parent plan ahead for educational experiences that would be most profitable, given the clarity of choice. Many times irrelevant requirements can be avoided if the course of study is well defined (VanTassel-Baska, 1981).

183

Mentorships

Much of the research on eminent persons clearly points to the profound influence of a single tutor/friend/family member on the gifted child (Bloom & Sosniak, 1981; Cox, 1926; Goertzel & Goertzel, 1962). Both as an aid to cognitive learning and for emotional support, the one-to-one relationship has provided special benefits for the development of exceptional potential.

Although the tutorial approach may be ideal, it is hardly practical for schools to consider for more than a few students and rather difficult for parents to implement on their own. But creating the opportunity for gifted children to experience a mentor relationship on a limited basis still can be facilitative to their development.

Creating a mentorship experience requires two fundamental steps: (1) developing a resource bank of adults in the community who have an interest in working with gifted students and who have high-level expertise in a particular area, and (2) identifying students who can profit from exposure to these adults and who share similar abilities and interests with the chosen mentor. A structured mentorship program can focus on a contract between student and mentor for completion of specific tasks or a project over a predetermined time period (Cox & Daniel, 1983; Ellingson, Haeger, & Feldhusen, 1986). Other collaborative opportunities can develop out of the working relationship that is established, such as an "apprenticeship" situation in a research laboratory, a joint publication, or a shared presentation at a professional meeting.

Key Issues in Development and Implementation of Curriculum

A curriculum for the gifted must be more than the sum of the components just discussed. It must represent an interaction among the content dimension, the instructional dimension, and the logistical dimension. Although the scope of this chapter concerns itself primarily with the content dimension, certain logistical issues that provide the framework and setting for the delivery of content merit comment.

Principles and Instructional/ Logistical Implications

The curriculum committee of the Leadership Training Institute has conceptualized seven principles that contain instructional and logistical implications in a curriculum for gifted students (Passow, 1982):

1. The content of curricula for the gifted should focus on, and be organized to include, more elaborate, complex, and in-depth study of major ideas, problems, and themes that integrate knowledge within and across systems of thought.
2. Curricula for the gifted should allow for the development and application of productive thinking skills to enable students to reconceptualize existing knowledge and generate new knowledge.
3. Curricula for the gifted should enable them to explore constantly changing knowledge and information and develop the attitude that knowledge is worth pursuing in an open world.
4. Curricula for the gifted should encourage exposure to, selection of, and use of specialized and appropriate resources.
5. Curricula for the gifted should promote self-initiated and self-directed learning and growth.
6. Curricula for the gifted should provide for the development of self-understanding and the understanding of one's relationships to persons, societal institutions, nature, and culture.
7. Evaluations of curricula for the gifted should be conducted in accordance with prior stated principles, stressing higher-level thinking skills, creativity, and excellence in performance and products.

Expanding on this list, VanTassel-Baska et al. (1988) cited the checklist of principles given in Table 12.1, some of which represent general curricular considerations as well as specific ones deemed appropriate for the gifted.

Scope and Sequence

Good curriculum must reflect progressive development in both skill and content arenas (Tyler, 1958) so that appropriate pacing and diversity are maintained. Student interest should be a prime input factor in modifying curricular units and teacher expectations with regard to the expansion of educational and cultural opportunities for gifted students.

The curriculum should reflect provisions for accelerating skill building in the areas of reading, writing, research, the use of computers and scientific apparatus, and mathematical problem solving. It should demonstrate well planned sequential development of increasingly difficult content and processes and include materials and activities that will provide for the development of skills in group and individual problem solving and decision making. Interdisciplinary curriculum units should provide for conceptual development over time. Themes such as humankind's search for identity, the question of authority, and the concept of unity could be explored at several grade levels with more sophisticated objectives in mind at each succeeding level.

185

TABLE 12.1
Checklist of Curriculum Principles
for Use in Developing Gifted/Talented Programs

General Principles

☐ 1. Continuity—a well defined set of learning activities that reinforce the specified curriculum objective
☐ 2. Diversity—provisions for alternative means to attain determined ends within a specified curricular framework
☐ 3. Integration—integrative use of all abilities, including cognition, emotion, and intuition
☐ 4. Substantive learning—inclusion of subject matter, skills, products, and awareness that are of consequence to the learner and to the discipline
☐ 5. Consistency with good teaching/learning methodologies—inclusion of varied teaching practices that allow for motivation, practice, transfer of training, and feedback
☐ 6. Interaction with peers and significant others—provisions to learn about and meet with individuals who share same and different talents/gifts
☐ 7. Value system—inclusion of consistent opportunities to develop and examine personal and societal values and to establish a personal value system
☐ 8. Communication skills—development of verbal and nonverbal systems and skills to dialogue, share, and exchange ideas
☐ 9. Multiple resources—provision of a variety of material and human resources as part of the learning process

Specific Principles for Gifted Curriculum

☐ 1. Appropriateness—curriculum based on assessment of abilities, interests, needs, and learning styles of gifted students
☐ 2. Openness—elimination of preset expectations that limit the learnings within the curricular framework
☐ 3. Independence—provisions for some type(s) of self-directed learning
☐ 4. Complexity—provision for exposure to systems of knowledge, underlying principles and concepts, and key theories about what students study
☐ 5. Interdisciplinary learning—provisions for transfer of learning to other domains of knowledge, new situations, and so on
☐ 6. Decision making—provisions for students to make some appropriate/relevant decisions regarding what is to be learned and how
☐ 7. Creation/re-creation—provisions to apply the creative process to improve and modify one's creations and to challenge prevailing thought and offer more appropriate solutions
☐ 8. Timing—appropriation of time span for learning activities that is consistent with characteristics of gifted learners for shorter/longer allotments
☐ 9. Accelerated/advanced pacing of content—provision for quickness and aptness of gifted students to master new material
☐ 10. Economy—compressed and streamlined organization of teaching material to match learning capacity of gifted students
☐ 11. Challenge—provision for a sophisticated level of learning experience that requires gifted learners to stretch their understandings

186

The scope of full-time curriculum for the gifted should be broad-based and as comprehensive as possible, given the level of ability and interest of the students. At the same time, curriculum experiences must be carefully structured to promote maximum learning in specific aptitude areas.

Differentiation

Most gifted programs, it is generally agreed, may be distinguished from regular programs by placing *more* emphasis on the following curriculum considerations:

1. *The principle of economy* seeks to delete or compress a gifted student's basic curriculum in content skills that he or she has mastered independently or can master quickly if the organization of content focuses on concept mastery. Thus, a student who comes to school reading holistically would not be expected to spend kindergarten and first grade in reading readiness programs or heavy phonics training. Rather, a reading program would be devised focusing on developmental reading skills such as vocabulary, comprehension, and interpretation. Phonics work would be organized into a set of skills for quick mastery by this student.

2. *Concentration on higher-level thinking skills* is an important tool for the gifted student as a producer rather than a consumer of knowledge. Application of skills such as critical and creative thinking are essential for meaningful work in any context.

3. *Concentration on the interrelationships among bodies of knowledge* focuses on depth in the curriculum plan developed for the gifted. Based on Ward's (1961) theory of differential education for the gifted, it establishes the concept of content integration by schemas and systems for the gifted as the highest order of importance.

4. *Exposure to nontraditional school subjects* provides gifted students challenging areas of traditional liberal arts curriculum not offered in elementary and secondary schools, such as logic, law, and philosophy. Early exposure and training in foreign language at the elementary level also could be an offering in this context.

5. *Self-directed learning* enables gifted students to develop responsibility and take charge of their own learning and growth. Upon demonstrating such responsibility, students will have access to more program options of an independent nature.

6. *Commitment to future learning.* Gifted students must become sensitive to the knowledge explosion and the impact of technology on the task of learning, with the view that learning will be a fulfilling, lifelong pursuit.

Grouping

Most educators who work with the gifted believe that the practice of putting young-sters of similar abilities, interests, and learning styles together for large portions of time is hard to equal. Gifted youngsters enjoy more than almost anything else the opportunity to exchange ideas among themselves without fear of being laughed at or scorned. Some programs group youngsters only periodically or for a certain time each day. In any case, extensive grouping by interest and ability is needed for gifted students to fully develop their potential. Recent research supports the con-tention that grouping together enhances achievement and a positive attitude toward the subject matter (Kulik & Kulik, 1983). An even more recent review of the group-ing studies shows favorable results from most forms of instructional grouping (Sla-vin, 1987).

Instructional grouping enables students to grow in ways that are not possible under other arrangements, and this approach allows a program to reveal effective-ness much more readily. The historical development of gifted programs highlights the strong relationship between the longevity of a program and its grouping pat-terns. Both the Cleveland Major Work Program and the Bronx High School of Sci-ence have survived more than 50 years and employ full-time grouping of gifted students in all academic areas. Comprehensive programs for the gifted should utilize instructional grouping strategies as frequently as possible to enhance con-tinuity of individual student progress as well as the continuity and effectiveness of the overall program.

Program Articulation

Any school district that takes on the task of developing a gifted program must care-fully consider an overall articulation plan that allows for identification of its gifted population at the kindergarten level and offers appropriate programming for that population on a K–12 basis. In many districts, funds do not exist to implement a total program in any given year, but total articulation can be accomplished within a reasonable span of time. An example might be a 3-year plan in which K–3 stu-dents and identified high school students receive programming during year 1, students in grades 4–6 in year 2, and 7–8 in year 3. In this way, all students iden-tified in year 1 will receive appropriate services from the point of identification, yet the district will have an opportunity to stagger its program implementation.

Program articulation of this kind is important for several reasons:

1. Once a student has been identified and offered a program at any given level, he or she has the right to expect that it will continue on the same basis.

2. Because content acceleration is and should be a facet of many gifted programs, students should not have to return to a level of work less than their state of advancement.
3. Growth gains and attitude changes can be adversely affected by programs coming too late in a student's career or stopping in the middle.

An Ideal Curriculum for the Gifted

Table 12.2 attempts to delineate and apply all the curricular components discussed in this chapter. It highlights the need for content specialization. It attends to the need for acceleration, enrichment, and other special services in educating the gifted. It recognizes the role of thinking skills in developing students' potential, and it provides appropriate experiences in the arts. It demonstrates progressive and sequential development of broad curriculum areas on a K–12 basis and suggests the need for comprehensive services across the span of school years. It highlights differentiation issues in an integrated fashion. I hope it will serve as a guide for schools and parents in making sound educational decisions around curriculum alternatives for gifted and talented students.

The table also provides provides examples of topics/courses that might be offered at a grade-level cluster. Sequence of a topic or content area is suggested across clusters by section. The intent of the table is to suggest ideas and principles discussed in this chapter, not to prescribe for any given school program.

Summary

This chapter has contended that a content-based curriculum is the core of any program for gifted and talented students. It has argued for including traditional subject matter areas taught from a process perspective with experiences in the arts. It has demonstrated that conceptual learning and enrichment in the content areas must be accompanied by appropriate content acceleration allowing for both pacing and depth. It has asserted the need for a facilitative grouping model to accommodate a full range of comprehensive articulated programs and services to gifted students at all grade levels.

References

Bloom, B., & Sosniak, L. (1981). Talent development versus schooling. *Educational Leadership, 39,* 86–94.

Bronowski, J. (1973). *Ascent of man.* Boston: Little, Brown.

TABLE 12.2
Essential Curriculum Components for Gifted Students

Acceleration, Compression, and Reorganization of Content Based on Proficiency (examples)

K–3	4–6	7–8	9–12
Reading Mathematics Science Social studies Literature/language arts	Reading Mathematics Science Social studies Literature/language arts	Access to high school coursework in selected content areas including mathematics, foreign language, English study, social studies, science	Access to upper-level high school and/or college courses Advanced Placement courses according to strength areas Foreign language instruction—third and fourth year of a foreign language

Infusion of Process Skills and Nontraditional Content (examples)

K–3	4–6	7–8	9–12
Problem-solving strategies Science experimentation via computers Expository and creative writing Creative dramatics Introduction of foreign languages Development of critical and creative thinking skills Learning of basic research skills on topics of interest	A computer literacy program Foreign language instruction Research projects Theater arts Junior Great Books Man: A Course of Study (MACOS)	Foreign language instruction (second year) A course in logic Selective reading and discussion groups Humanities course Writing computer programs Advanced research projects	Art appreciation Music appreciation Leadership Psychology Anthropology Urban planning Political science Law Creativity

Integration of Curriculum Experiences According to Ideas, Issues, and Themes (examples)

K–3	4–6	7–8	9–12
Change as reflected in the conventions of society (shelter, clothing, food) Signs and symbols that make up our world (words, traffic signs, language gestures)	Change as reflected in the development of major cultures in respect to art, language, inventive mathematics Symbol systems (languages, mathematics, sign language)	Change as reflected in the development of major cultures The development of a symbol system (codes, computer language)	Change as reflected in the development of major cultures Symbol systems as represented in the real world (abstract mathematics, genetic patterns, literary symbols)

Burke, J. (1978). *Connections*. Boston: Little, Brown.

Clark, B. (1980). *Growing up gifted*. Columbus, OH: Charles E. Merrill.

Clark, K. (1969). *Civilization*. New York: Harper & Row.

Cox, C. M. (1926). *Genetic studies of genius* (Vol. 2). Stanford, CA: Stanford University Press.

Cox, J., & Daniel, N. (1983, September–October). The role of the mentor, *G/C/T*, 54–61.

Durden, W. (1979). The Johns Hopkins program for verbally gifted youth. *Roeper Review, 2*(3), 34-37.

Eisner, E. (1984). *Educational Evaluation*. London: Falmer Press.

Ellingson, M., Haeger, W., & Feldhusen, J. (1986, March–April). The Purdue mentor program, *G/C/T*, 2–5.

Feldhusen, J., & Kolloff, M. (1978). A three-stage model for gifted education. *G/C/T, 1*, 53–58.

Gallagher, J. J. (1975). *Teaching the gifted child* (2nd ed.). Boston: Allyn & Bacon.

Goertzel, V., & Goertzel, M. (1962). *Cradles of eminence*. Boston: Little, Brown.

Hall, T. (1956). *Gifted children, the Cleveland story*. Cleveland: World Publishing.

Hollingworth, L. (1926). *Gifted children*. New York: World Book.

Hoyt, K., & Hebeler, J. (1974). *Career education for the gifted and talented*. Salt Lake City: Olympus.

Kaplan, S. (1979). Language arts and social studies curriculum in the elementary school. In H. Passow (Ed.), *The gifted and talented: Their education and development* (78th yearbook of the National Society for the Study of Education, Part 1). Chicago: University of Chicago Press.

Keating, D. (1976). *Intellectual talent: Research and development*. Baltimore, MD: Johns Hopkins University Press.

Kulik, E. & Kulik, J. (1983). Effects of ability grouping on secondary school students: A meta-analysis of evaluation findings. *American Educational Research Journal, 19*(3), 415–428.

Maker, C. J. (1982). *Curriculum development for the gifted*. Rockville, MD: Aspen Systems.

Meeker, M. (1969). *The structure of intellect: Its interpretations and uses*. Columbus, OH: Charles E. Merrill.

Passow, A. H. (1982). *LTI committee report*. Unpublished report, National/State Leadership Training Institute of the Gifted and Talented.

Renzulli, J. (1975). *The enrichment triad*. Wethersfield, CT: Creative Learning Press.

Slavin, R. (1987). *A synthesis of research in grouping*. Baltimore, MD: Johns Hopkins University, Center for Research on Policy.

Stanley, J. (1980). On educating the gifted. *Educational Researcher, 9*, 8–12.

Stanley, J., Keating, D., & Fox, L. (1974). *Mathematical talent: Discovery, description, and development*. Baltimore, MD: Johns Hopkins University Press.

Tyler, R. (1958). *Principles of curriculum and instruction*. Chicago: University of Chicago Press.

VanTassel-Baska, J. (1981). A comprehensive model of career education for gifted and talented. *Journal of Career Education*, 325–331.

VanTassel-Baska, J. (1983). *A practical guide to counseling the gifted in a school setting*. Reston, VA: Council for Exceptional Children.

VanTassel-Baska, J., Feldhusen, J., Seeley, K., Wheatley, G., Silverman, L., & Foster, W. (1988). *Comprehensive curriculum for gifted learners*. Boston: Allyn & Bacon.

Ward, V. (1961). *Educating the gifted: An axiomatic approach*. Columbus, OH: Charles E. Merrill.

Study Questions

1. What is meant by the term *comprehensive curriculum*? Why is such a curriculum needed for gifted learners?

2. What aspects of a curriculum should be differentiated for gifted learners? Provide a rationale for each.

3. In what ways could grouping be considered a curriculum issue?

4. Evaluate the importance of articulating a curriculum for K–12.

5. What if you were to select appropriate curriculum for a given group of gifted learners? What would be the most important criteria to consider in the process?

6. Why has traditional content-based curriculum for the gifted been less popular than other areas of learning?

7. Evaluate the efficacy of organizing curriculum for the gifted, using all models rather than selecting one.

13

Mathematics and Science for the Gifted

Joyce VanTassel-Baska

The general concerns about mathematics and science curriculum in our schools are felt even more deeply by educators of the gifted. Since the barrage of national reports on education in the early 1980s, deficiencies in these content areas have been widely recognized, reported, and discussed. Problems center on three key areas:

1. A teaching force unable to provide appropriate level content in math and science areas
2. Use of textbooks that are not up to date in respect to new technological and scientific discoveries; in mathematics, for example, textbooks that primarily stress computation at the elementary level
3. Little science education at the lower elementary levels; mathematics work at these levels focused on drill and practice and dominated by worksheets

Consequently, one of the first issues we must address in mathematics and science curriculum for the gifted is how to combat these generic problems and infuse the curriculum with appropriate content and methodology. Three strategies are crucial in this regard: first, identifying teachers, particularly at the elementary

193

level, who can teach math and science to the gifted; second, developing a differentiated staffing model that will allow the teachers to work with the gifted in these areas; and third, adapting existing materials and developing others that are appropriate for these learners.

The idea of linking mathematics and science curriculum for the gifted together may be appropriate from several vantage points. First, students who are gifted in one area tend to be very able in the other and have strong interests in both areas. Second, gifted students tend to enjoy mathematics and science classes more than other subject areas, especially by the time they reach junior high school, where they overwhelmingly select such courses as number one and two choices (VanTassel-Baska, in preparation). Third, the nature of mathematics as an applied area allows for much natural interdisciplinary overlap. Most science study requires a fundamental knowledge of mathematical topics; furthermore, scientific research is aided considerably by student understanding of probability and statistics—which are important mathematical topics for the gifted. Thus, the discussion of mathematics and science curriculum for the gifted that follows interweaves these two critical areas of intervention for gifted learners.

Ideas for integrating math and science programs for the gifted abound. The following list is meant to be suggestive of successful approaches to such a merger:

1. Team teaching among math and science teachers
2. Organization of curriculum according to themes or issues to accommodate both curriculum areas (for example, conservation, ecology, space travel)
3. Block scheduling of math and science options for the gifted
4. Use of special projects that have a math and a science component
5. Organization of seminars on careers in math and science using biographies of eminent scientists and mathematicians as the basis for the curriculum study
6. Development of units of study on the philosophy and history of mathematics and science for the purpose of analyzing relationships between the two areas
7. Teaching of the "doing" of science and math as art forms to enhance students' appreciation of these areas

Even when mathematics and science are addressed as separate domains of inquiry, the natural ties between the two are still obvious. Educators of the gifted may wish to find ways to offer appropriate curriculum in each area to gifted learners as well as to accommodate a more integrated learning context that blurs some of the distinctions between the two domains.

Mathematics for the Gifted

Given the state of mathematics education in this country, it is essential that special provisions be made for gifted students. Their needs cannot be met within the scope of regular school mathematics. During the 1980s, we were bombarded by national reports decrying the level of mathematical competency in U.S. schools, especially compared to other countries (Wirsup, 1986).

A mathematics curriculum for gifted students should be fast-paced, emphasize concepts rather than procedures, encourage individuals to construct ideas for themselves, and make full use of technology. Five broad goals of school mathematics identified by the National Council of Teachers of Mathematics (1987) are:

1. Becoming a mathematical problem solver
2. Learning to communicate mathematically
3. Learning to reason mathematically
4. Learning to value mathematics
5. Becoming confident in one's own ability

Clearly these goals are important for the gifted learner.

New views of teaching and learning mathematics also have stressed the importance of early and sustained exposure to key elements or strands in a mathematics curriculum. These strands include:

1. Counting, calculation, and approximation
2. Likelihood and chance (probability theory)
3. Algebraic manipulation techniques
4. Spatial awareness and geometric considerations
5. Logic, reasoning and inferential systems (statistics)
6. Algebraic structures and analysis
7. Modeling and problem solving

Special emphasis for the gifted within these strands should be on early access, in-depth opportunities for real-world applications, and use of mathematical concepts in other domains of inquiry as well as in research.

Early Access Issues

The Study for Mathematically Precocious Youth (SMPY), developed by Stanley, Keating, and Fox (1974), embodies the important aspects of allowing the gifted learner early access to significant mathematics topics. This model has the following characteristics:

1. Identifying gifted students with an off-level, high-powered mathematical aptitude test (SAT)

195

2. Using a diagnostic-prescriptive approach to mathematics instruction that allows students to move at a fast pace (for example, completion of 2 years of high school mathematics in 6 weeks) and not be subject to instruction in skills already learned

3. Utilization of existing precalculus curriculum and text materials to move students through the school-accepted scope and sequence in mathematics

4. Employing teachers who are adept at setting appropriately high learning expectations and then allowing students to meet those expectations in an individualized manner

Such an approach, which has been used extensively in talent search programs around the country (Sawyer, 1985; Stanley, 1980; VanTassel-Baska, 1983) uses the learner's readiness for advanced mathematics as the turnkey variable for determining the level of the intervention. This method has been very successful with highly precocious youth. It also puts a premium on the completion of advanced placement calculus, often before the senior year of high school, and college entrance with advanced standing. This method implies that gifted students should study a concept-rich elementary school mathematics curriculum and begin college preparatory courses as early as possible. Such radical acceleration offers the gifted student the possibility of making significant contributions in the field, typically while the individual is still in his or her 20s.

The early access opportunity is an important modification for gifted learners from kindergarten on because many of these students have grasped mathematical concepts well before the time they are usually presented in the curriculum (VanTassel-Baska, 1983). A recent study of mathematics textbooks revealed that more than half of such basal materials are review of previously taught material (Hirschhorn, 1986). Without opportunities for fast-paced study of school mathematics, a major disservice will have been done to the gifted.

Conceptual Emphasis Linked with In-Depth Opportunities

Simply rushing gifted students through chapters in mathematics textbooks does not guarantee that they will fulfill the aforementioned goals. Students should have the opportunity to construct powerful ways of thinking. Problem-centered learning (see chapter 17) using the topics recommended by the National Council of Teachers of Mathematics (NCTM) allows gifted students to conceptualize at a high level not dictated by fixed-paced courses. Conventional textbooks do not provide the integrated and relational treatment of mathematics that gifted learners need, and thus alternative sources of instructional materials must be sought. Topics not adequately addressed by current procedurally oriented texts are:

1. Problem solving
2. Estimation and mental arithmetic
3. Statistics and probability
4. Discrete mathematics
5. Mathematical structure
6. Mathematical connections
7. Use of technology

The mathematics envisioned by NCTM is organized conceptually. For example, in algebra, although an appropriate level of skill proficiency remains a goal, NCTM suggests a move away from a tight focus on manipulative facility to place a greater emphasis on conceptual understanding, with algebra viewed more as a means of representation. Algebra should include the study of matrices and be viewed as a problem-solving tool. Similar shifts must be made in geometry, trigonometry, and calculus. Programs for gifted learners at all grade levels should include attention to the foregoing topics in a setting that challenges students to rise to the high level of thought of which they are capable.

Problem Solving

Another approach is an intensive focus on problem-solving techniques that allows the gifted to experiment freely in areas of mathematical interest and desired competence. Infusing the curriculum for the gifted with small-group or cooperative learning experiences that use a set of problem-solving strategies, such as the following, as an organizer for student work would seem most advisable:

1. Look for a pattern.
2. Make a list.
3. Guess and test.
4. Search randomly.
5. Set up an equation.
6. Work backward.

Mathematical Contests

Another problem-solving approach that has gained acceptance is composed of various mathematics competitions that provide challenging nonroutine problems. Programs such as Talent Search, Math Counts, Math-Letes, and others are becoming increasingly popular and serve to focus attention on excellence in mathematics. Participation requires students to have a well developed conceptual base and an excellent problem-solving ability.

Use of Technology

Computers and scientific calculators have a significant place in mathematics programs for gifted students. They facilitate problem solving by freeing students to focus on heuristics rather than on computational procedures. Technology also aids in conceptualization. Equations for conic sections can be explored and related to the geometric representation using graphic programs available on computers (and now on some inexpensive calculators). Programs such as MuMath, Maple, and Macsyma, which perform algebraic operations, solve equations, differentiate, and integrate, are changing the very face of mathematics instruction. By using technology, gifted students can build powerful mathematical schema and rise above the routine of laborious paper-and-pencil computations.

It is important that gifted students construct relationships between mathematical topics. The 14th standard of the NCTM proposal (NCTM, 1987), called Mathematical Connections, suggests the following topics:

Relations and functions
Systems of equations and matrices
Function equations in standardized form and transformations
Complex numbers as a + bi or r(cos + sine) and ordered pairs (a,b) in the complex plane
Right-triangle ratios, trigonometric functions, and circular functions
Circular functions and series
Rectangular coordinates and polar coordinates
Explicit and parametric representations of equations
Function and its inverse, such as the logarithmic and exponential functions
Statistical procedures and their requisite probability concepts
Finite graphs and matrices
Recursive and closed form definitions of the same sequence

By building the relationships among these topics, which are traditionally learned separately, gifted students will gain greater mathematical proficiency as well as be able to apply mathematics in other disciplines, especially physics.

Relationship of Mathematics to Other Fields

It is useful to delineate skills essential for quantitative literacy in conceptualizing ways to link mathematical concepts to other domains. These skills are:

1. Graphing
2. Measurement techniques

3. Computing of descriptive statistics
4. Interpretation of graphic material
5. Pictorial displays of data
6. Preparation of written descriptions of data tables and results
7. Decisions about statistical tests and graphs, depending upon type of data
8. Use of the scientific process

These literacy skills are highly transferable to project work in other curricular areas of interest and are important interdisciplinary connectors if we view mathematics as a tool skill.

Nevertheless, mathematics is a powerful field of inquiry in its own right, with linkages to other domains, primarily at the abstract level of overarching themes. VanTassel-Baska and Feldhusen (1981) used four ideas from the *Syntopicon* to organize an elementary curriculum for gifted learners. Within that curriculum, mathematics was linked to science, social studies, and language arts via the concepts of change, signs and symbols, reasoning, and problem solving. These themes had relevance both within and across each of the curricular areas cited.

Mathematics materials such as MEGES (formerly titled CEMREL math) and Unified Math take yet a third direction in mathematics programming for the gifted. These programs, organized by mathematicians, focus on the structure of mathematics. Students are exposed to real mathematics introduced as a logical system rather than put together in the traditionally determined sequence. Such programs have worked well with gifted students but frequently have collided with the conventional iron-clad precalculus sequence in schools; here, the approach has usually had a short half-life.

A last area of focus for mathematics programs for the gifted has been on practical applications, on providing linkages for gifted students to the functional world of mathematics through mentorships and internships with adults who use mathematics in a significant way in their professional lives. Understanding the relevance of mathematics learning in diverse career areas helps to encourage gifted learners to take and stay with advanced coursework well into college.

Other integrative topics appear to be important in developing a powerful mathematics curriculum for the gifted. VanTassel-Baska, Olszewski, and Landau (1985) recommended the development of scope and sequence in mathematics that infuse the following topics into preexisting school-defined topics:

History of mathematics
The development and codification of mathematical ideas
The creative process in mathematics, problem finding, and problem solving
The use of technology
Applications of mathematics in the sciences
Mathematical modeling

199

Mathematics as a symbol system (issues of power and economy)
An understanding of limits, infinity, and infinitesimals

In that way, gifted learners might learn to appreciate mathematics as a field of study with integral ties to science, technology, and the social sciences.

Table 13.1 discusses the major advantages and disadvantages of each approach as it would affect school district planners in considering a comprehensive mathematics program for gifted learners. I believe that inclusion of all these models will best address the comprehensive needs of the mathematically talented in our schools.

Science for the Gifted

A science curriculum for the gifted is, in a sense, the foundation of their learning if they are to become knowledge producers rather than knowledge consumers. Fundamental internalization of scientific skills, such as observation, experimentation, and measurement, as well as adoption of an attitudinal mindset that views the world through the lens of a scientist provides a framework necessary for productive research in any field of inquiry. Consequently, ensuring that gifted learners have access to the following key components in a science curriculum from kindergarten through high school is essential:

1. Opportunities for laboratory experimentation and original research work
2. High-level content-based curriculum
3. Opportunities for interactions with practicing scientists
4. A strong emphasis on inquiry processes
5. Inclusion of science topics that focus on technological applications of science in the context of human decision making and social policy (VanTassel-Baska & Kulieke, 1987)

What are some elements of exemplary science programs for the gifted that differ from a generally excellent science program for all learners? Although one might make the usual observations that such programs take students further in science and expose them to more in-depth work, it may be useful to delineate some other factors that differentiate such programs.

Science as Process

In the world of science, discoveries are made slowly and painfully (Bruner, 1983). This principle must be simulated in experiments in gifted science programs. Some

TABLE 13.1

A Synopsis of Advantages and Disadvantages of
Implementing Key Mathematics Models for the Gifted

Acceleration of Content
Exemplum: Study for Mathematically Precocious Youth (SMPY) (Stanley, Keating, & Fox, 1974)

Advantages	*Disadvantages*
Embodies a mastery-level learning and continual progress model	Ignores the potential in constructing a conceptually based curriculum that is richer than what exists in the schools
Uses the current school curriculum and existing textbooks	Promotes an attitude of valuing *fast* over *deep*
Employs a diagnostic-prescriptive teaching strategy	Does not allow a diversified mathematics curriculum that develops appreciation
Creates advanced learning opportunities for younger students	Can promote the "more problems" syndrome

Conceptual Organization of Mathematics Content to Promote High Level of Understanding and Appreciation
Exemplum: The CEMREL (now termed MEGES) Program for Gifted Students in Grades 7–12

Advantages	*Disadvantages*
Developed by mathematicians who know and understand the important mathematical ideas that should be taught	Difficult to implement because of level of expertise in math required of teachers; district commitment needed to establish new framework from grades 7–12
Organized around a unified approach to mathematical systems rather than traditional school subjects	Does not mesh well with existing math curriculum at earlier levels
Presents a holistic program that has scope-and-sequence, materials, and training components	The whole package has to be adopted; not flexible for partial usage

Focus on Problem Solving and Heuristics
Exemplum: Cumberland Mathematics Project (Hersberger & Wheatley, 1980; Wheatley, 1984)

Advantages	*Disadvantages*
Focuses on important process skill development within a content area	Does not value highly the intellectual content of mathematics curriculum
Allows for individual and small-group learning rate to be flexibly determined	Focuses on one learning strategy to the exclusion of other (constructing knowledge for oneself)
Represents a current trend in general mathematics teaching	Deemphasizes formal mathematics learning according to scope-and-sequence continuum
Focuses on applications of mathematics through computer and calculator activities	Creates articulation problems across all levels

Integrated Perspective on Teaching Mathematics
Exemplum: University High School Mathematics Curriculum Project, University of
Illinois (Davis, 1984)

Advantages	*Disadvantages*
Considers *all* the characteristics of mathematically able students in its design	Requires high-level teacher talent to implement effectively
Considers and incorporates new trends in mathematics teaching but does not embrace any one approach	Requires systematic access 7–12 to high-level, mathematically talented students
Developed with a K–12 planning model in mind	Requires a team approach and "consistent vision" around program goals
Developed, field-tested, and researched during an 8-year period in a controlled setting	
Uses a "content expert" model for development and implementation	

of the best gifted programs in science, such as the Bronx High School of Science and the North Carolina School of Math and Science, clearly work with students so that they thoroughly understand scientific endeavor as an ongoing process whose goal is to make incremental progress in a well defined area.

One way to exemplify this is through engaging students in original research—an approach used in many laboratory-linked programs for the gifted (VanTassel-Baska & Kulieke, 1987). Through the preparation of research proposals as well as follow-up long-term projects, students can begin to internalize the act of doing science rather than merely simulating such activity through canned experiments. Use of a scientific paradigm such as the following may be helpful in encouraging gifted students to develop scientific investigation skills at early ages:

1. Define the problem.
2. Conduct a literature search.
3. Make hypotheses.
4. Collect data to test hypotheses.
5. Analyze data.
6. Interpret data.
7. Make conclusions.
8. Draw implications.

Through structuring activities that use such a process paradigm, gifted students may engage and practice the process skills of a scientist: observation, experimentation, and communication.

Teachers can also enhance an understanding of scientific process by asking many open-ended questions about what students see, such as: What do you observe? How might you classify what you observe? What inferences can be made about this? These questions, and others like them, provide the chance for students to think through what they see and respond to stimuli creatively. DeVito and Krockover (1979) have suggested the following way to improve the teacher's questioning techniques in science classrooms:

- Limit yourself to one question in a 15-minute period.
- Never answer your own questions.
- Eliminate "yes-or-no" response questions.
- Do not ask questions that invite aimless or guessing responses.
- Ask each child in your class at least one meaningful question a day.
- Ask narrow- and broad-response questions.
- Limit memory questions to one per hour.
- Let the students ask the questions.
- Mix up your questions (thought-provoking questions, what-if questions, evaluation questions, and so on).

Science as Collaboration

We know that given the nature of the knowledge explosion, probably no single person since Leibniz has been capable of correlating all content knowledge for purposes of generating new knowledge. Consequently, an important model of science for the gifted learner to understand is that of collaboration. In the world of scientific research today, real breakthroughs are made by scientific teams made up of individuals with specialized backgrounds but with a scheme for working together on current scientific problems that requires combinational knowledge from several areas. Work in biochemistry is a good example of this. Even the trend in awarding the prestigious Nobel Prize in the sciences is toward a joint award to a team that has made a major contribution. Several books also chronicle the importance of a team of people working arduously toward scientific discovery (Goodfield, 1981).

Ways in which collaborative work in science might be enhanced include the following approaches:

1. Structuring of small group investigations rather than individual ones
2. Use of cooperative learning principles
3. Use of creative problem-solving strategy in groups
4. Peer tutoring
5. Establishment of science mentorships
6. Organization of science centers in the classroom

Science as Interdisciplinary

One of the most powerful ideas that emerged out of a study by Shane (1981) of 120 scholars was the recognition among leading scientists in the group that students must understand the important role of human beings in the scientific process. Scientists in geology, physics, chemistry, and the natural sciences cited the following ideas as the most powerful organizers for a science curriculum for the year 2000:

Doctrine of limits	Evolution
Interdependence	Unity of nature
Entropy-conservation	Humans as change agents
Population explosion	Unpredictability of humans
Nature of the scientific method	Plate tectonic theory

Firmly embedded within this list is a concern for the relationship of science and people, an important area of exploration in science programs for the gifted. The teaching of ecology, for example, as a fundamentally interactive process of humans in nature that can be viewed from the perspective of a scientist as well as the perspective of a social scientist is one example of a natural interdisciplinary connection.

At the elementary level, many science activities can be made interdisciplinary. DeVito and Krockover (1976) suggested the following types of activity:

Mixing colors—Isaac Newton invented the color wheel to explain to his students what he had discovered about refracting light through a prism. Have the children mix colors both in a dry and in a wet state. Try using two basic colors and do a fingerpainting by intermixing the colors. (p. 142)

Symmetry and asymmetry—A discussion of equality, gravity, balance of nature, and mirror images can lead to art activities that differentiate between symmetrical and asymmetrical balance. These activities, in turn, can easily lead to crystallography activities. (p. 143)

Collages with natural materials—Have the children collect various plants (living or dead), bark, seashells, rocks, minerals, seeds, and anything else. This activity involves observation and possibly classification, depending on the direction in which you wish to move the lesson. Encourage overlapping and balancing the size and texture of the materials used to construct the collages. (p. 144)

Spider webs—Spiders weave webs with such mathematical exactitude that one species is actually called the "geometric spider"! Honeycombs, beehives, nests, and tunnels are all examples of the clever way in which insects and animals use geometry and artistry in their struggle for existence.

The globe—Try studying the position of the earth in relation to the sun, the solar system, the galaxy, the universe; the motion of the earth, such as rotation and revolution; the shape, volume, and density of the earth; the speed of rotation and revolution of the earth; the inclination of the earth's axis and the resultant seasons and distinct geographic regions; the history of man's exploration of the world.

Mapping—The orientation of oneself on the globe involves science and mathematics. The implementation of a grid system, with base meridian and equator lines and the establishment of lines of longitude and latitude, is of prime importance in mapping. Aspects of declination, magnetic inclination, and compass directions are also science topics. Can you design a set of mapping activities for children?

Science as Problem Finding

Clearly the work of Getzels and Csikszentmihalyi (1977) did much to raise our awareness of the critical role of problem finding in making original contributions in the world of art. It is also an important skill in the research paradigm of objective science. Hitting upon the right topic and asking the right questions about it are central to meaningful research. Helping gifted learners form such questions is a critical part of their science education. One way of focusing our problem finding is to provide scientific events for students, who then must decide on a question that might begin to focus on that event. Teaching research design techniques early on also can help the gifted focus better on this specific skill. Moreover, teaching creative problem solving, especially the stage of problem generation and definition, is a useful way to get students to consider a problem more intently. For example: After brainstorming several ideas, choosing three, then choosing one, illustrate the problem—provide specific examples of it; elaborate on the problem—cite other problems that occur as a result; state the problem many ways—very specifically, very generally—and develop "what if" scenarios to describe various manifestations of it; restate the problem as a single question. By following such techniques in a small group, students learn to discuss a problem in greater depth and rework it based on peer discussion.

Science as Experimentation

Everyone has heard of the unusual ways in which scientists have hit upon key discoveries—by accident or while looking for something else. What has not been sufficiently explained is the nature of the great experiments that have influenced our view of the world. What were the variables under investigation, and how did scientists proceed with their ideas? Gifted learners can benefit from a close look at the history of scientific discoveries and the people who made the breakthroughs. In this way, eminent scientists and their science become real. One excellent resource for this purpose is *Great Scientific Experiments* by Rom Harre. In his book, Harre treated 20 key experiments as case histories of scientists who used their creativity to understand nature. Among the experiments described are Aristotle's study of the embryology of the chick, Pasteur's preparation of artificial vaccines, and Jacob and Wollman's discoveries about genetics.

205

Science in Relation to Morality and Ethics

In recent decades, we have come to recognize the awesome connection among scientific discovery, technological development, and direct impact on society. Perhaps the development of the atom bomb was the first time this connection was truly etched on our collective consciousness. Since that time, however, the connections have been repeated over and over again. Consequently, to teach science as a totally objective set of processes is to misrepresent the role of science in today's world. Gifted students need to be exposed to the social issues surrounding the scientific enterprise and to develop a philosophy of science and a code of ethics that include concerns for the moral and ethical dimensions of doing science. Thus, topics such as pollution, ecology, and conservation of natural resources deserve special attention in the context of science programs for the gifted.

Supplementary resources that use such topics as organizers are available (VanTassel-Baska, 1987). One unit uses Jean Dorst's book *Before Nature Dies* as a major reference.

> This is a comprehensive and detailed book which treats the entire earth as a single unit. Dorst explores the unforeseen ramifications of men's actions throughout nature—for example, the historical process of soil degradation, through bad agricultural practices and accelerated erosion, and the uncontrollable ravages of animals. He brilliantly illuminates the side effects of the Industrial Revolution—the progressive poisoning of the earth's seas, rivers, and atmosphere by vast quantities of industrial waste—and of the Scientific Revolution—the disruption of delicate biological balances caused by the indiscriminate use of pesticides.
>
> In many ways man's understanding of his fragile environment remains as rudimentary as that of an early nomad, and yet his technological advances have made it possible for him to have a far greater effect on his environment. He may deplore the wanton slaughter of the huge herds of buffalo of the American West in the last century, but at the same time he continues to poison the world with chemicals and industrial effluents.
>
> The preservation of wildlife is only one of the most obvious aspects of man's need to protect the world's dwindling natural resources from man's stupidity. The population explosion makes the continuation of man's present pattern of behavior suicidal. Nature preserves and national parks are not enough. Man must develop an international policy of restraint and a program of land management and environmental control. This book suggests ways in which man can learn to live in harmony with nature, before nature dies. (p. 89)

The purpose of this unit is for students to gain an awareness of the problems and issues in conservation and how advances in technology have created, and continue to create, imbalances in the earth's ecosystems that permanently change the earth's ecosystem. Students also should become aware of the ways in which modern technology can be used to help correct the imbalances that already have occurred. Students should understand that with the new capacity we have to change the earth, we must now assume a responsible role of stewardship over the planet's resources, before we destroy the planet's very ability to sustain us.

Science as a Set of Powerful Ideas

In his wonderful book *Search for Solutions*, Judson (1974) listed eight major ideas that will influence science for its next 500-year history: change, modeling, prediction, patterns, feedback, chance, theory, and evidence. His explication of these ideas illustrates well how they permeate present as well as past scientific and social thought. A content outline of Judson's treatment of the idea of prediction follows to illustrate the connectedness of the concept across time, culture, and area of inquiry.

A. Ancient methods of prediction
   patterns of smoke, patterns in tortoise shells, palm reading, handwriting, tea leaves, astrology
B. Predictions in Physics and Astronomy
   Halley's comet, eclipses, prediction of existence of the planet Neptune
C. Predictions in Geology
   prediction of earthquakes
D. Predictions in Medicine
   prediction of existence of blood vessels
   modern-day prediction—for example, the effect of radiation on cancerous tumors, effects of drugs
E. Predictions in Economics
   prediction of economic growth
   prediction of future supply and demand
F. Predictions in Social Science
   prediction of achievement or adjustment

Common concepts: measurement, theory, inference, technology

Science and Technology

Recent statements from the National Science Teachers Association (1985) have iterated the importance of integrating science study with technology. Many of the newly developing science materials attempt to infuse technology into the required student text (Biological Sciences Curriculum Study Group, 1988). These events clearly demonstrate the importance that has been attached to this linkage. Gifted students are capable of appreciating the applications of basic science to the current and proposed technology and can profit from having technological applications embedded early in their curriculum experiences in science. One resource that sets the stage for understanding the relationship of science to technology is the book, and television series, entitled *Connections* (Burke, 1978). This opus traced common tools of technology today back to their original roots in science and illustrated well the nature of the relationship as it evolves in different ways.

Another idea for infusing technology into a science curriculum for the gifted is through special units of study. A unit outline on space travel, given in Table 13.2, was developed for use with junior-high-age gifted students (VanTassel-Baska, 1987).

Summary

Gifted learners have the capacity to do original work in science that can have a beneficial impact on society as a whole. Consequently, it is crucial for them to receive an enriched, high-powered set of learning experiences. Understanding what science is and how it works in the real world is essential to that education. Such science education, however, must be balanced with a healthy concern for the implications of scientific discovery in an ethical context.

References

Biological Sciences Curriculum Study Group. (1988). *Science for life and living: Integrating science, technology, and health*, Washington, DC: National Science Foundation.

Bruner, J. (1983). *In search of mind*. New York: Harper & Row.

Burke, J. (1978). *Connections*. Boston: Little, Brown.

Davis, R. (1984). Presentation to class at Northwestern University, Evanston, IL.

DeVito, A., & Krockover, G. (1976). *Creative sciencing*. Boston: Little, Brown.

Getzels, J., & Csikszentmihalyi, M. (1977). *The creative vision*. Chicago: University of Chicago Press.

Goodfield, J. (1981). *An imagined world: A story of scientific discovery*. New York: Harper & Row.

Harre, R. (1981). *Great scientific experiments*. Oxford: Oxford University Press.

Hersberger, J., & Wheatley, G. (1980). A proposed model for the mathematics education of gifted elementary school pupils. *Gifted Child Quarterly, 24*, 37–40.

Hirschhorn, D. (1986, November). The University of Chicago School Mathematics Project (UCSMP). Presentation to National Association of Gifted Children, Las Vegas.

Judson, H. (1974). *Search for solutions*. Bartlesville, OK: Phillips Petroleum.

National Council of Teachers of Mathematics. (1987). *Curriculum and evaluation standards for school mathematics: Working draft*. Reston, VA: Author.

National Science Teachers Association. (1985). *Science-technology-society: Science education for the 1980's*. Washington, DC: Author.

Sawyer, R. (1985). The early identification and education of brilliant students: The Duke model. *College Board Review, 135*, 13–17, 31.

Shane, H. (1981). *A study of curriculum content for the future*. New York: College Entrance Examination Board.

Stanley, J., Keating, D., & Fox, L. (1974). *Mathematical talent*. Baltimore, MD: Johns Hopkins University Press.

TABLE 13.2

Outline for Special Unit on Space Travel

I. History of Our Conception of the Cosmos
   - Ancient Greek and Babylonian perceptions
   - Stonehenge
   - Medieval Astrology
   - Invention of the telescope
   - Galileo and the Copernican revolution
   - Growth of modern astronomy through bigger and better telescopes and space probes

II. The Human Dream to Fly
   - Early myths: Daedalus; Bellerophon; Skidbladnir, the magic ship of the Norse god Grey that could sail over land or sea
   - Jules Verne's visions of flying and space travel
   - Hermann Oberth's *The Rocket into Interplanetary Space*
   - Invention and early uses of the airplane

III. Time and Distances in Space
   - Measuring distances in space (experiment)
   - The question of destinations: Calculate how long it will take to go to the moon at presently attainable speeds. The planets? The closest star? How fast would a spaceship have to travel to reach the closest star within the lifetime of a human being?

IV. Rocketry
   - History: From Chinese rockets to Goddard and Von Braun
   - Streamlining and rocket design (experiment)
   - Powering a spaceship
     To escape earth's gravitational pull
     In space
     The problem of fuel weight

V. The Problems of Living in Space
   - Cosmic rays; meteors
   - Temperature control (experiment: how color changes an object's ability to absorb or reflect heat)
   - Pressure in space (experiment: differences between internal and external pressure)
   - Gravity (experiment: using centrifugal force to simulate gravitational force)
   - Problems of vertigo due to weightlessness
   - Sources of food and water
   - Mental strain of spending long periods in cramped quarters

VI. Unmanned Space Probes
   - Above the earth's atmosphere
   - To the Moon
   - To Venus and Mars
   - Voyager II's close encounters with Jupiter and Saturn
   - Prospects for the future

VII. Manned Space Missions
  — Orbiting the earth
  — Landing on the Moon
  — The space shuttle
  — Skylab
  — Future space travel

VIII. Space-Age Technology
  — Monitoring space probes from earth
  — Controlling space probes from earth
  — Calculating speed, direction, and power: Everything is relative
  — Back-up systems
  — Troubleshooting when things go wrong
  — Earth-bound uses for space technology

IX. Do Sentient Extraterrestrial Creatures Exist?
  — Conditions necessary for intelligent life
  — Probabilities for these conditions being met
  — Our attempts to contact and communicate with ETs

Stanley, J. (1981). Using the SAT to identify mathematically precocious students. *College Board Review, 4.*

VanTassel-Baska, J. (in preparation). *Perceptions of counseling needs among gifted students and their parents.*

VanTassel-Baska, J., & Feldhusen, J. (1981). *Concept curriculum for the gifted.* Matteson, IL: Matteson School District #162.

VanTassel-Baska, J., & Feldhusen, J. (1981). *Concept curriculum for the gifted.* Matteson, IL: Matteson School District #162.

VanTassel-Baska, J. (in preparation). *Perceptions of counseling needs among gifted students and their parents.*

VanTassel-Baska, J., & Kulieke, M. (1987). The role of the community in developing scientific talent. *Gifted Child Quarterly, 31*(3), 115–119.

VanTassel-Baska, J., Olszewski, P., & Landau, M. (1985). Toward developing an appropriate mathematics and science curriculum for gifted learners. *Journal for the Education of the Gifted, 8*(4), 257–272.

Wheatley, G. (1984). Instruction for the gifted. In J. Feldhusen (Ed.), *Toward excellence in gifted education* (pp. 31–44). Denver: Love.

Wirsup, I. (1986). The current crises in math and science education: A climate for change. In J. VanTassel-Baska (Ed.), *Proceedings from the 9th Annual Research Symposium.* Evanston, IL: Phi Delta Kappa.

Study Questions

1. What should be the goals of appropriate mathematics and science programs for the gifted? Can the areas share some common goals?

2. Evaluate the effectiveness of various teaching strategies in working with the gifted in math and science that might be the most effective.

3. What might be the role of computers in enhancing the inter-relationships between math and science?

4. Can science and math be taught effectively to the gifted at the primary level? What factors influence the debate?

5. How can the curriculum ideas presented in this chapter become a part of school programs?

14

Social Studies and Language Arts for the Gifted

John F. Feldhusen
Joyce VanTassel-Baska

Verbally gifted youth have special need for enriched and accelerated learning experiences in social studies and in the language arts. Gifted students are concerned about political and social problems, values, and moral issues. Social studies and language arts offer unusual opportunities for these students to experience intellectual activity of a high order in dealing with issues, problems, and momentous events in our times and culture. Of course, students need historical, political, psychological, and philosophical perspectives as well as the aesthetic view derived from literature. This chapter presents an overview of these two areas of the curriculum and shows the opportunities for truly challenging learning experiences for the gifted and talented in social studies and the language arts.

Social studies and English often are linked in school programs as a core curriculum or in programs of American studies. These programs provide excellent opportunities for the gifted to experience interdisciplinary study of major themes and concepts cutting across disciplines and to engage in in-depth independent research activities. Higher-level courses of this nature often are offered as electives for high-ability students who are capable of intensive discussions and of making presentations to peers of the results of research projects.

Teachers of core courses in English and social studies or in American studies must be very well trained in their disciplines, and they must have a good grasp of the characteristics and needs of the gifted and talented as well as knowledge of the special methods and materials needed for effective teaching of the gifted and talented. This chapter therefore offers guidelines for the teacher of the gifted and talented in social studies and language arts.

Social Studies for the Gifted

Social studies programs for the gifted at the elementary level may be embedded in full-time special classes, in a pullout/resource room model, or in a cluster grouping approach in an otherwise heterogeneous classroom. Social studies activities also may be presented in special after-school or Saturday classes for the gifted. Wherever and whatever the program setting, curricular activities are apt to focus on broad themes, issues, problems, or concepts; substantial involvement of the students in research and independent study; curricular goals that stress the learning of thinking skills; and highly interactive classroom sessions involving discussions, problem solving, simulations, and student presentations of their own work.

At the secondary level, special opportunities for the gifted in social studies may be provided through special seminars (Kolloff & Feldhusen, 1986), honors classes, acceleration in which gifted students take advanced social studies courses ahead of schedule, concurrent enrollment in college-level social studies courses while in high school or through College Board Advanced Placement (1983) classes. Advanced Placement courses in social studies currently are in American history, European history, American government and politics, and comparative government and politics. Courses in macro and micro economics are to be introduced in 1989.

All of these arrangements are, or should be, associated with a differentiated curriculum that focuses on higher-level concepts and themes, stresses development of critical thinking skills, involves students in research and writing, includes much discussion and active interaction in class, and provides opportunities for students to present the results of their research to fellow students and to real-world audiences beyond the school setting. In all of these special class formats, the emphasis shifts from learning basics to experiencing much higher-level cognitive growth. The College Board (1983) suggested that students should have the following basic knowledge and skills by the time they leave high school:

- The ability to understand basic information developed by the social sciences, including statistical data and other materials
- Familiarity with the basic method of the social sciences—that is, with the framing and empirical testing of hypotheses

- A basic understanding of at least one of the social sciences and of how its practitioners define and solve problems
- Familiarity with how to explore a social problem or social institution by means of ideas drawn from several social sciences

To develop a realistic program that will prepare the gifted for the real world in which the social studies become operative, Schug (1981) recommended that the whole community serve as a laboratory for social studies learning experiences. For the study of history, he recommended the following activities:

- Arrange field trips to local museums, historical societies, or historical sites.
- Develop oral history collections by doing tape-recorded interviews with senior citizens.
- Do volunteer work at local museums or historical societies.
- Write local histories based upon written records, photographs, and interviews with resource people.
- Find and analyze historical artifacts such as weapons, tools, kitchen utensils, arrowheads, toys, clothing, letters, diaries, books, catalogs, or photographs (junkyards, garages, junk shops, and attics are often valuable sources of historical artifacts).
- Arrange a field trip to an old cemetery, where students record dates of births and deaths and make inferences about past life spans, epidemics, and health care.
- Do videotaped interviews with senior citizens talking about life in the past.

Schug proposed that a community advisory committee be organized to include representatives from business, agriculture, labor, the professions, the arts, and the political parties. They can help define real issues and problems to be studied and suggest ways to involve community agencies, organizations, and groups in developing community-based activities for the gifted. As an illustration of activities that might emerge from such planning with members of the business-economic community, he recommended the following:

- Develop a local consumer price index to measure inflation.
- Interview labor leaders and business people about collective bargaining.
- Produce videotaped documentaries about community economic problems.
- Arrange for field trips to a local bank, factory, or human service agency.
- Interview bankers, real estate salespeople, or stockbrokers about savings and investment.
- Establish an economic enterprise, such as manufacturing and selling products or providing community services.
- Interview student employers about the operations of their businesses.
- Develop and conduct consumer tests of products purchased at local stores.

215

- Develop land use maps to identify the relationships among resources, transportation, and the location of industrial and commercial firms.
- Develop a price comparison survey of products of interest to young people.
- Invite business people in multinational corporations to serve as guest speakers to discuss economic interdependence.

Example Programs

Social studies programs for the gifted can begin at the early childhood or primary level. Gifted children at the primary level can be engaged in discussion of basic concepts and participate in independent project activities that they plan and carry out themselves with teacher guidance. Flachner and Hirst (1976) developed one such program in New York City for the Astor Program for primary-level gifted children. Titled "200 Years, A Study of Democracy," the program uses quotations from great literature, such as Walt Whitman's *I Hear America Singing,* as vehicles for discussions.

Pioneering work in the development of social studies curricula for the gifted at the upper elementary, middle school, and high school levels has been carried out at Ball State University's Burris Laboratory School by Professors Carl Keener, Penny Kolloff, and others (Keener, undated). Their work utilizes the seminar as a classroom delivery model to engage gifted youth in high-level discussions, project and research activity, presentations to real audiences, and learning of higher-level thinking skills. The curriculum guides that have been developed in their project stress a global and futures orientation. Here, for example, are some of the concepts dealt with in one of the courses:

Systems	Populations
Interdependence	Scarcity/Allocations
Culture	Energy
Lifestyle	Habitat
Dignity of Humans	Institution
Conflict	Sovereignty

Some of the activities or investigations proposed for youth in this program are:

- Individual or small-group investigation of an alternative global future
- Delineation of the global futures investigation
- Report on research on global futures and individualized research projects/products

- Simplification of a demographic abstraction
- Nuclear holocaust survival skills
- Appropriate technologies for developing economies—role playing

Inquiry Approach

In developing social studies programs for the gifted, the major direction of activity is often the inquiry approach. This seems particularly appropriate for the gifted because inquiry implies the achievement of deep understanding through active search and investigation and the use of techniques of critical thinking. Taba was a principal advocate of the inquiry method, especially in the teaching of social studies. Taba's thoughts about teaching for thinking were presented in the volume *Curriculum Development* (1962). Her later work toward a specific inquiry-oriented teaching model was presented in a number of publications and summarized by Maker (1982) in *Teaching Models in Education of the Gifted*. Maker suggested that four fundamental strategies characterize the Taba inquiry model:

1. *Concept development.* In this strategy students engage in the acquisition and organization of information and the development and naming of key concepts in an area of study. In a sense, this is the content acquisition stage, but Taba stressed that it must not be simply a transmission of predigested content from teacher to student but, rather, a generatively acquired grasp or understanding of content as key concepts through student interaction with basic information or data in the field of inquiry.
2. *Interpretation of data.* This strategy involves students in a number of higher-level thinking activities through which they achieve a still higher level of disciplined understanding in a field. In a first approach to interpretation, students engage in listing relevant and irrelevant information and otherwise organizing the available information. At a second stage, they are led to infer causes and effects within the phenomenon under study. In a third stage, they infer prior causes and subsequent effects. The fourth step provides experiences in drawing sound conclusions based on data. Finally, students engage in generalizing and transferring their knowledge to new situations.
3. *Application of generalizations.* In this strategy students are guided to apply facts, concepts, and principles in new and real-life situations through the activities of predicting, inferring, concluding, and examining generalizations.
4. *Resolution of conflicts.* In this strategy students deal with the affective experiences of attitudes, feelings, and values in conflict situations. Students learn how to deal with the feelings, attitudes, and values that underlie the documents or content under study.

217

These inquiry strategies, often based on the research and theory of Bruner (1960), provide high-level and challenging cognitive experiences for gifted youth. They demand a new range of teaching skills quite unlike the usual presentation-and-lecture approach that characterizes much teaching. The payoff in cognitive growth for the gifted, however, can be substantial.

Questioning Skills

Productive learning in the social studies through inquiry, discovery, concept induction, and deductive reasoning calls for effective questioning skills on the part of both teacher and students. Through a mutual questioning process, they can clarify the accuracy of information, understand concepts better, delineate the true issue or problem, analyze complex situations, and better understand values involved in a complex situation. Torrance and Myers (1970) offered a comprehensive framework for conceptualizing teachers' and students' questions that facilitates inquiry and creative syntheses or production:

1. Interpretation (What is meant by "conspicuous consumption"?)
2. Comparison-analysis (How are lakes and oceans different?)
3. Synthesis (How could you combine . . . ?)
4. Redefinition (What is a clock other than a timepiece?)
5. Open-ended (Suppose that. . . .)
6. Evaluation (Did the United States reveal moral bankruptcy in Cambodia?)
7. Sensitivity to problems (What are the U.N.'s problems?)
8. Clarify problems (What problem does OPEC pose for Western nations?)
9. Provocative questions (What if all violence were barred from TV?)
10. Hypothetical questions (What if Cortez had been killed by Montezuma?)
11. Questions to stimulate thoughtful reading (Why was Mozart called the "boy wonder?")
12. Questions to stimulate thoughtful listening (Why does the speaker dwell on political confrontation?) (pp. 149–221)

A number of writers (e.g. Hunkins, 1985; Sanders, 1960) have used the Bloom taxonomy as a theoretical model to guide students and teachers in formulating questions for inquiry:

1. Knowledge
   Teacher: Can you describe the land formation patterns along the river?
   Student: How far inland from the river should we go?

2. Comprehension
   Teacher: What are the authors really trying to tell us in this passage?
   Student: Are you saying that you want us to go beyond the literal message?
3. Application
   Teacher: Can you solve this problem using the concepts of simultaneous equations?
   Student: Does this problem have a single solution?
4. Analysis
   Teacher: How are estuaries and bays alike, and how are they different?
   Student: Must a bay always run off from a large body of water?
5. Synthesis
   Teacher: Using the concepts of geography that we have learned, can you design a new method of mapping?
   Student: Can such a map have live or animate components?
6. Evaluation
   Teacher: Which of the countries of southern Africa has the greatest potential for economic growth because of its geography?
   Student: Should we use historical factors as a part of our decision-making process?

This pattern of questioning by teachers and students illustrates an interactive inquiry situation in which students engage in higher-level thinking activities and deal with significant, real-world issues and problems. Hunkins (1972, 1985) gave further guidelines for teaching students how to ask good questions so that they can become effective in inquiry and self-directed in learning.

Language Arts for the Gifted

Descriptions of the gifted often seem to stress their verbal abilities. Early word recognition and reading, rapid and easy learning, large vocabulary, ability to deal with complex and abstract concepts, verbal expressiveness, voracious reading, and precocious reading comprehension frequently are listed as characteristics of gifted children. At the same time, programs for the gifted have been criticized for overemphasizing language arts activities and neglecting mathematics and science. The field of gifted education clearly is oriented to verbally gifted youth.

Nevertheless, how to provide for verbally gifted youth remains a big challenge. Despite their evident precocity and the resultant need for instructional activities at a high, abstract, complex, and challenging level, programs, especially pullout–resource room-type programs, stress enrichment projects and activities

219

that often are not presented at a high or fast-paced level. The term *enrichment* often is used to characterize programs in which there may even be purposeful avoidance of higher-level content because of complaints from teachers at higher grade levels that they will have nothing left to teach if content and skills are introduced earlier.

The ideal language arts program for the gifted will have to overcome such problems and will offer curricular experiences that are enriching and accelerated. The good sense of enrichment is that it offers instruction that extends beyond normal offerings to accommodate the wider and more diverse interests of the gifted and that it does so at a higher level of abstraction and complexity to fit the precocity of the gifted child's capacity to learn rapidly.

Reading and the Study of Literature

The gifted child's major contact with the world of ideas is through literature. Books stimulate thought and provide the knowledge base required for creative thinking and problem solving. Intellectual growth in gifted children depends on their access to and regular involvement in the reading process. From the time of their earliest ability to read, they need access to a rich variety of fiction and nonfiction literature and opportunities to respond actively and creatively to what they are reading. With parents and teachers there should be abundant opportunities to discuss, analyze, and share the joy of what is real and, above all, to be guided by adults who model the processes of analyzing, discussing, and joy in reading.

Several authors provide excellent guidance to good literature for the gifted and how to teach it to optimize learning and love of literature. In *Books for the Gifted Child*, Baskin and Harris (1980), suggested the following criteria for finding the right books for the gifted:

1. The language used in books for the gifted should be rich, varied, precise, complex, and exciting, for language is the instrument for the reception and expression of thought.
2. Books should be chosen with an eye to their open-endedness, their capacity to inspire contemplative behavior, such as through techniques of judging time sequences, shifting narrators, and unusual speech patterns of characters.
3. Books for the gifted should be complex enough to allow interpretative and evaluation behaviors to be elicited from readers.
4. Books for the gifted should help them build problem-solving skills and develop methods of productive thinking.
5. Books should provide characters as role models for emulation.
6. Books should be broad-based in form, from picture books to folktale and myths to non-fiction to biography to poetry to fiction. (p. 46)

Polette (1982) and Polette and Hamlin (1980) also offered a wealth of ideas for structuring and conducting literature programs for the gifted. Polette and Hamlin have suggested the following guidelines for teachers of literature for the gifted:

220

There are many times when the gifted child will be alone in an opinion or belief. Encourage the child to support or deny the concepts held through the use of a wide variety of materials. At the same time, work patiently with the child in helping him or her cope with differing opinions.

Gifted children often want to explore areas that society says are not within normal expectations because of age or because of sex. Such exploration should not be discouraged if resources are available or can be found.

Encourage creative thought. The great minds of the ages are those that would not accept the idea that a thing could not be done. Science fiction of fifty years ago is science fact today. Do not dismiss an idea simply because it does not seem possible given the limits of our present knowledge.

Allow these children, within the limits of safety, to experience the consequences of their behavior, both acceptable and unacceptable behavior. Help children to examine consequences before behavior choices are made.

Let children test their ideas without threat of evaluation. Assign grades only when absolutely necessary. Parent/child/teacher conferences are far more valuable than a letter grade. Encourage the child to read, read, read! As author Scott Corbett says, "Reading gives one an entire second life and two lives are certainly better than one." (pp. 22–23)

They went on to delineate the following guidelines for the teacher of the gifted:

The major requirements of the teacher of the gifted in a literature program include knowledge, creativity, a love of books and of reading, a respect for children and their ideas, and a high risk taking potential. The teacher must know both the positive characteristics and the prevailing negative attitudes of the students with whom he or she will work, being able to capitalize on the positive and deal effectively with the negative. Finally, the teacher must know precisely the teaching strategies that are more suited to gifted students than to the average or below average student. (p. 23)

The majority of the book is devoted to topics such as character and plot development, setting and mood, themes and values, fairy tales, folk tales, fantasy, and gifted authors.

In *3 R's for The Gifted*, Polette (1982) showed how thinking skills can be developed through reading experiences and presented guidelines for curriculum development in the literature program. She proposed the following 15 components for the language arts program for the gifted:

1. Emphasis on process rather than content
2. Emphasis on product
3. Emphasis on the higher cognitive levels of Bloom's taxonomy: Application, Analysis, Synthesis, Evaluation
4. Development of critical reading skills and critical judgment
5. Expanded vocabulary development
6. Development of literature skills and understanding
7. Emphasis on productive thinking skills: Fluency, Flexibility, Originality, Elaboration
8. Emphasis on critical thinking skills: Planning, Forecasting, Decision-Making, Problem-Solving, Evaluation

221

9. Use of resources beyond the classroom and the school
10. Exposure to a wide range of imaginative literature
11. Development of skills in visual literacy
12. Assured competency in basic research skills, including: Location, Acquisition, Organization, Recording, Evaluation, Verification
13. Planned experiences for younger children in development of Piaget's cognitive tasks: Conservation, Seriation, Classification, Reversibility
14. Planned experiences for older children in exploration of values through literature
15. A high level of skills competency in reading, writing, speaking, listening, research, and all related communication skills. (p. 17)

A number of learning modules also are presented in this book for the teaching of literature.

Literature programs at the high school level should involve gifted students in reading high quality adult literature and should help them develop skill and enthusiasm in the intellectual and aesthetic experience of literature. The California State Department of Education (1978) published a guide for *Teaching Gifted Students Literature and Language in Grades Nine Through Twelve*. It offered the following description of the secondary literature program for the gifted:

> Gifted students read more widely and more perceptively than do the nongifted, and they enter high school having been exposed to a variety of literary types; for example, stories, myths, tall tales, and fantasy. Their response has been primarily emotional and superficial, their feelings deriving from vicarious or personal experience. They have given little heed to design or structure. It follows, then, that the task of the English teacher of gifted high school students is to open other literary doors. The teacher must broaden the scope and increase the depth of the students' reading by examining in specific selections the philosophies encountered and the techniques of the artist's craft. In short, the teacher must try to effect a total engagement of the learners with mature literary experience.
>
> No single organization of literary study will accomplish the objective of total engagement. Each type of organization can, however, make a significant educational contribution, and the adoption of one type as a frame should not exclude the use of other types. The four basic organizational approaches that are most prevalent are (1) history and chronology; (2) genre; (3) textual analysis; and (4) theme or idea. (p. 6)

This guide stressed gifted students' need to be actively engaged in discussions of literature with teacher guidance as they deal with character, plot, mood, major ideas, conflict, authors' points of view, and so on.

Writing and Composition

Writing programs for the gifted should begin as soon as they enter school and should provide an abundance of opportunities to write. Writing is a thinking process, and through writing experiences the gifted child can develop excellence in capacity to think as well as to write. Very young children who may lack the motor coordination to write may nevertheless be engaged in writing-related activities through the following teaching techniques (VanTassel-Baska, 1988):

222

1. Have the child compose a story and translate it for him or her as it is being developed. Read it back for editing changes or additions and elaborations. Share stories in class.
2. Encourage parents to transcribe stories at home and bring to school for sharing.
3. Have students draw pictures to illustrate their stories and then develop titles for them.
4. Use tape recorders to initially record the story and then transcribe it later.
5. Have students compose a story at the computer or typewriter if they have mastered the device adequately enough.
6. Encourage free story building; provide students with a set of givens (characters, plot pieces, a setting).
7. Have students respond in writing to a piece of music, a picture, or a poem presented in class.
8. Allow young students the freedom to write without requiring accurate spelling and grammar.

By the time gifted students reach the intermediate grades, they should begin to **master the basic skills of language and writing. Collins (1985) suggested some** strategies to get gifted students acclimated to writing and composition:

1. Provide opportunities for students to discuss and clarify writing assignments before they begin writing.
2. Provide opportunities for students to get more information about a topic before they begin writing.
3. Provide specific information about the criteria you will use to correct each assignment.
4. Provide opportunities for students to review and revise written work completed earlier in the year.
5. Encourage students to edit each others' papers before they are handed in.
6. Provide opportunities for students to read written work out loud to individuals or to small groups of students.

The fundamental skills of writing to be mastered are:

Prewriting
Paragraph development
Theme development
Development of introductions and endings
Work on supporting details
Effective use of figures of speech
Editing
Revising
Rewriting

223

Foreign Language Study

Gifted children can benefit a great deal from the study of a second language to enhance their grasp of the structure and semantics of their own language. Foreign language study should begin as early as kindergarten or first grade and be continual throughout high school and into college. Mastery of a second (and third) language gives the gifted student a comprehensive understanding of the comparative structure of languages and their related cultures. VanTassel-Baska (1987) suggested that gifted students ideally should learn Latin as well because:

1. Sixty percent of English words are derived from Latin; thus, the study of this language greatly heightens vocabulary power in English.
2. Syntactic understanding, a major goal in the learning of Latin, enhances linguistic competence in English and in other languages.
3. The complexity of the language and its logical consistency make it a challenge to gifted students who enjoy learning new symbol systems, analyzing, and using deductive logic in solving problems.
4. The cultural heritage of the Western world is based on Greco-Roman traditions in art, music, and literature, as well as language. Thus, to study Latin is to gain invaluable insight into the Western cultural system.
5. Modern language tends to stress oral/aural skills with a focus on language fluency. Latin learning, on the other hand, stresses logical reasoning and analysis through an emphasis on translation and study of form changes at increasing levels of difficulty. In that respect, Latin is a verbal analog to the teaching of mathematics as a cumulatively organized subject area that is amenable to fast-paced instruction. Thus, Latin is an easy subject to modify for precocious students.
6. Unlike most languages, Latin has few irregularities.

She concluded that the major goals of a foreign language program for the gifted should be to develop proficiency in reading, speaking, and writing in two languages; to learn the culture and traditions that shape language; to be challenged by the interrelationships across languages in respect to form and meaning; and to appreciate and understand language systems.

The English Language

The language arts program for the gifted should offer opportunities to study the English language. VanTassel-Baska et al. (1988) suggested that the goals for an English language program should be to understand the syntactic structure of English (grammar) and its concomitant uses (usage); to promote vocabulary development;

to foster an understanding of word relationships (analogies) and origins (etymology); and to develop an appreciation for semantics, linguistics, and the history of language. The programs of study for the English language can profit immensely from the existence of a concurrent foreign language study program.

Because gifted children have extreme individual differences in their mastery of the language skills of grammar, usage, and vocabulary, these segments of a program for the gifted must be highly individualized to accommodate individual levels of proficiency. Pretesting of skills and vocabulary always should be carried out, and instructional activities and materials should be determined diagnostically on the basis of pretest results. Gifted youth find particularly onerous instruction that covers material they already know or that is adjusted to the pace of the slowest student in a class.

Oral Language Arts

Oral mastery and use of language are critical parts of the language arts program. The thinking processes involved in experiencing literature and in writing are linked intimately to and can be enhanced by oral language experience. Through planned experiences in discussion, debate, oral reading and interpretation, oral reports, dramatics and panel presentations, gifted youth can learn to think effectively in and through the language, and they can learn to write more effectively.

At the primary and elementary levels, gifted children can learn to read aloud from storybooks with expressiveness, can learn to verbalize ideas through creative dramatics, and can begin to give oral reports and presentations. Beginning at the fourth or fifth level, they can engage in the more cognitively demanding activities of debate, acting, and research reporting. Middle school and high school classroom discussions can become strongly analytical, theoretical, and abstract and can deal with values and judgment. Improvisation and extemporaneous presentations, as well as formal debate, can provide high-level oral language experiences for the gifted.

Programs and curricula for the gifted should be planned carefully to incorporate these oral language experiences in the total language arts program. Teachers of the gifted also should make a continuing effort to help gifted students see the linkages among the language arts experiences of literature, writing, language, foreign language, and oral language. In all language arts program experiences, gifted youth should have access to higher-level content presented at a fast pace (acceleration), much dynamic cognitive interaction with content, and a wider variety of language arts experience than characterizes the regular school language arts program (enrichment). All of their language arts experiences should be linked to thematic and conceptual content and should stress the use and learning of higher-level thinking skills. Through modeling by parents, teachers, and peers of their enthusiasm

225

for language arts experiences, gifted children should develop a true love of literature, writing, and symbolic language experiences.

Summary

Experiences in social studies and language arts are essential in all programs for the gifted and talented. In these two domains, the gifted and talented can experience high-level challenges to think and grow intellectually through in-depth research, group projects, and classroom discussions. The social studies and language arts programs should be differentiated for the gifted from K–12. Cultural literacy is essential to full actualization of the gifted and talented, and experiences in these two domains provide the base of knowledge to achieve it.

References

Baskin, B. H., & Harris, K. H. (1980). *Books for the Gifted Child*. New York: R.R. Bowker.

Bruner, J. S. (1960). *The process of education*. Cambridge, MA: Harvard University Press.

California State Department of Education. (1978). *Teaching gifted students literature and language in grades nine through twelve*. Sacramento: California State Department of Education.

College Board. (1983). *Academic preparation for college*. New York: Author.

Collins, J. (1985). *The effective writing teacher: 18 strategies*. Andover, MA: Newwork.

Flachner, J., & Hirst, B. (1976). 200 years, a study of democracy. New York: Astor Program (490 Hudson Street, New York, NY 10014).

Hunkins, F. P. (1972). *Questioning strategies and techniques*. Boston: Allyn & Bacon.

Hunkins, F. P. (1985). Helping students ask their own questions. *Social Education, 49*, 292–296.

Keener, C. (Undated). *A curricular approach for global studies*. Muncie, IN: Ball State University (Burris-Ball State School Corporation, 2000 University Avenue, Muncie, IN 47306).

Kolloff, P. B., & Feldhusen, J. F. (1986). Seminar: Instructional approach for gifted students. *Gifted Child Today, 9*(5), 2–7.

Maker, C. J. (1982). *Teaching models in education of the gifted*. Rockville, MD: Aspen Systems.

Polette, N. (1982). *3 R's for the gifted: Reading, writing and research*. Littleton, CO: Libraries Unlimited.

Polette, N., & Hamlin, M. (1980). *Exploring books with gifted children*. Littleton, CO: Libraries Unlimited.

Sanders, N. M. (1960). *Classroom questions: What kinds?* New York: Harper & Row.

Schug, M. C. (1981). Using the local community to improve citizenship education for the gifted. *Roeper Review, 4*(2), 22–23.

Taba, H. (1962). *Curriculum development, theory and practice*. New York: Harcourt, Brace & World.

Torrance, E. P., & Myers, R. E. (1970). *Creative learning and teaching*. New York: Dodd, Mead.

VanTassel-Baska, J. (1987). The case for teaching Latin to the verbally talented. *Roeper Review, 9*(3), 159–161.

VanTassel-Baska, J., Feldhusen, J., Seeley, K., Wheatley, G., Silverman, L., & Foster, W. (1988). *Comprehensive curriculum for gifted learners*. Boston: Allyn & Bacon.

226

Study Questions

1. What are major current social studies issues and problems that could be related to historical events?

2. What are major ways of organizing a classroom to facilitate discussion of social studies topics?

3. What could you all do in a seminar for gifted and talented youth?

4. What is the essence of inquiry activity in the social studies?

5. What are some activities you could use in teaching literature to gifted youth?

6. How could you involve gifted youth in writing to build their motivation for reading and writing?

7. Why should gifted youth study a foreign language?

8. What are some good oral language arts activities?

15

Arts and Humanities
for the Gifted

Ken Seeley

The approach we often use for curriculum for the gifted is to extend and expand from the core content areas. But the arts and humanities present a unique challenge because they are not as well developed as the regular curriculum in most schools. Indeed, the curriculum areas of arts and humanities often are given short shrift. Content areas within the arts and humanities are taught as separate disciplines in most school curricula. For example, students are taught history as if it were unrelated to philosophy, language, geography, anthropology, and political science. A humanities approach necessarily implies integration among the social sciences, literature, and foreign languages.

The same is true for the arts. Although visual art, writing, speech, and music often are organized as credit courses, rarely is any attempt made to integrate these courses except as extracurricular projects, such as school plays or musicals. Frequently absent from the curricula are dance, sculpture, music composition, and aesthetics.

Given the weak base of arts and humanities in the regular curriculum, we have to develop new curricula for gifted learners that ultimately could be adapted into the core curriculum. This chapter will focus on the need for this curriculum development, a philosophy to guide its development, humanities approaches, and integration of the arts through collaboration.

Why Arts and Humanities for the Gifted?

The arts and humanities offer gifted learners a unique opportunity to subject to the most rigorous scrutiny the knowledge, experience, and values they derive from all of their studies and to use these as bases for an individual world view. To achieve this goal, education should contain the following three elements:

1. Learning should be *interpretive or integrative* of the students' knowledge and experience.
2. Learning also should be *normative*; it should move the students toward an understanding of the common culture and the students' own position relative to that culture through the study of art history, aesthetics, and philosophy.
3. Learning should develop *critical thinking* by strengthening the students' ability to question, confront, deliberate, judge, and create alternatives.

The arts often are thought to be of value only for students who have exceptional talent in the fine or performing arts. Nevertheless, exposure to the arts is important for all gifted students. They have greater sensitivities and depths of emotion than do more typical students (Clark, 1979; Hagen, 1980; Wallach & Kogan, 1965) and therefore need corresponding experiences. Because of this, the arts provide an excellent medium to address these needs. Albert Einstein (1954) eloquently described the importance of an arts and humanities role in development:

> It is not enough to teach man a specialty. Through it he may become a kind of useful machine but not a harmoniously developed personality. It is essential that the student acquire an understanding of and a lively feeling for values. He must acquire a vivid sense of the beautiful and of the morally good. Otherwise he—with his specialized knowledge—more closely resembles a well trained dog than a harmoniously developed person. (p. 172)

Dabrowski (in Piechowski, 1979) first articulated a paradigm to describe giftedness, which was later interpreted by Piechowski (1979) in his work on developmental potential. He defined developmental potential as "the original endowment which determines what level of development a person may reach under optimal conditions" (p. 28). Developmental potential has five components: intellectual, psychomotor, sensual, imaginational, and emotional. The latter three can be addressed through the arts.

The humanities are important, particularly for gifted learners, because they are by nature integrative, interdisciplinary, paradoxical, and cultural, as a humanities approach to curriculum and instruction for gifted learners must be. The humanities offer an epistemological view of information, which in its highest form can offer gifted learners opportunities to generate new theories. According to Piaget (in Gruber, 1981), the epistemological point of view acknowledges

230

how the construction of a new theory is far from being reducible to the accumulation of data, but necessitates an extremely complex structuring of interpretive ideas which are linked to the facts and which enrich them by framing them in a context. But as the ideas which have guided even the discovery of the observables, every alteration at one point gives rise to a modification of the system as a whole. This process maintains both the coherence of the system and at the same time the adequacy of its fit to the data of experience and observation. (p. viii)

In its simplest form, epistemology is the study of the structure of knowledge. By using a humanities approach to teaching the gifted, we expose them to a holistic notion of knowledge and allow for an interpretation of ideas that links factual information in the respective disciplines.

How Do We Differentiate an Arts Curriculum?

The term *arts* refers to the major fine and performing arts, including music, visual art, creative writing, dance, and theater. As indicated earlier, public school offerings in the arts are widely disparate. The secondary schools usually have more highly developed courses of study in these disciplines than does the elementary level. Typically, larger school districts have more arts instruction in the core curriculum than smaller districts have. In any event, teachers of gifted students are not expected to teach all of these disciplines. Rather, the expansion and enrichment of existing offerings from the core curriculum are best served when teachers act in a facilitating role. This usually occurs when a combination of the following approaches is used:

1. Organize field trips to arts facilities for all gifted students, using whatever community resource people are available to provide the expertise.
2. Arrange for artistically talented students from the elementary level to attend secondary arts classes.
3. Have artistically talented students hold seminars or group discussions with other gifted students to share products or performances as well as their approaches, thoughts, and feelings in the creative process.
4. Arrange for mentorships in the arts that provide ongoing relationships between gifted students and artists in the community.
5. Cluster-group artistically talented students together by discipline, and arrange for master classes, magnet schools, and individual instruction.
6. Generate outlets for the students' work or performances through contacts with commercial galleries, dance companies, and music or theatrical groups; submit creative writing for publication.

In addition to the facilitator role, teachers of the gifted can make a unique curriculum contribution by promoting the idea of collaboration. Other means of inte-

231

gration are possible through study in areas such as art appreciation, art history, and aesthetics.

What Is Collaboration in the Arts?

Collaboration implies a search for a common ground, a common vocabulary, a place or framework where different artistic disciplines intersect. Once this dialogue has begun, the artists proceed to create a work that goes beyond a mere layering of disciplines to an interweaving that produces a whole greater than the sum of its parts. In the process, each discipline retains a quality and an integrity of its own.

The steps to create collaboration begin with cross-disciplinary study. This typically is limited to the study of two, or a maximum of three, artistic disciplines. Specifically, this means to:

1. Develop a common vocabulary that applies across the disciplines (for example, space, light, tone, rhythm, improvisation, centering).
2. Encourage experimentation, exploration, and risk taking in each of the disciplines for all of the students.
3. Develop the idea that the students are the source of their art, through self-expression and self-discovery, as they experiment and explore the disciplines (differentiate between the external environment and the internal environment).
4. Introduce the concept of critique through a focus on performances or products with suggestions for improvement.
5. Develop a clear understanding of the importance of revision after critique. First performances of products are merely "rough drafts" from which artists work together to critique and revise their collaborative work.

To meet the standards for a collaborative effort as opposed to a layering of disciplines, the following questions should be posed as the work is in progress and in its final form:

1. *Does the collaboration find common elements in each discipline?* A successful collaboration somehow identifies an idea, a theme, a word, or a concept about which each discipline has something to contribute.
2. *Can the separate elements from each discipline stand on their own?* A successful collaboration is made of parts from each artistic discipline that have their own integrity and quality.
3. *Are the separate elements of each discipline even better for being a part of the collaboration as a whole?* The collaboration should be greater than the sum of its parts.

232

The collaboration itself will take on a life of its own and will carry the students along with the momentum of its creative energy. The final product will not likely look much like the teacher's ideas, but a substantial amount of guidance is necessary throughout its creation. The students will believe that they can claim a great deal of ownership of the collaboration for they have been swept along in the excitement and satisfaction of developing the idea to fruition.

How Does a Humanities Approach Develop?

The first step in developing a humanities program for gifted students is to mobilize the human resources around the philosophy and goals of integration of knowledge and epistemology. Although teachers often view the integration of subject areas as overwhelming, beginning with two disciplines can be exciting and satisfying for teachers and students alike. Involving the students as partners with teachers in planning a humanities program is an excellent way to develop a sense of ownership.

Gifted students feel empowered by their own use of knowledge and experience. This empowerment affirms that the arts and humanities are an intrinsic component of their intellectual and emotional development and, as such, must be a part of any well rounded education. Many gifted students apply their knowledge and experience to situations in unique ways. This may be the essence of "creativity," which can serve as a broad-based theme for study. Through biographical examination of famous creative people, students can understand and experiment with their own creative ideas. They can see the influences of personal interest, knowledge, emotion, and intellect interacting in the lives of major contributors to a field of study. A good example of this is *Mathematical People* (Albers & Alexanderson, 1985). This book presents interviews with 25 of the most famous living mathematicians in the world and gives personal vignettes that provide insights into the lives of these creative thinkers. Gifted students can use this book as a model to interview teachers, community members, or each other.

Teachers of the gifted again can act in the facilitator or convenor role by bringing subject-area teachers together to begin planning. Interdisciplinary seminars for gifted students can be organized around themes. Such seminars usually require administrative support for scheduling and arranging credit at the secondary level. At the elementary level, teachers usually have more flexibility in scheduling and implementing interdisciplinary studies. Some programs for the verbally gifted are based on a humanities model using seminars and independent study.

Two examples are presented to illustrate these ideas across the grade levels. Table 15.1 shows a theme-based curriculum that was developed in the state of Hawaii. Table 15.2 presents a curriculum for the verbally gifted developed by Joyce VanTassel-Baska (in VanTassel-Baska, Feldhusen, Seeley, Wheatley, &

233

TABLE 15.1
Sample Themes, Concepts, and Generalizations from a Curriculum Scope and Sequence

Overarching Theme: Humankind and the Universe

Overarching Concepts: The universe and all things in it are in a constant state of flux. Humans continually search for meaning and knowledge. Humans affect and are affected by their environments. All people, past and present, have adapted their beliefs and behavior in the face of universal needs and problems.

Grade-Level Themes and Generalizations

K–3	4–6	7–8	9–12
Interaction/Reaction	*Laws of Nature vs. Laws of Humans*	*Conflict/Harmony*	*Independence/ Interdependence*
1. Humans are a product of their beliefs and environment.	1. Interaction of people has necessitated setting up rules and forming governments.	1. Humans deal with conflict and harmony as they search for meaning.	1. All knowledge is interrelated.
2. Different people and cultures have different environmental concerns.	2. Human control and modification of nature results in changes in environment.	2. Conflict can be a positive force.	2. People search for meaning and knowl-edge by discovering patterns in what they know and then using, transforming, extending, breaking, or relating these patterns in new ways.

Note: These themes, concepts, and generalizations were developed by a team of teachers representing all island districts in the State of Hawaii under the direction of C. June Maker, using a process presented by the National/State Leadership Training Institute on the Gifted and Talented.

234

TABLE 15.2
Sequence of Curricular Foci in Verbal Programs

Key Element	K–3	4–6	7–8	9–10	11–12
Literature	Selected biographies *Junior Great Books series* Oral reading of children's literature Selected rhymes and poems	Baskin & Harris's *Books for the Gifted Child* NCTE's *Literature for the Gifted*	Interrelated arts Fry's *Man the Myth-Maker The Perilous Journey* Selected readings by genre	AP literature selections Literature club (genre/author approach) Humanities	AP literature World literature (thematic approach)
Broad-based reading skills	Vocabulary development Reading comprehension Discussion skills of listening, questioning, interpreting Readings in all content areas	Critical reading (inference, evaluation, arguments) Group discussion skills Readings in all content areas	Analysis and interpretation Use of symbols and analogies (10 SATs)		
Composition	Writing stories (prereading) Journal writing Writing to explore new forms	Writing skills paragraphs themes structure Journal writing	Expository writing Critical review and editing	AP composition Creative writing	Technical/research writing
Verbal/nonverbal discourse	Oral reports Creative dramatics Role playing Puppet plays	Panel discussions Skits Play production	Debate Oral interpretation Speech	Debate Dramatics Theatrical productions	
Language	Vocabulary play Foreign words and idioms (5 languages) Sentence patterns	English grammar and usage Foreign language offering (4 years)	Linguistics Etymology	Semantics Second foreign language (4 years)	History and development of language

Note: From *Comprehensive Curriculum for Gifted Learners* by J. VanTassel-Baska, J. Feldhusen, K. Seeley, G. Wheatley, & L. Silverman, 1988, Boston: Allyn & Bacon.

Silverman, 1988). Both programs are based on a humanities approach to understanding, drawing upon knowledge from a broad base. They are only two examples that might serve as starting points for planning.

Summary

The approaches to arts and humanities presented here are intended to be starting points for planning curriculum for gifted students. They are liberating to the students, who too often are exposed to right-answer learning. These approaches provide for individual growth through an understanding of the interrelatedness of different disciplines.

References

Albers, D. J., & Alexanderson, G. L. (Eds.). (1985). *Mathematical people: Profiles and interviews.* Cambridge, MA: Birkhauser Boston.

Clark, B. (1979). *Growing up gifted.* Columbus, OH: Charles E. Merrill.

Einstein, A. (1954). *Ideas and opinions* (p. 172). New York: Crown.

Hagen, E. (1980). *Identification of the gifted.* New York: Teachers College Press.

Piaget, J. (1981). In H. Gruber, *Darwin on man* (2nd. ed., p. 97). Chicago: University of Chicago Press.

Piechowski, M. M. (1979). Developmental potential. In N. Colangelo & R. T. Zaffrann (Eds.), *New voices in counseling the gifted* (pp. 25–57). Dubuque, IA: Kendall-Hunt.

VanTassel-Baska, J., Feldhusen, J., Seeley, K., Wheatley, G., & Silverman, L. (1988). *Comprehensive curriculum for gifted learners.* Boston: Allyn & Bacon.

Wallach, M.A., & Kogan, N. (1965). *Modes of thinking in young children.* New York: Holt, Rinehart & Winston.

Study Questions

1. How might you use a broad-based theme to combine a history and literature unit?

2. Using two common arts areas, such as visual art and music, how might a teacher of the gifted work with the music and art teachers to develop a collaborative production for an entire school?

3. How does epistemology relate to the teaching of higher-level thinking skills?

4. How could you use professors from a nearby college to supplement a humanities unit for gifted students?

5. How might you use a humanities approach to have gifted students critique their own experience with education in the schools?

16

Thinking Skills for the Gifted

John F. Feldhusen

Gifted students, and in fact *all* students, should be taught how to think or to think more effectively. Although there is little baseline data on proficiency in thinking among the gifted or among children in general, many teachers and educational researchers believe that children are weak or woefully deficient in thinking ability and that these skills, whatever they are, could be measurably improved. Some recent research reviewed by Feldhusen and Clinkenbeard (1986) confirms the teachability of cognitive skills (Feuerstein, Miller, Hoffman, Mintzker, & Jensen, 1981; Savell, Twohig, & Rachford, 1986; Sternberg, 1985b). We have no evidence, however, that instruction in thinking skills is particularly needed by the gifted, and some evidence even indicates that they are superior in thinking ability at the point of their first identification as gifted (Anderson, 1986; Devall, 1982; Spitz, 1982; Ward, 1979; Woodrum, 1978).

Perhaps a sense that the gifted should be capable of achievements in thinking at advanced levels leads to the special concern for development of their thinking skills. It also may be the case that because many of the gifted are likely to be future leaders in the professions, business, and the arts, we want them to be highly effective thinkers, creators, and problem solvers so that they will provide optimum leadership for our society. Thus, we endeavor to build strength in thinking in students who show promise of high-level cognitive attainment, and we assume that strength in thinking will transfer to a wide variety of problem situations. Furthermore, our goal in teaching thinking skills to the gifted is to carry such instruction to much higher and more complex levels than we do for children of average ability, and to introduce the higher-level thinking skills earlier in the educational programs.

Several movements from psychological and educational research also are converging and reporting results that have heightened our interest in thinking skills. One is the field of metacognition research and theory development (Flavell, 1985; Sternberg, 1985a). Another is the shift in psychology from behaviorism to cognitive science (Gardner, 1985). Still another is the active subfield of research and theory development focusing explicitly on thinking skills (Nickerson, Perkins, & Smith, 1985). Studies of cognitive style (Witkins, 1976), and to some extent learning or productivity styles (Dunn & Price, 1980), also have generated new interest in the domain of thinking skills. Finally, popular training packages, such as De-Bono's (1970) *CoRT* program, the Purdue Creative Thinking Program (Feldhusen, 1983), and Taylor's (1968) Talents Unlimited, have generated optimism about the need for and value of thinking skills in the general curriculum and in the gifted curriculum in particular.

Closely related to the movement for the teaching of thinking skills is the renewed emphasis on higher-level content in curriculum in general, but particularly in curriculum for gifted youth. From Bruner (1960) in *The Process of Education*, a major curriculum movement came to American schools. After a decade, it waned but left a legacy of concern for the teaching of major concepts. Phenix (1964), in *Realms of Meaning*, and Ward (1961), in *Educating the Gifted*, both echoed this critical need for a curriculum based on major concepts, themes, or issues, especially in instruction for the gifted. Nevertheless, Sizer (1985) pointed out in his study of American high schools, *Horace's Compromise*, that in a majority of American secondary classrooms, transmission of information remains the major goal of instructors.

There is also a great concern for the knowledge base in relation to the development of thinking skills (Glaser, 1984) and a concern for the nature of thinking skills in various disciplines (Raths, Wasserman, Jonas, & Rothstein, 1986; Nickerson, et al., 1985). Emerging research evidence suggests that the nature of thinking may differ from discipline to discipline and that the nature of thinking differs depending on the thinker's level of expertise (Glaser, 1984).

This review of methods for teaching thinking skills will focus on general systems as well as specific applications of those systems in separate disciplines. I shall focus particularly on practical systems that have potential for application in K–12 programs for the gifted and talented. Thus, the major domains of thinking for attention here will be critical thinking, creative thinking, the cognitive operations of the Bloom taxonomy (1956), inquiry, problem solving, and metacognitive processes.

240

Creative Thinking

Interest in teaching creative thinking dates from the early work of Guilford (1959), Taylor (1964), and Torrance and Myers (1970), as well as from the work of Osborn (1963) and Parnes (1977). These researchers paved the way for development of creativity instructional programs and techniques that now are widely used in general school programs and that are stressed in enrichment programs (Feldhusen & Treffinger, 1985). Osborne's "brainstorming" and Parnes' creative problem-solving models now are well known in school programs, as are Torrance's familiar concepts of fluency, flexibility, originality, and elaboration, either in verbal or nonverbal forms.

Fluency

Fluency refers to the modes of thinking in which ideas are generated or recalled without regard to producing specific answers or solutions. The typical fluency activity in the classroom asks children to produce as many ideas as possible within a relatively broad framework:

> What are all the ways you can think of to remove the skin from an orange?
> What are all the alternatives the United States might have considered when
>   faced by the U-boat (submarine) threat to shipping in World War II?
> List as many character traits as you can think of for a story character.
> What are practical uses of the dye properties of certain chemicals?

All of these tasks can be done individually or in groups. Students are typically urged to strive for quantity of ideas, avoid self- or group criticism, and feel free to build upon or extend their own ideas or those contributed by others.

Flexibility

Flexibility refers to the capacity to generate solutions or ideas that break away from or are alternative to conventional ideas. The classroom stimulus can set the stage for flexible thinking by calling for alternatives to the conventional:

> Rewrite this equation to include two equal signs and no parentheses.
> How would our lives be different today if the South had won the Civil War?
> How could medical science carry on research if animals could not be used?
> Develop an alternative orthographic system.

In all efforts to evoke and develop flexible thinking, we can structure the task to call for approaches that look from new viewpoints. We hope also that rigidity or inflexibility can be overcome. One of the major programs designed to facilitate this thinking in new and fresh ways is the *synectics approach* (Gordon, 1961; Gordon & Poze, 1980). In synectics, metaphors are used to tease out alternative ways of looking at problems. Following is an example of a classroom activity in synectics: Faced with the problem of creating a new type of society, students draw analogies from ant colonies. By observing ant behavior in colonies, students can be led to see ways of developing leadership and worker roles in a new society.

Originality

Originality of response implies that an idea is unusual or unique in addition to its value or practicality. Originality often is thought to be the essence of creative thinking. The link among fluency, flexibility, and originality also should be obvious. Fluency means producing ideas without fear of evaluation; flexibility means looking for new or alternative connections or associations, and originality means seeking the unique or unusual. Originality obviously calls for an evaluative function in that the original thinker must be able to judge an idea or response as fitting the stimulus demand and yet as new, novel, or unusual.

Elaboration

The fourth creative mode of thinking, elaboration, is the process of taking the new idea, which has been recognized as unique and potentially valuable, and developing it into something useful or practical. For example: A new idea is a television show that is highly entertaining for adolescents and promotes love of learning. Finding the situation, developing characters, outlining plots, and writing dialogue are all parts of the process of elaboration. A student who can take an idea and add details, integrate various correlated elements, and produce a good story or essay is an effective elaborator.

All of these skills of fluency, flexibility, originality, and elaboration should be called into play in the more complex form of creative activity called *creative problem solving*. The many models of creative problem solving (Parnes, 1981; Torrance & Myers, 1970; Treffinger, 1982) offer excellent opportunities for the gifted to learn how to combine a number of aspects of creative thinking into a sequence of problem-solving steps. Several models of problem solving will be discussed in depth later in this chapter.

The field of creative thinking is characterized by packaged training programs. Feldhusen and Clinkenbeard (1986) reviewed the training programs and methods, including those for creative problem solving, and derived some positive evidence for the teachability of creative thinking. Good training programs of the future, however, probably will move from relatively abstracted forms of training in artificial contexts to applications of principles and methods in realistic contexts and in disciplines such as science, mathematics, literature, and social studies. Training for the gifted in creative thinking should begin at the kindergarten level and continue through high school, when it is applied in all academic disciplines.

Critical Thinking

Ennis (1985) defined critical thinking as "reflective and reasonable thinking that is focused on deciding what to believe or do." Note that there are creative activities covered by this definition, including formulating hypotheses, questions, alternatives, and plans for experiments" (p. 45). Ennis (1962) published one of the early guides to the teaching of critical thinking, and Harnadek (1980) authored a widely used set of instructional materials for teaching critical thinking skills. Ennis proposed the following list of 12 critical thinking skills:

1. Grasping the meaning of a statement
2. Judging whether there is ambiguity in a line of reasoning
3. Judging whether certain statements contradict each other
4. Judging whether a conclusion follows necessarily
5. Judging whether a statement is specific enough
6. Judging whether a statement is actually the application of a certain principle
7. Judging whether an observation statement is reliable
8. Judging whether an inductive conclusion is warranted
9. Judging whether the problem has been identified
10. Judging whether something is an assumption
11. Judging whether a definition is adequate
12. Judging whether a statement made by an alleged authority is acceptable

In a more recent publication, Ennis (1985) restructured the critical thinking skills into the following three major categories:

1. Define and clarify:
    - Identify central issues and problems.
    - Identify conclusions.
    - Identify reasons.
    - Identify appropriate questions to ask, given a situation.
    - Identify assumptions.

243

2. Judge information:
   - Determine credibility of sources and observations.
   - Determine relevance.
   - Recognize consistency.
3. Infer—solve problems and draw reasonable conclusions:
   - Infer and judge inductive conclusions.
   - Deduce and judge deductive validity.
   - Predict probable consequences.

Ennis (1985) further identified a set of 13 dispositions of the critical thinker, as follows:

1. Be open-minded.
2. Take a position (and change a position) when the evidence and reasons are sufficient to do so.
3. Take into account the total situation.
4. Try to be well informed.
5. Seek as much precision as the subject permits.
6. Deal in an orderly manner with the parts of a complex whole.
7. Look for alternatives.
8. Seek reasons.
9. Seek a clear statement of the issue.
10. Keep in mind the original or basic concern.
11. Use credible sources and mention them.
12. Remain relevant to the main point.
13. Be sensitive to the feelings, level of knowledge, and degree of sophistication of others.

The teaching of critical thinking skills probably can be addressed best in gifted programs in the upper elementary grades, middle school, and high school, and predominantly in the context of subject matter or the disciplines. Although some aspects of critical thinking, particularly those related to logic, can be taught in abstracted formats (for example, if all A are X, does it follow that all X are A?), it seems likely that early generalization of the skills to meaningful contexts will best assure transfer of the critical thinking skills to real settings. Here is an example of a problem in critical thinking:

> The city council discussed calling for bids for a new trash truck. Alderman Henry Alexson argued that our city was the only one in the area still using the old Mack model. The mayor countered by arguing that the cost would probably be prohibitive. Alderman John Ordevay suggested that they were not identifying the central issue or problems. What do you think are the basic issues or problems?
>
> After deciding on the basic issues or problems, identify which of Ennis' thirteen dispositions might be appropriate behaviors for the mayor and alderman as they discussed the trash truck problem.

Here is another illustration of a situation in which students' critical thinking skills might be developed:

> Mayor Smith urged the local TV station not to run spot commercials on AIDS prevention because they would offend the religious views of many citizens. An attorney urged that they be run during breaks in the station's airing of "soaps." Mayor Smith then argued that that would not be acceptable either. Can you detect any contradictions or inconsistencies in the arguments?

All gifted youth should develop strength in the skills of critical thinking, and the skills should be practiced and made useful in all of the major academic areas of the curriculum.

Cognitive Skills Represented in the Bloom Taxonomy

In a publication in 1956, *Taxonomy of Educational Objectives, Cognitive Domain*, a committee of the College Board chaired by Benjamin Bloom sought to delineate levels of cognitive functioning that could be used to classify the intellectual demands of standardized test items or teaching objectives (Bloom, 1956). Since that time, the taxonomy has come to be used widely as a system for conceptualizing levels of thinking skills or abilities in teaching.

Acquisition and Transmission

At the low end of the taxonomy are teaching and learning activities that stress the *acquisition* of knowledge or the *transmission* of information:

Students will be able to identify all the bones of the foot.
Students will be able to specify the major characters in Shakespeare's plays.
Students will be able to describe the order of the Milky Way.

Maker (1982) described the student role as a passive receiver and the teacher's role as provider of information.

Comprehension

At the second level, *comprehension,* instruction focuses on producing understanding. The learning process now becomes interactive and strives for meaning. Appropriate objectives at this level are:

245

Students can explain the meaning of all passages in Lincoln's Gettysburg address.
Students can explain the metaphors in a poem.

Maker described the student role as active participant and the teacher as questioner, organizer, and evaluator at this level.

Application

The next higher level is *application*. At this level, the student learns how to use rules, principles, methods, or formula in new situations. For example:

The student will be able to use the methods of solving simultaneous equations to solve complex story problems.
Given a series of complex political problems, students will be able to select the best methods to solve them.

Clearly, the application level involves students and teachers in practical use of theoretical concepts and principles.

Analysis

The fourth level of the taxonomy, *analysis,* is a cognitive process of taking ideas or phenomena apart so as to identify the parts and to delineate relationships among the parts. Analysis is also the process of detecting patterns, ascertaining the structure, or clarifying underlying principles. Here are some illustrative objectives:

Students will be able to identify and show the relationship among the elements of a complex chemical compound.
Students will be able to identify the main elements of character, mood, and setting in a spy novel and show how these interact in development of the plot.

The analysis level of thinking calls for the teacher's close monitoring of student actions to provide feedback concerning the students' accuracy in specifying parts and their interrelationships.

Synthesis

The next higher, and more complex, level of thinking to be learned by students is called *synthesis.* This is the creative process of integrating ideas, information, and theories to create a new or unique whole. This might mean learning to write a play, planning a new political system, creating a new compound, or proposing a new theory. Some illustrative objectives are:

Students will be able to design a new form of city government.
Students will write original essays on the relationship between social trends and economics.

The synthesis level requires students to use creative thinking along with all the preceding levels of thinking represented in the taxonomy. It is also likely that critical and evaluative thinking are involved in creating synthesis of ideas.

Evaluation

The final level of thinking, *evaluation,* is a process of making judgments, selecting criteria for making judgments, and applying criteria in decision making. Several of the lower levels of the taxonomy undoubtedly are involved in the evaluation process. A knowledge base and analytical skill are undoubtedly essential in evaluation. Here are some illustrative objectives:

Use a set of 10 criteria to select employees for a new civic enterprise.
Debate the justifiability of U.S. involvement in a war in the Persian Gulf.

The case study is one form of instruction for the evaluation level of thinking and learning. Making decisions about best courses of action or judgments about a process in a realistic case setting reflects evaluation in action.

It is critical to see that the taxonomy is used to conceptualize cognitive or thinking activities that often seem to be problems to be solved. The tasks or problems afford students an opportunity to learn the thinking process or algorithm involved. The teacher may structure the problems for students or help them discover problems to be solved. During the thinking activities, the teacher monitors the process, provides feedback, and often models the effective thinker in action. Students must experience successes in the thinking tasks to provide reinforcement of the skills to be learned. They often work in small groups, thinking together, and reinforcing one another as they move through a task.

These thinking skills, particularly the higher levels, are the appropriate domain for much instruction of the gifted. Gifted students have the potential to achieve much higher levels of thinking ability even though they begin new lessons with advanced levels of thinking skill as compared to children of average or low ability. The teachers' task, then, is to challenge these students to the limits of their ability, to model the thinking process, to guide them in acquiring appropriate

247

knowledge bases in disciplines, and to provide accurate feedback as they practice on structured problems. For the gifted this means much time spent exploring ideas, testing the applicability of theories, synthesizing ideas into new inventions or solutions, and judging the quality of solutions.

Problem Solving

Perhaps all teaching of thinking skills can be viewed as teaching students to solve problems. Thinking is always an adaptive process in which the thinker must be able to utilize his or her current knowledge base to deal with new and novel situations that call for some decision or action. Some recent research also suggests that our task is not simply to teach students how to solve problems but also to help them become sensitive to problems, to see problems that should be solved, to understand disciplines or domains of knowledge well enough to develop an awareness of the gaps or the unexplained, and to formulate hypotheses that can in turn lead to problem-solving activities (Getzels & Csikszentmihalyi, 1975).

Related Behaviors

After reviewing the problem-solving research literature, Feldhusen, Houtz, and Ringenbach (1972) concluded that 12 cognitive components or related behaviors had been identified through research:

1. Sensing that a problem exists
2. Asking questions about the problem
3. Noticing relevant or critical details of the problem situation
4. Defining the problem specifically
5. Guessing or speculating about causes
6. Clarifying solution goals
7. Judging whether sufficient information is available to solve the problem or whether more information must be sought
8. Redefining common objects to serve as solution elements
9. Foreseeing consequences or implications of alternative courses of action
10. Seeing a way to test or verify a possible solution
11. Selecting a correct solution when only one solution is possible
12. Selecting the best or most creative solution when several are possible

Feldhusen et al. (1972) also developed a comprehensive measure of problem-solving ability in children and found it to be correlated with other tests of logical thinking, concept formation ability, language skills, perceptual acuity, reading ability, intelligence, and general school achievement. Thus, problem solving possibly involves a complex set of cognitive operations that are basic components of several types of thinking skill.

Problem Finding

Getzels and Csikszentmihalyi (1975) investigated the process of "problem finding" and presented a continuum of eight levels of initial problem confrontation ranging from the fully presented problem to the discovered problem situation. Problem finding focuses particularly on the discovered problem situation. They claimed that problem finding may be a more creative function than solving problems that already have been formulated. In their observations of art students who were formulating the problem of a drawing, they found that artists who considered more problem elements, explored those elements more thoroughly, and selected the most uncommon ones to use in a picture were the most creative problem finders. Their conclusion was that the processes involved in problem finding are crucial in determining the creativity of solutions and that problem finding is really central in the problem-solving process.

Superior Problem Solving

In a recent review of the research literature on gifted or superior problem solvers, Hoover (1987) concluded that the following were components or characteristics of their problem-solving ability:

1. Able to reason at an abstract conceptual level (Anderson, 1986; Holzman, Pellegrino, & Glaser, 1983)
2. Able to structure ambiguous tasks (Ward, 1979)
3. Can identify the specific problem to be solved (Anderson, 1986)
4. **Effective in monitoring their own problem-solving behavior and in verifying solutions (Klausmeier & Laughlin, 1961; Wong, 1982)**
5. Have a number of effective strategies or cognitive routines to use in problem solving (Scruggs, 1986)
6. Adept at formulating concepts of problem elements or conditions (Blodgett, 1961).
7. Utilize short-term memory effectively (Ludlow & Woodrum, 1982)
8. Spend more time on initial planning (Ludlow & Woodrum, 1982)
9. Able to encode relevant information in a problem statement (Scruggs, 1986)
10. Can synthesize information in solving a problem (Davidson & Sternberg, 1984)
11. Able to use relevant, similar, or related information in solving a problem (Cohn, Carlson, & Jensen, 1985)

249

Creative Problem-Solving Model

A number of researchers have attempted to develop training sequences to assist students in the development of problem-solving ability. The most widely used model in the United States is the creative problem-solving model pioneered by Osborn (1963), Parnes (1981), Torrance and Myers (1970), and Treffinger and Huber (1975). Feldhusen and Treffinger (1985) summarized the creative problem-solving model as follows:

> *Mess-Finding* involves considering your goals and concerns and your own personal orientation or "style" of dealing with problems in order to determine the most important or immediate starting point for your problem solving efforts. In Mess-Finding, your major concern is to determine a broad goal or area of concern towards which your CPS efforts will be directed.
>
> *Data-Finding* involves examining all of the information and impressions available about the "Mess." In this stage, you will be "sifting through" all of the data surrounding your Mess—the facts, the feelings, the questions, and the hunches and concerns that you feel—to help you to understand the "Mess" better. In Data-Finding, you are attempting to clarify the most important directions you should follow during the subsequent CPS steps.
>
> *Problem-Finding*. In this stage, your major task is to take the most important information that you located in the previous stage, and begin to formulate specific problem statements; you are defining the problem. In any Mess on which you're working, there may be many different problems that might be solved; in Problem-Finding, we are trying to state as many different problems or sub-problems as possible, so we can better select an appropriate problem on which to work.
>
> *Idea-Finding*. Once you have formulated an appropriate and workable problem statement, the next step is to generate as many ideas as possible. You are trying to generate or produce as many possible solutions as you can for the problem. During this stage, you may use many different techniques or strategies for producing new and unusual ideas. The principle of deferred judgment (Osborn, 1963) is very important to remember. Since you are attempting to find as many solution ideas as possible, evaluating too soon or too much may inhibit your thinking and cause you to overlook very unusual or promising ideas. It is much easier to go back later and evaluate your ideas than it is to try to retrieve one really imaginative idea that was lost or held back by evaluation.
>
> *Solution-Finding*. After a list of ideas has been developed, you will want to determine which ones are the most promising solutions for the problem. Solution-Finding helps you to do this. In this stage, you will first generate possible criteria to use in evaluating the ideas on your list; then, you will use those criteria to conduct a detailed and systematic evaluation of the ideas. You are not simply trying to select one idea and eliminate all the rest, nor are you looking only for "perfect" ideas. You are attempting to locate, from among all the ideas you have generated, the ones that you believe have the greatest potential for solving the problem.
>
> *Acceptance-Finding*. A good idea is not worth much unless it is put to use. In Acceptance-Finding, you will take the promising ideas that you identified in Solution-Finding, and decide how they can best be implemented. What help will you need? What obstacles might need to be overcome? What specific steps will need to occur? Acceptance-Finding is primarily concerned with helping good ideas become useful ideas. (pp. 66–68)

250

Treffinger and Huber (1975) suggested the following six objectives for creative problem solving:

1. Be sensitive to problems.
   Given a "mess," the student should be able to:
— describe many specific problems that could be appropriately attacked;
— describe many elements of a situation;
— employ a checklist to extend analysis of possible problems.
2. Be able to define problems.
   Given a perplexing situation, the student should be able to:
— recognize the "hidden" or "real" problem that may underlie the stated question;
— broaden the problem, or redefine it by asking "why";
— redefine or clarify the problem by changing verbs;
— identify several possible sub-problems.
3. Be able to break away from habit-bound thinking.
   Given a description of a common situation, the student should be able to:
— describe habitual ways of responding;
— evaluate the effectiveness of those responses;
— develop several possible alternative ways of responding;
— select promising alternatives;
— develop and implement a plan for using new responses.
4. Be able to defer judgment.
   In viewing a perplexing situation, the student should be able to:
— produce many responses;
— give responses without imposing evaluations;
— refrain from evaluating others' responses.
5. Be able to see new relationships.
   Given perplexing situations or stimuli, the student should be able to:
— identify similarities among objects or experiences;
— identify differences among objects or experiences;
— list ideas for relating or comparing objects/experiences.
6. Be able to evaluate the consequences of one's actions.
   Given a situation calling for decisions, the student should be able to:
— identify a variety of criteria for evaluation;
— develop many possible criteria for a problem;
— demonstrate deferred judgment with respect to criteria.

Psychological Processes

Feldhusen (in Feldhusen & Treffinger, 1985) also presented a model of the problem-solving process. This model attempts to show the underlying psychological processes at each stage of problem solving. It stresses a strong role for problem

251

generation by the problem solver and a strong role for creative syntheses of ideas generated in an idea-finding stage. The model is presented in Table 16.1.

Problem solving consists of a complex set of skills that probably are carried out in varying sequences according to the styles and habits of the individual problem solver or the group of solvers. Grouping gifted children into clusters of four to seven for problem-solving instruction is now quite common, as in the quality circle mode of problem solving (Harshman, 1982). The component skills of problem

TABLE 16.1
Model of Problem-Solving Process

Process	Problem-Solving Stages
	I. Problem Generation
Fluency	A. What are some problems our country faces as a result
Flexibility	of the energy crisis? Brainstorm problem
Originality	identification.
Deferred judgment	
Evaluation	B. What are the most critical and general problems?
	II. Problem Clarification
Analysis	A. What are illustrations of the problem?
Evaluation	B. What are things that cause the problem?
	C. What are further problems caused by the problem?
	D. What are attributes, characteristics, or dimensions of the problem?
	III. Problem Identification
Synthesis	State the problem, in light of stage II discussion, as precisely as possible.
	IV. Idea Finding
Fluency	Brainstorm for solutions
Flexibility	1. What could we do?
Analysis	2. What could be changed?
Originality	
Deferred judgment	
	V. Synthesis of a Solution
Synthesis	A. Pick out the best elements from stage IV.
Elaboration	B. Develop an integrated solution.
Evaluation	C. Does it fit the problem statement?
	VI. Implementation
Synthesis	A. Who will do what?
Evaluation	B. How will it be done?
Originality	C. What temporal sequence will be followed?
Flexibility	D. What precautions and obstacles must be watched for?
	E. How can we overcome obstacles?

252

solving probably can be taught by first sensitizing students to the components and helping them to gain control of each component. Initial training can be in relatively abstract conditions with artificial problems or puzzles, but training should move toward application of the component skills and automatic use of a sequence of skills with applied problems in practical situations or in the disciplines. As noted earlier, students will show some unique problem-solving talents within particular disciplines, and these can be discovered and developed only through knowledge and experience in these disciplines.

Problem solving is a "generative" (Wittrock, 1977) experience through which gifted students can develop their own understandings of phenomena in disciplines or in real-world settings. Students can become more effective problem solvers through awareness and mastery of the cognitive components of problem solving.

Metacognitive Skills

Metacognition is a process of becoming aware of one's own thinking processes and gaining control over, or skill in using, orienting processes to think more effectively. Metacognition means cognitive awareness of one's own cognition or knowledge of one's own knowledge production processes. According to Flavell (1985), metacognition is "any knowledge or cognitive activity that takes as its object, or regulates, any aspect of any cognitive enterprise. It is called *meta*cognition because its core meaning is cognition about cognition" (p. 104). Flavell went on to suggest that metacognitive knowledge is knowledge about persons, tasks, and strategies. The person category refers to *beliefs* about humans as cognitive processors. The task category has to do with beliefs about the nature of the content, material, or discipline with which one must deal cognitively. Strategies are beliefs or skills one has learned in achieving cognitive goals.

There is a set of skills or cognitive orienting functions that can be brought under one's control or that can be taught. Students who acquire metacognitive skills can do a better job of controlling their thinking, problem solving, conceptualizing, reasoning, remembering, synthesizing, analyzing, and both creative and critical thinking. Teachers have long been aware that children who know the Bloom taxonomy well, who know the process of creative thinking, and who are aware of the elements of critical thinking can do a much better job of thinking or reasoning within cognitive frameworks.

Sternberg (1981) proposed six higher-order cognitive control or orienting processes:

1. Decision as to just what the problems are that have to be solved
2. Selection of lower-order components of problem solving
3. Selection of strategies for solving problems

253

4. Selection of representations for information
5. Decisions regarding allocation of componential resources in problem solving
6. Solution monitoring in problem solving

For example, the students in an American history course are trying to specify the problems faced by the South prior to the Civil War (1); they decide to focus on lower-order problems faced by some Southern states (2); they move on to decide on some strategies for solving the problems that Southerners might have used (3); they decide to represent the problems with charts (4); they divide up into groups to work on solutions to different subproblems (5); and they appoint a committee to evaluate emerging solutions (6). Gifted individuals are likely to excel in becoming aware, mastering, and controlling those processes of thinking or cognition.

Sternberg (1981) also described six metacognitive performance components:

1. *Inference* is detecting relations between objects.
2. *Mapping* is relating aspects of one area of study to another.
3. *Application* is making predictions on the basis of perceived patterns or maps.
4. *Comparison* involves the examination of a prediction in relation to alternative predictions.
5. *Justification* is a process of verifying options.
6. *Response* is communicating a solution.

As an example, sixth graders may examine the relationship between atoms and molecules (1); compare the world of atoms and molecules to the solar system (2); predict the response when two chemicals are combined (3); compare the prediction to alternative hypotheses or predictions that could be formulated (4); argue the case for the alternative (5); and communicate the resulting chemical reaction to an audience of peers (6). Finally, Sternberg identified three knowledge-acquisition components that otherwise have been identified as insight skills:

1. Selective encoding—identifying information that is relevant to a problem
2. Selective combination—combining selectively encoded information to form an integrated whole
3. Selective comparison—relating new information to information acquired in the past

Sternberg asserted that gifted students can develop these metacognitive skills to high levels of cognitive efficiency. All are skills that can be learned, and all are skills that can be exercised more effectively when students are aware of their efficacy and have gained control over their operations (Sternberg, 1986a).

Feuerstein and Jensen (1980) developed a training program called instrumental conditioning that is designed to develop a set of metacognitive skills. The framework of those skills is presented in Table 16.2.

A review of the research on Feuerstein's instrumental enrichment cognitive training programs by Savell et al. (1986) indicates that the program is teachable and that students make substantial gains in these cognitive operations after exposure to a training program. Metacognitive skills play important roles in all areas of human learning. Gifted children can learn complex metacognitive processing skills that can be used in all areas of thinking or cognitive functioning.

Summary

Through the cognitive processes of creative thinking, critical thinking, the Bloom taxonomy, problem solving, and metacognition, I have suggested that the thinking skills of gifted students can be developed to help them become effective information processors. These thinking skills can best be developed when children know or understand the thinking processes they are using, when they are guided by teachers who are themselves effective and knowledgeable thinkers, and when gifted students are given ample time to practice the skills and get feedback in artificial, realistic, and discipline-based contexts. Children can learn the subject matter of all the disciplines most effectively through dynamic, generative, cognitive interaction with subject matter or content.

References

Anderson, M. A. (1986). Protocol analysis: A methodology for exploring the information processing of gifted students. *Gifted Child Quarterly, 30*(1), 28–32.

Blodgett, E. D. (1961). A comparative study of intellectually gifted and intellectually average children in a problem solving situation. *Dissertation Abstracts International, 21*(12), 3699–3700.

Bloom, B. S. (1956). *Taxonomy of educational objectives: Cognitive domain* (Handbook I). New York: David McKay.

Bruner, J. S. (1960). *The process of education.* Cambridge, MA: Harvard University Press.

Cohn, S. J., Carlson, J. S., & Jensen, A. R. (1985). Speed of information processing in academically gifted youths. *Personality and individual differences, 6*, 621–629.

Davidson, J. E., & Sternberg, R. J. (1984). The role of insight in intellectual giftedness. *Gifted Child Quarterly, 28*(2), 58–64.

DeBono, E. (1970). *Lateral thinking: Creativity step by step.* New York: Harper & Row.

Devall, Y. L. (1982). Some cognitive and creative characteristics and their relationships to reading comprehension in gifted and non-gifted fifth graders. *Journal for the Education of the Gifted, 5*(4), 259–273.

Dunn, R., & Price, G. E. (1980). The learning style characteristics of gifted students. *Gifted Child Quarterly, 24*(1), 33–36.

TABLE 16.2

Instrumental Conditioning Framework

I.   Gathering all the information we need (input)

     1. Using our senses (listening, seeing, smelling, tasting, touching, feeling) to gather clear and complete information (clear perception)
     2. Using a system or plan so that we do not skip or miss something important or repeat ourselves (systematic exploration)
     3. Giving the thing we gather through our senses and our experience a name so that we can remember it more clearly and talk about it (labeling)
     4. Describing things and events in terms of where and when they occur (temporal and spatial referents)
     5. Deciding on the characteristics of a thing or event that always stay the same, even when changes take place (conservation, constancy, and object permanence)
     6. Organizing the information we gather by considering more than one thing at a time (using two sources of information)
     7. Being precise and accurate when it matters (need for precision)

II.   Using the information we have gathered (elaboration)

     1. Defining what the problem is, what we are being asked to do, and what we must figure out (analyzing disequilibrium)
     2. Using only the part of the information we have gathered that applies to the problem and ignoring the rest (relevance)
     3. Having a good picture in our mind of what we are looking for or what we must do (interiorization)
     4. Making a plan that will include the steps we need to take to reach our goal (planning behavior)
     5. Remembering and keeping in mind the various pieces of information we need (broadening our mental field)
     6. Looking for the relationship by which separate objects, events, and experiences can be tied together (projecting relationships)
     7. Comparing objects and experiences to others to see what is similar and what is different (comparative behavior)
     8. Finding the class or set to which the new object or experience belongs (categorization)
     9. Thinking about different possibilities and figuring out what would happen if we were to choose one or another (hypothetical thinking)
    10. Using logic to prove things and to defend our opinion (logical evidence)

III.   Expressing the solution to a problem (output)

     1. Being clear and precise in our language to be sure that there is no question as to what the answer is; putting ourselves into the "shoes" of the listener to

be sure that our answers will be understood (overcoming egocentric communication)
2. Thinking things through before we answer instead of immediately trying to answer and making a mistake, and then trying again (overcoming trial and error)
3. Counting to 10 (at least) so that we do not say or do something we will be sorry for later (restraining impulsive behavior)
4. Not fretting or panicking if for some reason we cannot answer a question even though we "know" the answer; leaving the question for a little while and then, when we return to it, using a strategy to help us find the answer (overcoming blocking)

Ennis, R. H. (1962) A concept of critical thinking. *Harvard Educational Review, 32*(1), 81–111.

Ennis, R. H. (1985). Logical thinking. *Educational Leadership, 43*(2), 44–48.

Feldhusen, J. F. (1983). The Purdue creative thinking program. In I.S. Sato (Ed.), *Creativity research and educational planning* (pp. 41–46). Los Angeles: Leadership Training Institute for the Gifted and Talented.

Feldhusen, J. F., & Clinkenbeard, P. M. (1986). Creativity instructional material: A review of research. *Journal of Creative Behavior, 20*(3), 153–182.

Feldhusen, J. F., Houtz, J. C., & Ringenbach, S. (1972). The Purdue elementary problem solving inventory. *Psychological Reports, 31*, 891–901.

Feldhusen, J. F., & Treffinger, D. J. (1985). *Creative thinking and problem solving in gifted education.* Dubuque, IA: Kendall-Hunt.

Feuerstein, R., & Jensen, M. R. (1980, May). Instrumental enrichment: Theoretical basis, goals, and instruments. *Educational Forum, 44*(4), 401–423.

Feuerstein, R., Miller, R. Hoffman, M. B., Mintzker, Y., & Jensen, M. R. (1981). Cognitive modifiability in adolescence: Cognitive structure and the effects of intervention. *Journal of Special Education, 15*, 269–287.

Flavell, J. H. (1985). *Cognitive development.* Englewood Cliffs, NJ: Prentice-Hall.

Gardner, H. (1985). *The mind's new science: A history of the cognitive revolution.* New York: Basic Books.

Getzels, S. W., & Csikszentmihalyi, M. (1975). From problem solving to problem finding. In I. A. Taylor & J. W. Getzels (Eds.), *Perspectives in creativity* (pp. 90–116). Chicago: Aldine.

Glaser, R. (1984). Education and thinking: The role of knowledge. *American Psychologist, 39*(2), 93–104.

Gordon, W. J. J. (1961). *Synectics.* New York: Harper & Row.

Gordon, W. J. J., & Poze, T. (1980). SES: Synectics and gifted education today. *Gifted Child Quarterly, 24*(4), 147–151.

Guilford, J. P. (1959). Three faces of intellect. *American Psychologist, 14*(8), 469–479.

Harnadek, A. (1980). *Critical thinking.* Pacific Grove, CA: Midwest.

Harshman, C. L. (1982). *Quality circles: Implications for training.* Columbus, OH: Clearinghouse on Adult, Career, and Vocational Education.

Holzman, T. G., Pellegrino, J. W., & Glaser, R. (1983). Cognitive variables in series completion. *Journal of Educational Psychology, 75*, 603–618.

257

Hoover, S. M. (1987). *Review of the research on problem solving*. Unpublished manuscript, Purdue University, Department of Education.

Klausmeier, H. J., & Laughlin, L. T. (1961). Behavior during problem solving among children of low, average, and high intelligence. *Journal of Educational Psychology, 52*(3), 148–152.

Ludlow, B. L., & Woodrum, D. T. (1982). Problem solving strategies of gifted and average learners on a multiple discrimination task. *Gifted Child Quarterly, 26*(3), 99–104.

Maker, C. J. (1982). *Teaching models in education of the gifted*. Rockville, MD: Aspen Systems.

Nickerson, R. S., Perkins, D. N., & Smith, E. E. (1985). *The teaching of thinking*. Hillsdale, NJ: Lawrence Erlbaum Associates.

Osborn, A. (1963). *Applied imagination*. New York: Scribners.

Parnes, S. (1977). Guiding creative action. *Gifted Child Quarterly, 21*, 460–476.

Parnes, S. (1981). *The magic of your mind*. Buffalo, NY: Bearly Limited.

Phenix, P. H. (1964). *Realms of meaning*. New York: McGraw-Hill.

Raths, L. E., Wassermann, S., Jonas, A., & Rothstein, A. (1986). *Teaching for thinking*. New York: Teachers College Press.

Savell, J. M., Twohig, P. T., & Rachford, D. L. (1986). Empirical status of Feuerstein's "instrumental enrichment" (FIE) as a method of teaching thinking skills. *Review of Educational Research, 56*(4), 381–410.

Scruggs, T. E. (1986). Learning characteristics research. *Journal for the Education of the Gifted, 9*(4), 291–301.

Sizer, T. R. (1985). *Horace's compromise: The dilemma of the American high school*. Boston: Houghton-Mifflin.

Spitz, H. H. (1982). Intellectual extremes, mental age and the nature of human intelligence. *Merrill-Palmer Quarterly, 28*, 167–192.

Sternberg, R. J. (1981). A componential theory of intellectual giftedness. *Gifted Child Quarterly, 25*(2), 86–93.

Sternberg, R. J. (1985a). *Beyond IQ: a triarchic theory of human intelligence*. New York: Cambridge University Press.

Sternberg, R. J. (1985b). *Intelligence applied*. New York: Harcourt Brace Jovanovich.

Sternberg R. J. (1986). A triarchic theory of intellectual giftedness. In R. J. Sternberg & J. E. Davidson (Eds.), *Conceptions of giftedness* (pp. 223–243). New York: Cambridge University Press.

Taylor, C. W. (Ed.). (1964). *Creativity: Progress and potential*. New York: McGraw-Hill.

Taylor, C. W. (1968). The multiple talent approach. *Instructor, 77*, 27.

Torrance, E. P., & Myers, R. E. (1970). *Creative learning and teaching*. New York: Dodd, Mead.

Treffinger, D. J. (1982). *Encouraging creative learning for the gifted and talented*. Ventura, CA: Ventura County Supt. of Schools/LTI Publications.

Treffinger, D. J., & Huber, J. R. (1975). Designing instruction in creative problem solving. *Journal of Creative Behavior, 9*, 260–266.

Ward, M. G. (1979). Differences in the ability levels and growth gains in three higher cognitive processes among gifted and non-gifted students. *Dissertation Abstracts International, 39*, 3960-A.

Ward, V. (1961). *Educating the gifted: An axiomatic approach*. Columbus, OH: Charles E. Merrill.

Witkins, H. A. (1976). Cognitive style in academic performance and in teacher-student relations. In S. Messick (Ed.), *Individuality in learning*. San Francisco: Jossey-Bass.

Wittrock, M. C. (1977). Learning as a generative process. In M. C. Wittrock (Ed.), *Learning and instruction* (pp. 621–631). Berkeley, CA: McCutchan.

Wong, B.Y.L. (1982). Strategic behaviors in selecting retrieval cues in gifted, normal achieving, and learning disabled children. *Journal of Learning Disabilities, 13*, 33-37.

Woodrum, D. T. (1978) A comparison of problem solving performances for 4th, 5th, 6th grade children classified as normal, gifted or learning disabled and by focusing level and conceptual tempo. *Dissertation Abstracts International, 38*, 6708–6709.

Study Questions

1. Is it important for children to learn how to think? Why?

2. What special needs do gifted students have in learning to think?

3. What is creative thinking?

4. What is critical thinking? In what subjects is it best taught?

5. At what levels of the Bloom taxonomy should we concentrate instruction for the gifted?

6. Can problem solving be taught in all subjects? Explain.

7. What is metacognition? How can we teach it?

8. What are impediments to teaching thinking skills, and how can we overcome them?

17

Instructional Methods
for the Gifted

Grayson H. Wheatley

As you enter Mr. Foerster's sixth grade mathematics and science class for gifted, you immediately notice that the students are working in clusters, often gathered around a microcomputer. Some are moving around the classroom. Karen and Coleen are writing a computer program using matrices to analyze data collected from a class survey. David and Eugene are heatedly discussing the best way to solve the problem: The sum of three numbers is 57 and the sum of their cubes is 21,033. What are the numbers? Other groups of students are gathered around computers, developing programs to achieve goals they have set. Chris and Gray are writing a computer graphics program to simulate a basketball program. They are discussing the merits of writing a subroutine in machine language rather than BASIC because it would be faster. Sally and Pat have just approached Mr. Foerster to ask for assistance in selecting a problem to solve. He directs them to a resource file, they return later with three possibilities, and he helps them make their final selection. Brian and Bob are discussing plans for constructing a kite they will enter in the kite flying contest next week. Winners will be recognized for highest flying, longest flying time, and most acrobatic flying. The two boys are considering building a tetra-kite formed from tetrahedrons. Clearly, all of these students are absorbed in their tasks and the teacher is a resource.

Teaching Metaphors

Metaphors are powerful ways of knowing. As Lakoff and Johnson (1980) stated: "Our ordinary conceptual system, in terms of which we both think and act, is fundamentally metaphorical in nature" (p. 3). Consider the metaphorical views of teaching we hold. As teachers, we often think of teaching as a conduit. We transmit knowledge; students receive information. We often believe our method is effective or correct because our actions match our idea of teaching as tacitly defined by the conduit metaphor. Our methods of direct instruction are based on the belief that students are containers to be filled, that students receive messages and store those messages as received to be utilized at a later time.

But Bruner (1986), Goodman (1984), and von Glasersfeld (1983) argued that students do not just take in information from a "real" world; rather, they construct meaning in their own idiosyncratic ways. As instructors, we may have developed a clever explanation for a complex set of ideas and be quite proud of our teaching when we present that conceptualization to a class. But our explanation makes sense to *us* in the world we have constructed and yet may have little meaning for the learners in *their* mental world. Metaphors influence our actions in ways we may fail to realize. Perhaps the reason we hold so firmly to our teaching methods in the face of their ineffectiveness is that they follow from the beliefs we have about learning embodied in our educational metaphors.

Operating from the transmission view of education is particularly troublesome when we work with young children, those who have not reached what Piaget called formal operational thought. Such children cannot reflect on abstractions as the teacher can; they literally live in a different conceptual world. They have not constructed meanings for the symbols we use, including the language itself. To assist children in learning, we must try to look at the world as they do. "Teachers and students are viewed as active meaning-makers who continually give contextually-based meanings to each other's words and actions as they interact" (Cobb, in press). We might call this the teacher-as-researcher metaphor. The teacher-pupil interaction is viewed as a process of negotiating meaning rather than imposing fixed procedures (Bishop, 1985). As Kozmetsky (1980) stated, "Each student must . . . be encouraged to build his/her own conceptual constructs that will permit the ordering of knowledge into useful problem-solving schema" (p. 152). Thus, the teacher's role is to provide stimulating and motivational experiences through negotiation and act as a guide in the building of personalized schema.

Much of current school practice, as determined by textbooks, reflects a behavioristic set of assumptions. In such materials, learning is seen as the process of making associations or building bonds. Associations are strengthened through repetition with prompt reinforcement of correct responses and the extinction of "wrong" responses. The learner is assumed to be, in the John Locke tradition, a *tabula rasa*. Learning is the slow accumulation of knowledge through practice.

Thus, content is broken down into small units and carefully sequenced for the learner by an "expert." We are exhorted to write behavioral objectives and tell learners what they will learn. The emphasis is on observable behavior rather than on mental activity and competence.

Primarily because of behavioristic influences, school learning is rule-oriented. Based on analysis of classrooms, Eisner (1980) found that most of the time pupils are applying rules or memorizing facts. Students spend most of their in-school time practicing skills. In mathematics this has meant memorizing facts and practicing computational procedures. In English it has meant emphasis on grammatical rules and spelling. In social studies it has meant learning names, dates, and places.

A behavioristic approach has been reflected in every discipline of the school curriculum. Although much has been written about teaching for meaning, textbooks still emphasize, in the Bloom (1956) sense, lower-level objectives. Thus, building an effective program for gifted students is difficult if existing basal textbooks are used.

Problem-Centered Learning

Favorable conditions for learning exist when a person is faced with a task for which no known procedure is available—that is, when the learner finds himself or herself in a problematic situation. Problematic situations are a function of the learner's conceptual level; what is a problem for one person may not be for another. There is nothing inherent in any task that classifies it as a problem per se; on the other hand, a seemingly routine task can pose a problem for a learner at a particular time in his or her life. To identify potential problematic situations the teacher must focus on students' understandings. Rather than trying to persuade students to "see it the teacher's way," we must strive to understand the thought patterns of students so we may frame tasks that students will consider problematic. As Dewey (1945) said,

> It is also essential that the new objects and events be related intellectually to those of earlier experiences, and this means that there be some advance made in conscious articulation of facts and ideas. It thus becomes the office of the educator to select those things within the range of existing experience that have the promise and potentiality of presenting new problems which by stimulating new ways of observation and judgment will expand the area of further experience. He must constantly regard what is already won not as a fixed possession but as an agency and instrumentality for opening new fields which make new demands upon existing powers of observation and of intelligent use of memory. (p. 75)

Mathematics is considered the most "factual" of subjects. Beliefs abound that students must become proficient with a set of facts and skills before problem solving can take place. But 13 + 49 is problematical for a first grade child who has not developed a procedure for addition with two-digit numerals. It has been shown that children faced with problems such as 13 + 49 will develop their own meaningful procedures (algorithms) for this task and, in the process, build meanings that provide the foundation for rapid advancement in mathematics learning (Cobb & Wheatley, 1988; Cobb, Wood, & Yackel, in press). Mathematics can be taught from a problem-centered perspective with considerable benefit to the students.

Problem-centered learning is effective for all disciplines. In an English class the problem might be to interpret a passage of literature. After students have read the passage, they can meet in groups to discuss their interpretations; this is followed by a class discussion in which groups present their views. In social studies the problem might be to interpret an historical event such as why the Panama canal was built and why control was eventually turned over to Panama. In science, the students might observe a candle as it stops burning when a jar is placed over it and be asked to formulate explanatory hypotheses, which then could be tested. Procedures, and, in fact, all aspects of knowledge, are best learned in context, so that they become a part of children's thinking. The knowledge is then available for more encompassing constructions.

Such an instructional format communicates several important messages to students. First, it sanctions natural instincts to construct meaning. Students come to realize they are capable of problem solving and do not have to wait for the teacher to show them a procedure or give the official answer. Students come to believe that learning is a process of meaning-making rather than the sterile game of figuring out what the teacher wants. In any instructional mode, whether it be lecture, practice, discussion, or problem solving, students are solving problems; it is a natural phenomenon.

Unfortunately, the students' "problem solving" often consists of determining how to get a good grade, to please the teacher, to avoid looking stupid—all of which are part of an academic game that children play in direct instruction environments. In these settings student motivations are extrinsic—for example, to get an "A." Problem-centered learning has the potential to help students become task-oriented rather than ego-oriented (Nicholls, 1983) and thus to focus on learning for its own sake. The use of small groups provides opportunities for students to explain and defend their views, a process that stimulates learning.

Whether the subject is grammar or mathematics, showing students efficient methods for getting answers rather than allowing them to make meaning in their own way has many undesirable effects. It may rob them of the opportunity to succeed on their own. It also robs them of the thrill of insight and communicates an image of learning as codified by others and accessible only through a mediator. In the long run, problem-centered learning is clearly more effective and even more efficient. The extensive time devoted to reteaching in our schools is an indication of the ineffectiveness of teacher-dominated direct instruction. The process of learning is one of formulating methods to solve problems, which then are revised in light of new encounters.

264

As Goodman (1984) said, "Knowing [understanding] is conceived as developing concepts and patterns, as establishing habits, and as revising or replacing the concepts and altering or breaking habits in the face of new problems, needs, or insights" (p. 19). Students develop methods for solving a particular problem that have to be revised or abandoned in the light of new problems. Even as adults, we elaborate and revise our concepts in the light of new experiences.

Gifted students have a greater capacity to become engaged in problem-solving activities because of their advanced levels of cognitive ability and vocabulary (Bloom, 1985). These students are able to analyze and solve more complex problems and to develop more elaborate and theoretical conceptions or schema. What counts as a problem for them may be considerably more abstract and general than for students with lesser ability. Thus, the practice of having gifted students work from a textbook written for average-ability students at a later age is inappropriate; gifted students need to consider larger issues. In short, teachers of the gifted must give careful thought to what will be problematical for them in light of their understandings. This will require the teacher to decenter and become a student of learning.

Problem Solving

The preceding section made a case for problem-centered learning, and this would seem to encompass problem solving. In one sense it does, but there is more to the story. When students are engaged in problem-centered learning, they are essentially building their intellectual world. In this setting students are engaged in real problem solving. It could be called learning *through* problem solving. At other times it is helpful to learn *about* problem solving. The literature on problem solving is extensive. Krutetskii (1976) provides many insights into the problem-solving characteristics of students who are gifted mathematically. Feldhusen, Houtz, and Ringenbach (1972) identified 12 components of problem solving; Hoover (1987) isolated characteristics of successful problem solvers; and Feldhusen (1985) developed a model of problem solving that contains the following components:

Problem generation
Problem clarification
Problem identification
Idea finding
Synthesis of a solution
Implementation

Significantly, Feldhusen associated specific thought processes with each of these components. Polya (1957) formulated the following four steps in problem solving:

1. Understand the problem.
2. Devise a plan.
3. Carry out the plan.
4. Look back.

The two lists have considerable similarity. During problem solving it is important to lead students to reflect on the activity of solving a problem. The foregoing steps are useful in obtaining this goal.

In using these models, we must recognize that students do not apply the steps sequentially. Even when we attempt to understand a problem before we devise a plan, it rarely works that way. Normally we grasp some aspects of the problem, try a tentative plan, increase our understanding based on the experience, formulate a new plan, and so on. Furthermore, we do not evaluate our work only at the end; we are constantly monitoring our progress and the appropriateness of methods and partial solutions.

According to Wheatley and Wheatley (1982), a key to problem solving is *exploration*. In a research study with sixth grade pupils, those researchers found that successful problem solvers made many more exploratory moves. They tried several approaches, not expecting any one of them to produce a solution; rather, this strategy was a way of getting to know the problem. Poor problem solvers made few if any exploratory moves; they typically performed a single computation and expected the result to be the answer. The solver's intentions are crucial in interpreting student actions.

In all knowledge domains there are heuristics we use in problem solving. Some heuristics are quite general and apply in all domains, but others are discipline-specific. In mathematics, heuristics such as draw a diagram, look for a pattern, take the problem as solved, work backward, and try a special case are particularly useful. Students should be encouraged to identify heuristics and become aware of their use. Naive problem solvers have a tendency to get caught up in applying the first method that comes to mind; they often fail to reflect on the problem in a broad sense and consider other solution methods. Although students should be encouraged to think about heuristics, care must be taken to avoid teaching the heuristics as new rules. It is best if the heuristics evolve during the problem-solving process rather than being introduced prior to problem-solving activities.

Metacognition is a process of becoming aware of one's own thinking and problem-solving processes and bringing those processes under personal control so the individual can think, solve problems, and derive meanings more effectively. Gifted students have high capacity to understand and develop control of their own thinking processes. Teachers of the gifted can expect much more rapid development of awareness and control on the part of gifted students when they are given opportunities for inductive, discovery, and problem-solving experiences.

There is some controversy about the value of teaching specific heuristics (Silver, 1985). The danger is always present that heuristics may become new rules and that students may interpret their task as naming the heuristic used, which may detract from problem conceptualization. Although direct teaching of heuristics such as look for a pattern, generalize, and make a table may or may not be effective, students, given the power of language in thought, do benefit by having names for heuristics. These names can be assigned to heuristics as they arise in student explanations. In this way there is a signified for the signifier.

During the past several years, methods of encouraging problem solving with gifted students have been developed (DeBono, 1970; Feldhusen & Treffinger, 1985; Hersberger & Wheatley, 1980; Polya, 1957). Such programs have proven effective with gifted students and are an important component of quality gifted education programs. These programs were deemed necessary because problem solving was not part of conventional instruction. Even as teachers develop problem-centered instruction, these materials will continue to be useful. The processes, components, and strategies can be integrated into subject matter courses rather than being an alternative unit of study. Thus, teachers will find much assistance in building problem-centered courses from these materials.

For example, from time to time it is important to reflect on the reasoning process we use in making meaning. Students gain greater power and control as they are stimulated to reflect on their thinking (metacognition). In addition to providing opportunities for students to engage in problem solving and to apply a recommended problem-solving model, we should encourage reflection on the act of problem solving. At times shifting to the metacognitive level and reflecting on the process of problem solving can be useful. This can be accomplished during class discussions and by setting tasks that call attention to thinking about thinking.

One technique utilized by Clement (1984) to encourage students to reflect on their methods is assigning differential roles to individuals in a paired problem-solving format. One person solves a problem by thinking aloud while the other acts as a prompter and critic, encouraging the first student to verbalize his or her thoughts continually. In this way, one person focuses on the problem-solving *process* while the other is solving the problem. A similar method could be used with larger groups in which one person is assigned the role of prompter, critic, and analyzer. A class discussion in which the prompter/critic describes what the other was doing encourages all students to operate at the metacognitive level.

Problem Finding

A number of authors differentiate between problem solving and problem finding (Brown & Walter, 1983; Dewey, 1929; Getzels & Csikszentmihalyi, 1975; Mackworth, 1965; Polya, 1981). In problem finding, students generate their own questions, which become problems to be investigated; in problem solving, the teacher provides the problem to be solved. This distinction is clearly important in gifted education. Getzels and Csikszentmihalyi (1975) stated that problem finding

267

is central to the creative process. If we wish to see gifted children become productive adults, creativity surely will play an important role in their professional and personal lives. Yet many educational programs are thin on problem solving, not to mention problem finding. Even in inquiry and discovery learning (Bruner, 1963; Suchman, 1966), lessons may be structured for students to discover a principle the teacher had in mind before the lesson began. Students may interpret their task as one of figuring out what the teacher has in mind rather than addressing the intended relationships. This type of learning environment allows students little or no intellectual autonomy (Kamii, 1985); they are led to a particular goal by the teacher, and they sense the imposition. There is no atmosphere of freedom to reason independently and make decisions, a prerequisite atmosphere for problem finding to occur.

Problem finding is built into well designed problem-centered learning environments. As students attempt to solve problems posed by the teacher or their peers in an atmosphere of collaboration and trust, new problems arise naturally. In fact, a teacher-posed problem serves only as a catalyst for generating problems. Thus, what has been called problem finding is an integral part of problem-centered learning.

Academically rigorous programs, such as high school Advanced Placement courses, often contain so much material to be covered that teachers think they must present information in a fast-paced mode that seems to obviate the process of students' "finding" problems; the content must be covered. Teachers who agree with proposals that emphasize problem solving/finding frequently bemoan the pressures they feel that do not allow them to allocate time to such activities. In this line of reasoning, the underlying assumption is that lecturing is a more efficient mode of instruction than less direct teaching (small-group problem solving/finding). Yet efficiency is surely related to the evaluation method used. If scores on factual tests administered shortly after instruction are used as measures of learning, perhaps (but perhaps not) lecturing proves to be efficient. But if we consider the goals of gifted education, which include the ability to synthesize ideas, become creative, and deal with novelty, the transmission view of teaching is certainly inappropriate.

Hersberger and Wheatley (1980) developed a fifth and sixth grade mathematics program for gifted students, which included problem finding/problem solving. More than 25% of each year was allocated to computer problem solving. Students, working in small groups, selected problems to solve from resources or, as many did, formulated their own problems. Students wrote computer programs in BASIC to solve the problems. In these classes both the level of thinking and the level of excitement were high. Careful evaluation of the program showed the students engaged in surprisingly sophisticated reasoning. Statistical analyses revealed that on a mathematics achievement test these students outperformed an equivalent control group (Hersberger & Wheatley, 1980). Students can make quantum leaps in learning when given the opportunity to engage in problem finding.

268

Cooperative Learning

Gifted students can profit greatly by working together (Bishop, 1985). Once we as teachers abandon the "dispenser of knowledge" role and recognize that students construct knowledge in their own way regardless of whether we like it (it is often frustrating that we cannot put what we consider to be beautiful and powerful ideas directly in children's heads), other ways of operating in the classroom must be found. Although children make sense of ideas for themselves, this does not happen in isolation from others. Piaget and Inhelder (1969) included socialization as one of the four factors in cognitive growth. Participation in small-group problem solving can stimulate cognitive disequilibrium, which results in a measurable change over time in the structure of thinking (Haste, 1987). Doise and Mugny (1984) have demonstrated that children working in pairs and groups to solve logical problems produce more adequate solutions than when they are working alone. Thus, it makes sense for children to work together.

Cooperative learning has an important place in instruction for the gifted. When children work in small groups, they are stimulated by challenges to their ideas and thus recognize the need to refine and clarify their thinking. The very act of formulating an expression of their views promotes reflection, which then leads to revision (Haste, 1987). People often modify their position once it has been communicated to others in a small-group setting.

Cooperative learning can take many forms. Johnson and Johnson (1985) and Slavin (1983) described a variety of small-group organizations. In some of these models, competition between groups and extrinsic rewards play a major role; in others these factors are considered detrimental. If we wish students to become task-oriented (Nicholls, 1983), we should avoid awarding points on the basis of group performance and other extrinsic "motivators." Yackel, Cobb, and Wood (in preparation) described an instructional model with second graders in which the children, working in pairs, engage in activities that, given what is known about the students' level of development, are judged to be problematical for them. After the children have been engaged in this small-group activity for perhaps 25 minutes, the teacher leads a class discussion in which groups present their solution methods. During this discussion the teacher makes a conscious effort to be nonjudgmental and nonevaluative, encouraging a variety of methods and elaborations of methods. The teacher does not correct "wrong" answers but instead challenges students to come to consensus.

In this way the students do not look to the teacher/authority for sanctioning but, rather, accept responsibility for determining agreement. The teacher attempts to get many different views presented without imposing his or her view on the students. The teacher also puts the class under obligation to understand the explanations made by other students and indicate when they do not follow or they disagree. In this learning environment, students can develop intellectual autonomy. This instructional method has broad applicability at all academic levels. I have even used

269

this method in a senior-level university mathematics course with considerable success.

Although a fundamental principle of this chapter is that students must construct knowledge for themselves, they are not lonely voyagers in this process. Learning occurs in the social context of classrooms, which are heavily influenced by interactions among the members of this community. It may be accurate to say that students co-construct knowledge through social interactions with others. Through the exchange of ideas with teacher and peers, students develop shared meanings that allow group members to communicate with each other. The importance of the social setting in which learning takes place cannot be overemphasized.

Using the Proposed Instructional Model

The constructivist approach* to instruction for the gifted requires considerable restructuring of course materials as well as different teaching strategies. Conventional textbooks developed in the explain-practice mode require adaptation for use in problem-centered learning. In some cases implementation requires extensive preparation. The core of the approach is a set of problematic tasks that focus attention on the key concepts of the discipline that will guide students to construct effective ways of thinking about that subject. Thompson (1985) listed five components of constructivist-based curricula. Based on his recommendations, curricula for the gifted should:

1. Be problem based
2. Promote reflective abstraction
3. Contain (but not be limited to) questions that focus on relationships
4. Have as its objective a cognitive structure that allows the student to think with the structure of the subject matter.
5. Allow students to generate feedback from which they can judge the efficacy of their methods of thinking. (p. 200)

Identifying tasks that embody the central ideas of the discipline and will be problematical for students is quite challenging. It requires attention to the central ideas of the discipline and to students' understandings.

Teachers cannot make this paradigmatic shift (Kuhn, 1970) all at once. Just as students construct meanings by revising a previously accepted method, we as teachers will try the problem-centered approach and continually modify and refine our methods each time we teach the course. In so doing, however, the potential for student growth increases.

---

*By a constructivist approach, I mean a learning environment characterized by (1) tasks based on theoretical models of students' reasoning, (2) collaboration in problem solving, and (3) sharing of ideas in the intellectual community (the classroom). In this setting, intellectual autonomy resides in the students.

As in preparing for any course, the goals must be identified. But in this approach, the goal analysis is more critical because we are asking which ideas must be constructed, not what behaviors should be specified in objectives. We are concerned more with competence (what they know) than behavior (what they can do) (Goodman, 1984).

As a second consideration, we must understand gifted students' thinking; we must learn to look at the world through the students' eyes. Rather than being considered mistakes to be corrected, student errors are rich sources of information about children's thinking. They indicate the meaning children have given to the associated ideas. The issue is not what procedures and knowledge students have amassed. Rather, the issue is what concepts they have constructed, which cognitive level they are operating from, what their motivations and beliefs are. It is important for the teacher to observe students closely in problematic situations to determine their level of competence. Selecting problematic activities requires knowledge of the students' level of functioning. Identifying what we want students to learn is not enough. We must be clear on what students know and believe.

For example, a teacher of 9-year-old gifted students may wish to teach a unit on proportional reasoning, a topic that, in the way it usually is taught, requires formal operational thought. A lesson on the conventional procedures for manipulating equations that express proportional reasoning would be inappropriate, but consider the following alternative. The lesson opens with a drawing of a hand covering a large bulletin board. The teacher begins with the statement, "Last night we were visited by a giant. He left his hand print on the wall over there. How tall was the giant?" Nine-year-olds can approach this problem in a variety of ways, each compatible with their level of cognitive functioning. Some may attempt to draw a picture of the giant on butcher paper based on the size of the hand print and proceed to measure the proportional drawing constructed in an intuitive fashion; others may write numerical relationships; and still others may work from graphs.

In classes for the gifted, tasks are frequently too straightforward and thus fail to be problematical. We must make judgments about the appropriateness of activities by seeing if they require students to restructure their thinking and elaborate on what they already know. To use a Vygotskian term, we must determine students' "zone of proximal development" (Vygotsky, 1962) and assist them in navigating across it. This approach avoids the error of teaching material that gifted students already know and the error of presenting ideas that at that time are beyond gifted students' level of comprehension. Obviously, selecting just the right tasks is a challenging endeavor, and we will not always be successful in having gifted students work in their zone of proximal development. But we must try.

In judging the appropriateness of an activity, we perform a concept analysis and consider the task demands. We then compare this with what we know about the students' conceptual development and ultimately test the activity by having a group of students try it. If it is problematical but possible, then we have a good activity. If the discussion is flat or if the students propose only one solution, we look for better activities. In this way we refine and adjust based on our observations of students' actions. Just as students construct ideas for themselves, we must construct lessons based on our understanding of student actions.

Obviously students in a class for the gifted vary greatly in ability. A strength of the constructivist approach is that because activities are problem-centered, students can operate at their cognitive level using their preferred learning style. Some students may solve a problem using sophisticated methods; others may use methods that from an adult perspective seem strange or immature. But all will be making sense of the task in ways that are meaningful to them. During class discussions, students see alternative methods that prompt them to compare methods and develop a broader perspective, which subsequently will influence how they think about new tasks. Thus, good problems are ones that can be solved in a variety of ways by students at different cognitive levels.

Projects

If challenged, gifted students are capable of producing significant projects. Within the theoretical framework of problem-centered learning is the project method. Under the guidance of a skillful teacher, students working independently or in groups can pursue a major topic culminating in a report or product. An independent project can take many forms.

Sample Projects
1. Investigate the rate at which a liquid rises in a wick. Describe the relationship between height and time.
2. Investigate and write a report on Fibonacci Numbers.
3. Prepare a report on the uses and effects of advertising. Give particular attention to television. What are the nature and source of revenue for a television station? Think of the questions to be posed.
4. Prepare a report on the effects of acid rain. Consider the issue from a sociological, psychological, scientific, or philosophical perspective.

Summary

This chapter has described an approach to instruction for gifted students that stems from constructivism. This approach contrasts sharply with behaviorism, which emphasizes breaking knowledge down into skills and subskills, writing behavioral objectives, and judging mastery based on a skills test. As Bruner (1986) stated, "Emphasis shifted [during the cognitive revolution of the late 1950s] from performance (what people *did*) to competence (what they *knew*)" (p. 94). This mode of instruction differs from transmission teaching and views the learner more as a growing tree than a sponge. Thus, rather than using the explain-practice paradigm, the teacher establishes contexts for meanings and sets activities for students that force restructuring of ideas at a higher level. Problem-centered learning with cooperative groups and class discussions becomes a rich environment for students' meaning-making.

References

Bishop, A. (1985). The social construction of meaning—A significant development in mathematics education? *For the Learning of Mathematics, 5*(1), 24–28.

Bloom, B. (1956). *Taxonomy of educational objectives: Cognitive domain.* New York: Longmans, Green.

Bloom, B. (1985). *The development of talent in young people.* New York: Ballantine Books.

Brown, S., & Walter, M. (1983). *The art of problem posing.* Philadelphia: Franklin Institute Press.

Bruner, J. (1963). *On knowing: Essays for the left hand.* Cambridge, MA: Harvard University Press.

Bruner, J. (1986). *Actual minds, possible worlds.* Cambridge, MA: Harvard University Press.

Bruner, J., & Haste, H. (Eds.). (1987). *Making sense: The child's construction of the world.* New York: Methuen.

Clement, J. (1984). Basic problem solving skills as prerequisites for advanced problem solving skills in mathematics and science. In J. M. Moser (Ed.), *Proceedings of the Sixth Annual Meeting PME-NA.* Madison, WI: PME.

Cobb, P. (in press). Tension between theories of learning and instruction in mathematics education. *Educational Psychologist.*

Cobb, P., & Wheatley, G. (1988). Children's initial understanding of ten. *Focus, 10,* 1-28.

Cobb, P., Wood, T., & Yackel, E. (in press). A constructivist approach to second grade mathematics. In E. von Glasersfeld (Ed.), *Constructivism in mathematics education.* Dordrecht, Netherlands: Reidel.

DeBono, E. (1970). *Lateral thinking: Creativity step by step.* New York: Harper & Row.

Dewey, J. (1929). *The quest for certainty.* New York: Putnam.

Doise, W., & Mugny, G. (1984). *The social development of the intellect.* Oxford: Pergamon Press.

Eisner, E. (1980). Future priorities for curriculum reform. *Educational Leadership, 37*(6), 453–456.

Feldhusen, J. F., Houtz, J. C., & Ringenbach, S. (1972). The Purdue elementary problem solving inventory. *Psychological Reports, 31,* 891–901.

Feldhusen, J. F., & Treffinger, D. J. (1985). *Creativity and thinking in problem solving for gifted education.* Dubuque, IA: Kendall-Hunt.

Getzels, J. W., & Csikszentmihalyi, M. (1975). From problem solving to problem finding. In I. A. Taylor & J. W. Getzels (Eds.), *Perspectives in creativity.* Chicago: Aldine.

Goodman, N. (1984). *Of mind and other matters.* Cambridge, MA: Harvard University Press.

Haste, H. (1987). Growing into rules. In J. Bruner & H. Haste (Eds.), *Making sense: The child's construction of the world.* New York: Methuen.

Hersberger, J., & Wheatley, G. (1980). A proposed model for a gifted elementary school mathematics program. *Gifted Child Quarterly, 24*(1), 37–40.

Hoover, S. M. (1987). *Review of research on problem solving.* Unpublished manuscript, Purdue University.

Johnson, D. W., & Johnson, R. T. (1985). Cooperative learning and adaptive education. In M. C. Wang & H. J. Walberg (Eds.), *Adapting instruction to individual differences*. Berkeley, CA: McCutchan.

Kamii, C. (1985). *Young children reinvent arithmetic: Implications of Piaget's theory*. New York: Teachers College Press.

Kozmetsky, G. (1980). The significant role of problem solving in education. In O. Tuma & F. Reif (Eds.), *Problem solving and education: Issues in teaching and research*. Hillsdale, NJ: Lawrence Erlbaum Associates.

Krutetskii, V. (1976). *The psychology of mathematical abilities in school children*. Chicago: University of Chicago Press.

Kuhn, T. (1970). *The structure of scientific revolutions* (2nd ed). Chicago: University of Chicago Press.

Lakoff, G., & Johnson, M. (1980). *Metaphors we live by*. Chicago: University of Chicago Press.

Mackworth, N. H. (1965). Originality. *American Psychologist, 20,* 51–66.

Nicholls, J. (1983). Conceptions of ability and achievement motivation: A theory and its implications for education. In S. G. Paris, G. M. Olson, & H. W. Stevenson (Eds.), *Learning and motivation in the classroom*. Hillsdale, NJ: Lawrence Erlbaum Associates.

Piaget, J., & Inhelder, B. (1969). *The psychology of the child*. New York: Basic Books.

Polya, G. (1957). *How to solve it*. Garden City, NJ: Doubleday.

Polya, G. (1981). *Mathematical discovery*. New York: John Wiley & Sons.

Silver, E. A. (1985). Research on teaching mathematical problem solving: Some underrepresented themes and needed directions. In E. A. Silver (Ed.), *Teaching and learning mathematical problem solving: Multiple research perspectives*. Hillsdale, NJ: Lawrence Erlbaum Associates.

Slavin, R. (1983). An introduction to cooperative learning research. In R. Slavin, S. Sharan, S. Kagan, R. Hertz-Lazarowitz, C. Webb, & R. Schmuck (Eds.), *Learning to cooperate, cooperating to learn*. New York: Plenum.

Suchman, J. R. (1966). *Developing inquiry*. Chicago: Science Research Associates.

Thompson, P. (1985). Experience, problem solving, and learning mathematics: Considerations in developing mathematics curricula. In E.A. Silver (Ed.), *Teaching and learning mathematical problem solving: Multiple research perspectives*. Hillsdale, NJ: Lawrence Erlbaum Associates.

von Glasersfeld, E. (1983). Learning as a constructive activity. In J C. Bergeron & H. Herscovics (Eds.), *Proceedings of the Fifth Annual Meeting of PME-NA*. Montreal: PME.

Vygotsky, (1962). *Thought and language*. Cambridge, MA: MIT Press.

Wheatley, G., & Wheatley, C. (1982). *Calculator use and problem solving strategies of sixth-grade pupils*. Washington, DC: National Science Foundation.

Yackel, E., Cobb, P., & Wood, T. (in preparation). *Small group interactions as a source of learning opportunities in second grade mathematics*.

274

Study Questions

1. How does a constructivist lesson differ from an explain-practice lesson?

2. Interview a gifted student, and, based on what you learn, design a problematic task. Explain the reasons for your choice.

3. What are the differences between task orientation and ego orientation? Give an example.

4. What do you mean when you use the term *problem solving*?

5. Choose an academic discipline, and describe a problem-finding activity for gifted students.

6. Select a topic, and describe how you would teach a lesson compatible with constructivism.

HELPING THE GIFTED ACHIEVE EXCELLENCE

18

Facilitators for the Gifted

Ken Seeley

During the course of childhood, many significant persons impact on a child's development. In the case of gifted children, this array of significant people and roles they plan can have a great effect on the realization of the children's potential. These significant people involved in educating gifted children transcend formal education. In his landmark work, *Excellence*, Gardner (1961) stated:

> Education in the formal sense is only a part of the society's larger task of abetting the individual's intellectual, emotional and moral growth. What we must reach for is a conception of perpetual self-discovery, perpetual reshaping to realize one's best self, to be the person one could be. (p. 162)

In examining the role of significant persons in a gifted child's environment, this chapter addresses the facilitators of learning. The discussion is limited to certain major groups, even though others not included might have a significant role. Possibly, Einstein would never have reached his potential had he not had an uncle who played mathematics games with him as a child. Or the nontraditional teachers influenced by Pestalozzi, whom Einstein had in a special school, might have stimulated his success. Rarely does only one facilitator make the difference in the realization of potential. Rather, a network of individuals influences a child's learning both positively and negatively, as do a good deal of chance factors.

279

With this selective view of facilitators, the discussion here examines the roles of teachers, parents, mentors, and support personnel. Selection of the term *facilitators* is based on Gardner's premise of "perpetual self-discovery," which can be facilitated but not created. The ultimate responsibility for learning must rest with the child. The facilitators, however, must be sensitive to learning. As Piaget (1970) stated, "Remember also that each time one prematurely teaches a child something he could have discovered for himself, that child is kept from inventing it, and consequently from understanding it completely" (p. 271).

Teachers as Facilitators

What Are the Roots of Teacher Preparation For Gifted Learners?

The preparation of teachers in our country began with little awareness of the problems of special students. Modeled after the European pattern, knowledge of subject matter and criteria for mastery of content were key values for the first upper schools in our country. Teachers were academic specialists, and educational settings were highly competitive in nature (Wilson, 1958). This educational philosophy dominated the early years of our country and was

> only slightly affected either by the movement for the training of teachers that developed during the nineteenth century or by the anxiety of public schoolmen over the differences in learning ability among the children to be taught in the established system of free universal education. (p. 365)

While this emphasis was developing, the special needs of bright and able children were also surfacing. Pressures were mounting for their academic accomplishment. Gallagher (1960) later stated this growing concern:

> The present nation-wide concern about the education of gifted children apparently stems from three main sources. First, there is the American educational tradition of being concerned with individual differences of all types and adapting to them. Second, there is the undeniable impact of world crises that helped us to become aware that the country's future is related to the educational future of these children. Third, there are the needs of a complex society for a vast reservoir of highly educated and intelligent leaders in the arts and sciences. (p. 1)

Tannenbaum (1979) postulated that the half-decade following *Sputnik* in 1957 and the last half of the 1970s might be viewed as peak periods of interest in gifted education. Between these peaks were only occasional bright spots for gifted and talented students and their potential teachers. Teacher preparation institutions for the most part reflected society's interest in low-functioning, poorly motivated, and socially handicapped children.

280

This alternating or cyclical interest in the gifted was aptly described by Gardner (1961): "The critical lines of tension in our society are between emphasis on individual performance and restraints on individual performance" (p. 33). The conflict was rooted in society's dual commitment to excellence and equality in education. To foster excellence meant encouraging the gifted to work up to their potential ability, but if this necessitated special educational services or teachers, it was under fire for being elitist. Conversely, support for egalitarianism, while providing increased attention to lower-status students, threatened to deprive gifted students of full academic advantage to develop their own potentialities. "Perhaps because we cannot live exclusively with excellence or egalitarianism for any length of time and tend to counterpose rather than reconcile them, we seem fated to drift from one to the other indefinitely" (Tannenbaum, 1979, p. 6).

Teacher education institutions reflected this fleeting interest 3 decades ago. A 1951 survey of all teacher education institutions, conducted by Wilson (1953), attempted to determine the availability of gifted education courses. Of the 400 replies, 2% indicated "required" or "elective" special courses on gifted at the undergraduate level, and 5% reported courses in graduate programs. A little more than half of the responding universities stated that material dealing with the gifted was included in discussion of individual differences in courses such as education and child psychology, principles of education, and methods. Several universities utilized special summer session programs, particularly at the graduate level, to provide practicing teachers with courses in gifted education.

A follow-up study in 1956 revealed little change in the informal approach to teacher education for the gifted. Wilson (1958) summarized, "It seems doubtful that students by such limited attention are being supplied with the insights and skills suitable to the creative and potential natures of gifted and talented youth" (p. 367).

Davis (1954), Wilson (1958), and Snider (1960) found very few institutions offering a specific sequence of courses related to teaching the gifted. The programs at Kent State University, Hunter College, and Pennsylvania State University were exceptional at that time in that they included sequential coursework, advanced study, practica, and graduate degree offerings.

Abraham's (1958) study reported that of 4,601 persons majoring in special education, only 21 persons were concentrating on the gifted child. Only 2 of the 1,549 who were awarded degrees in special education majored in gifted child education. Abraham also found that of the 897 higher education faculty members working in special education, 1 was devoting full time to gifted instruction. He indicated that a trend toward greater interest was shown by numerous dissertations being completed in this field. Gowan and Demos (1964) stated, "One of the educational phenomena of our times which the future will find almost impossibly difficult to explain or account for is the almost total lack of attention to the selection and training of teachers of the gifted" (p. 382).

A more recent study by Parker and Karnes (1987a) reported that 134 colleges and universities in 42 states and the District of Columbia offer graduate-level training in education of the gifted for teachers. In contrasting these data to a previous survey the authors had completed in 1984, there was an increase of more than 33% in graduate programs and 47 of the universities were offering one or more doctorates in education with a major emphasis in gifted education. These findings clearly indicate the growing interest among teachers for advanced training, and this results in better qualified professionals.

What Are Teachers' Attitudes Toward the Gifted?

Researchers found that teachers with no special preparation or background were uninterested in or even hostile toward gifted students (Wiener, 1960). On the other hand, teachers with experience working in special programs for, or doing inservice presentations about, the gifted tended to be more enthusiastic about them (Justman, 1951; Wiener, 1960). Thomas (1973) found that regular classroom teachers' attitudes were frequently negative and filled with misconceptions concerning giftedness. They further implied that these biased attitudes were forcing gifted students to modify their classroom behavior, hide their real talents, and imitate the "less bright, more normal" child.

Reasons for teacher education undergraduates' electing a class on education of the gifted were surveyed by Lazar (1973) and Lazar and Demos (1975). Curiosity about the gifted and creative, personal interest, and the need for more knowledge were identified as key reasons for university students' selecting the courses. Lazar (1973) believed that his study pointed up the need for more course offerings on the gifted at the university level to train "the teacher who is capable of meeting student needs, interests, and highly individual intellectual abilities and potentials" (p. 278).

What Are Characteristics of Teachers of the Gifted?

Authorities generally agree that successful teachers of the gifted have the following personality characteristics:

Maturity and experience; self-confidence
High intelligence
Avocational interests that are intellectual in nature
High achievement needs; desire for intellectual growth
Favorable attitude toward gifted children

Systematic, imaginative, flexible, and creative in attitudes and responses

Sense of humor

Willingness to be a "facilitator" rather than a "director" of learning

Capacity for hard work; willingness to devote extra time and effort to teaching

Wide background of general knowledge; specific areas of expertise (especially secondary teachers)

Belief in and understanding of individual differences

(Abraham, 1958; Bishop, 1968; Davis, 1954; Gear, 1979; Gold, 1976; Gowan & Demos, 1964; Maker, 1975; Marland, 1971; Mirman, 1964; Newland, 1976; Torrance, 1963; Ward, 1961).

Even though these traits are seen as desirable for all teachers, they repeatedly are listed as *essential* for teachers of the gifted. Maker (1975) attempted to narrow the list and identified two absolute necessities for a successful teacher of the gifted: (1) a high degree of intelligence and knowledge about subject matter being taught, and (2) emotional maturity coupled with a strong self-concept. In his review, Gold (1976) identified the same two prerequisite characteristics (high-level ability and ego strength) and pointed out the direct relationship between them.

Much has been written concerning the skills and qualifications of good teachers in general and, in the past decade, about specific competencies for teachers of the gifted. Seeley (1979) conducted a national survey of teacher competencies needed for education of the gifted. In this study a questionnaire was sent to universities, principals, and teachers involved in gifted education. Of 21 choices, respondents placed the following 5 competencies as highest in importance:

1. Higher cognitive teaching and questioning
2. Curriculum modification strategies
3. Special curriculum development strategies
4. Diagnostic-prescriptive teaching skills
5. Student counseling strategies

Seeley also found agreement among his respondents that teachers of the gifted should have a master's degree in the field, experience in the regular classroom, and a variety of special competencies for teaching gifted children.

What Is the Nature of Training For Teachers of the Gifted?

"Students enrolled in gifted child education coursework need assurance that their training will be as qualitatively differentiated as the methodologies they are taught

283

to use with gifted children" (Hershey, 1979, p. 13). Literature indicates that preparation programs for teachers of the gifted should expect not only the mastery of concepts but also application to real situations and analysis, synthesis, and evaluation of current philosophical approaches (Feldhusen, 1973; Hershey, 1979; Newland, 1962; Rice, 1970; Waskin, 1979). In his description of teacher training programs, Schnur (1977) believed the programs should "reflect some features of prescription and some flexibility . . . some of pedagogy and some of content. Perhaps the real quest is to train the teacher of the gifted to become a true master teacher" (p. 9).

Preservice training options include both undergraduate and graduate-level university-based education programs for teachers preparing for direct service with gifted children. Periodically, surveys have been conducted to determine which colleges and universities offer courses or degree programs in gifted education (Guy, 1979; Laird & Kowalski, 1972; Seeley, 1979). Results have shown constant change, with a steady increase of opportunities available for teachers, both in numbers of courses offered and number of institutions offering training (Maker, 1975). The trend has been to offer graduate rather than undergraduate degree programs, with some emphasis on knowledge of gifted for all certified teachers (Maker, 1975; Seeley, 1979). This practice has ensured a solid background of liberal arts education before offering specialization.

The Special Education Report ("Teacher Training for the Gifted and Talented Is Essential," 1978) listed the areas generally covered in training programs for teachers of gifted and talented. These include:

1. Characteristics and identification of gifted and talented
2. Understanding of cognitive, affective, and psychomotor processes, higher-level thought processes
3. Teaching strategies, learning environments matched to gifted/talented interests and styles
4. Program organization and operation
5. Program evaluation.

The *Report* also recommended knowledge of research and its application to the classroom, as well as the ability to demonstrate teaching techniques and ideas.

What Are the Current Trends in Training?

During 1981, Seeley and Hultgren (1982) conducted a study of teacher competencies and training. The primary purpose of this research was to determine the competencies or skill areas essential for teachers of gifted children. The secondary purpose was to determine to what extent university course offerings and pre- and inservice training programs have prepared practitioners, currently active in the field of gifted education, in the recognized competency areas. Higher education programs for teachers/administrators of gifted programs existed in at least 140 colleges and universities in more than 40 states. The types of program option varied from one or two courses through entire degree programs at the master's, specialist, and doctoral levels. Most common was the master's program. Many responding universities indicated that their offerings presently were being expanded to include degree programs to meet certification standards. The number and types of professional program in gifted education appeared to be on the increase at the time of this study.

A large sample of practitioners (N = 528) representing 48 states provided information. Teachers of the gifted, administrators in gifted programs, and a variety of instructional, curriculum, and support personnel were represented. The most common training options for teachers were inservice and staff development classes and summer or workshop courses. Half the sample practitioner group (primarily the administrators and support personnel) held graduate degrees in education with emphasis on the gifted. On the whole, the group was experienced, primarily coming from the regular or special education classroom, and seemed to be adequately prepared to teach in gifted programs. The practitioners rated competencies for teachers of the gifted as follows:

1. Knowledge of nature and needs of gifted
2. Skill in promoting higher cognitive thinking abilities and questioning techniques
3. Ability to develop methods and materials for the gifted
4. Knowledge of affective/psychological needs of the gifted
5. Skill in facilitating independent research and study skills
6. Ability to develop creative problem solving
7. Skill in individualizing teaching techniques
8. Knowledge of approaches to extension and enrichment of subject areas
9. Supervised practical experience in teaching a group of gifted students

Effective inservice training of teachers is an important activity to raise skill levels of professionals to provide appropriate education for gifted children. Stedman (1987) reviewed the effective schools research of the mid-1980s and formulated some guidelines based on successful practice. He stated that:

> Most effective schools used practical, on the job training . . . tailored to the specific needs of staff members and students. Effective schools gave demonstration lessons to inexperienced teachers; provided extra preparation periods for novices during which the novices often observed experienced teachers; videotaped teachers' performances to help improve instruction and evaluations; and helped teachers (select) materials and teaching techniques. (p. 220)

These suggestions have strong implications for changing the typical inservice presentations and for building high-level gifted educators who could provide these types of training experiences for teachers.

What Training Should Be Required of All Teachers?

The Seeley and Hultgren research indicated that more than three fourths of university program directors and practitioners in gifted education believed all professionally trained and certified teachers should have exposure to education of the gifted. Respondents preferred a separate semester or quarter course addressing topics in gifted education, for all teachers, rather than a shorter unit within general education coursework, as is currently the more common practice. Hesitation on the part of some universities might reflect problems involved in adopting new curriculum requirements for existing programs or perhaps the desire to isolate gifted education as a separate program or graduate-level concentration.

With the current attention to gifted education, an introductory course addressing the major competency areas would seem desirable for all teachers. Practitioners were highly in favor of this concept, perhaps because a majority had first been classroom teachers themselves. Practitioners realized that unless full-time special programs exist for gifted students, regular classroom teachers must assume a great responsibility for the affective and cognitive needs of gifted students. When programs do exist, teachers outside the gifted classroom greatly benefit from increased understanding of identification procedures and special strategies for gifted students.

What Changes Are Needed in Training?

Institutions of higher education should offer a variety of quality program options to prepare teachers of the gifted. These programs should be taught by qualified faculty members and should address as many of the recognized competency areas as possible. Graduate degree programs with a variety of delivery systems are most appropriate. For institutions with established programs, new areas should be emphasized, including counseling, leadership training, cultural differences, current research, underachievers, parent/community relations, and educational technological developments. Universities must design programs for teachers of the gifted that are competency-based and sensitive to changing needs of the profession.

To ensure quality programs and professional security, practitioners working in gifted education should seek and demand high-level training. They should have available to them credit courses, degree programs, or inservice options based on relevant needs and competencies. Practitioners should continue to express concern about areas of training they deem important that have not been covered adequately in education programs. Program administrators should expect that new personnel would be of high caliber, would most likely be experienced teachers, and certainly should be especially trained to work with gifted students.

The competencies listed in the literature should be recognized as a minimal level of skill or knowledge to be required of teachers of gifted students. These lists of competencies, in addition to personal characteristics and experiences, might be used to evaluate prospective teachers according to specific program needs.

In 1983, the National Association for Gifted Children formed a Professional Training Institute to establish national standards for training and teacher certification. Feldhusen and Bruch (1985) reported on the development of this effort. The standards for training included these courses:

1. A survey of gifted and talented education
2. Program planning and development with attention to administration and supervision of gifted programs
3. Curriculum and instruction for the gifted
4. Counseling and guidance for the gifted
5. Practicum with supervision
6. Creativity: theories, models, and applications
7. Development of the gifted individual
8. Advanced leadership
9. Advanced research
10. Advanced practices
11. Courses in content areas

These course recommendations were accompanied by a list of teacher certification requirements at the master's degree level, which included:

1. A minimum of 12 semester hours of credit, including the following topics: nature and needs, assessment, counseling, curriculum development, strategies, creativity studies, program development and evaluation, parent education, special populations/problems, cognitive and affective processing
2. At least one graduate course in research procedures
3. A minimum of 9 semester hours in an approved content area as a specialization
4. A practicum with gifted students supervised by a university

These standards should be helpful to universities in planning training programs and to state departments of education for certification. Close coordination among schools, higher education, and state government is necessary to implement these standards effectively.

Parents as Facilitators

What Are the Characteristics of Parents of the Gifted?

Goertzel and Goertzel (1962) reported a number of characteristics of parents of eminent people in their work. This retrospective study revealed the following characteristics of families:

Tended to be small families
Usually had high socioeconomic status
Were Caucasian and lived in an urban area
Parents were professional
Family roots were English, German, Jewish, and Oriental
Were often troubled homes with interpersonal conflicts

The parents of the eminent people:

Placed high value on education and learning (not necessarily schooling)
Fostered an enjoyment for learning
Provided recognition and respect for their child's ability
Held strong opinions on social issues
Had little tolerance for rebellion in their child
Were dominating (mother or father)
Held negative attitudes toward school and teachers

We must review these characteristics with some caution. The subjects of these studies were a small representation of gifted persons. The vast majority of gifted children we see in schools will never achieve the same level of national or international eminence as those reported by the Goertzels. This is not to diminish their potential contributions to society but, rather, to indicate the limited generalizability of family characteristics of eminent persons.

General themes concerning parents as reported elsewhere in the literature tend to both support and contradict the Goertzels' work. Some of the common themes were (1) high degree of respect for the fathers who were professionals, (2) parents' sincere love of learning, and (3) stability of marriages (Roe, 1952; Terman, 1954).

In research by Bloom and Sosniak (1981), parents were found to have a great influence on talent development of young eminent persons. Bloom and Sosniak studied 120 persons who had distinguished themselves in three general areas: artistic talent, psychomotor talent, and cognitive talent. The groups included pianists and sculptors, Olympic swimmers and tennis players, and research mathematicians and research neurologists. Those authors reported common findings for the home and parenting styles of the majority of their subjects. These findings were that (1) a parent or relative had a personal interest in the child's talent area, (2) parents provided a model in valuing the talent, (3) parents encouraged and rewarded development of the talent through home activities, (4) parents "assumed that the children would wish to learn the talent emphasized by the parents" (pp. 87–88). These results tend to support the previously cited research of parents of eminent people. No aversive or negative influences, however, were reported in the research.

Recent research by Cornell and Grossberg (1987) used a family environment scale to report on family characteristics that differentiate gifted children from other children. These authors found a causal relationship between environment and the gifted child's personality adjustment. Specifically, they found that family members who interact cooperatively with minimum conflict and maximum freedom for personal expression were the most important dynamics in the environment. Furthermore, they found that neither the degree of structure imposed nor the subject of the family activities was as important to personality development as the cooperative interaction component. They stated that "we are led to the conclusion . . . that it is not what parents do with their children, but how they do it which is the most important to the child's personality adjustment" (p. 64).

How Should Parents Relate to Schooling?

One of the greatest myths in education is that "all parents think their child is gifted." Parents are often so intimidated by this myth that they are compelled to amass large amounts of evidence of precocity just to begin discussion of schooling for their child. Some parents seek formal psychoeducational testing privately to confront schools for appropriate programming. Others provide information from home activities to demonstrate high abilities. The 6-year-old child who routinely completes crossword puzzles in the *New York Times* and the 10-year-old who designs a laser machine to produce holographs are but two examples of children's home activities that parents have reported.

Schooling is often a frustrating experience for parents and their gifted children. Bloom and Sosniak (1981) nicely differentiated "schooling" from "talent development." They described schooling as:

> . . . highly formalized, even in the early grades. There are written guidelines for what is to be learned and when it is to be learned. . . . Each individual is instructed as a member of a group with some notion that all are to get as nearly equal treatment as the teacher and the instructional material can supply. (p. 89)

Talent development, however, is instruction that is usually on a one-to-one basis with the instructor, who individually sets standards and timelines for mastery. "In

289

talent development, each child was seen as unique . . . and there was continual adjustment to the child learning the talent" (p. 89).

Parents expect schools to provide "talent development," but their children usually get "schooling." Some schools come closer than others in individualizing instruction. Some have special programs for the gifted. But rarely do we find intensity of instruction in talent development when we look to schools. With varying degrees of success, parents have advocated and must continue to advocate accommodations for their children. Public schools have the best resources to do the job. Mobilizing these resources is the greatest challenge we face in educating the gifted.

What Should Schools Be Doing with Parents?

Parents can be either a formidable threat to teachers and administrators or productive partners in the evolution of schools. Schools should educate parents but should also be open to learning from parents. This education must provide a process for change that is evolutionary, not revolutionary. Schools can enlist parents' support through active involvement rather than passive paternalism. Parents can approach schools in a helping, rather than demanding, way.

Delp and Martinson (1975) offered some excellent suggestions for schools to involve parents. Some of their ideas are:

- Ask parents to provide information about their child to help determine interests, abilities, needs, and development.
- Have parents assist the teacher in organizing individual projects, mentorships, special interest groups, and field trips.
- Ask parents to serve on advisory committees to the school or district in creating and monitoring programs for the gifted.

These are just a few ideas for creating a climate in which parents can participate. We must listen to parents and seek their support if we are to have a significant impact on the child's potential.

Support Personnel as Facilitators

What Is the Role of Psychologists?

Psychologists can play a key role in identifying gifted children and in counseling them and their parents. Unfortunately, many psychologists receive little, if any, training related to the gifted. Psychologists usually are exposed to the medical model of looking for deficits through testing. Often they learn about gifted children on the job, and many become quite adept at examining children for strengths and special abilities. The deficit orientation of psychologists has to be overcome through training and experience. The emergence of more school programs for the gifted has necessitated new assignments and new approaches for psychologists. We now are seeing some changes that may be adopted for preservice and inservice training of psychologists.

Psychologists have good skills in intellectual assessment for their professional activity. Their expertise in this area is important to the testing and identification of giftedness. The intellectual assessment, coupled with good individual achievement testing, should culminate in a clear direction for parents and educators. This direction is usually a series of recommendations based on identified strengths and needs.

Psychologists also can serve an important role in counseling parents and gifted children. The psychologists' knowledge of development, learning theory, and interpersonal dynamics can assist in understanding the intellectual and personality characteristics of gifted children. Precocious behaviors on one hand and normal developmental growth on the other constitute a delicate balance. Psychologists should inform parents, educators, and children about coping with this balance in the most productive ways.

As we learn more through research and experience with gifted learners, psychologists must be involved—not only in inputting information to this knowledge base but also in translating it into improved assessment and programming. Understanding the uniqueness of gifted children as well as the implications for their normal development is an important role for psychologists.

What Is the Role of School Counselors?

Alexander and Muia (1982) described the special role of school counselors by stating, "Exceptionally bright learners, plagued at times by concomitant problems associated with their giftedness, require the warmth, support, and understanding of competent, caring persons—a job description suited to the school's guidance and counseling personnel" (p. 173). Counselors can provide a unique service in facilitating the growth of gifted students in the school context. Counselors are usually familiar with the academic programming and resources of the school. They can work closely with other support personnel in carrying out the psychologist's recommendations in planning for the gifted child's academic and social life.

To become "environmental engineers," counselors must be sensitive to the unique needs of the gifted. Scheduling appropriate classes, matching student needs with teacher styles, and counseling parents are just a few key roles counselors serve in creating a growth environment. They also must be concerned with

291

the long-term implications of educational and career planning. This is indeed a complex task for these busy professionals. Counselors often are burdened with heavy caseloads, which necessitates special approaches to organizing services for special populations of learners such as the gifted.

Realizing the limitations of time, counselors must marshal all the help they can get from a variety of resources. Some approaches counselors use to extend their services include:

1. Setting up a teacher-adviser program for gifted students, in which a key teacher the student likes, who teaches in an area of interest of the student, serves as the adviser in planning courses, activities, and perhaps mentorships
2. Organizing groups for the gifted, wherein these students come together periodically to discuss problems and share experiences concerning the academic and social life of the school
3. Establishing a career education resource center so that gifted students can explore careers through guided reading and can identify appropriate community mentors for visitations
4. Providing a special information file for the gifted to explain programs such as Advanced Placement, CLEP exams, National Merit Scholarships, universities' honor programs, and so on
5. Organizing gifted students to create a "survival package" for new gifted students entering the school that gives insights into "good" teachers, special access to labs and computers, special clubs and extracurricular activities, and names and phone numbers of other gifted students available as personal resources

All of these things can help counselors extend their services through self-directed, peer-directed, and teacher-directed activities. The organizing will take time, but once the processes are in place, the investment should pay off.

Buescher (1987) presented an excellent model for a counseling process for the gifted (Figure 18.1). The model includes curriculum considerations as well as group and individual counseling. By focusing on the critical issues in adolescence, the model gives the counselor or teacher intervention strategies for all students as well as for the gifted learner.

Unfortunately, the services of counselors usually are restricted to the secondary level. Schools that have elementary counselors are in a good position to utilize vertical planning for gifted students. The counselor's role is an important one for all schools to utilize in programming for the gifted. The challenge lies in mobilizing these resources productively.

FIGURE 18.1
A Counseling Process Model

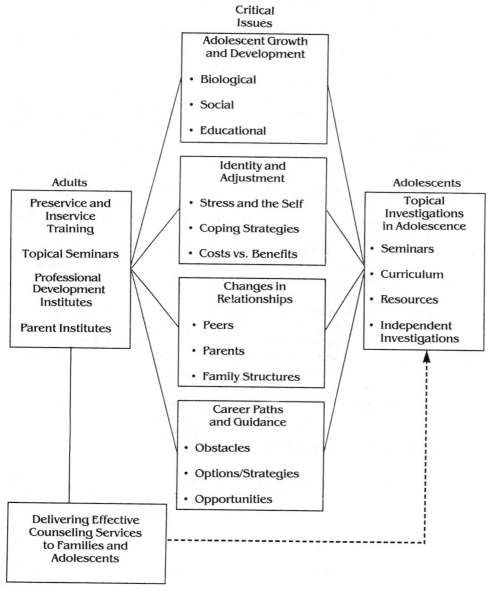

Note: From "Counseling Gifted Adolescents" by T. M. Buescher, 1987, *Gifted Child Quarterly,*
31(2), 90–94. Used by permission.

293

Mentors as Facilitators

Who Are Mentors for the Gifted?

Anyone can be a mentor to the gifted child. Teachers and parents are constantly surprised at whom the child will identify as a mentor. In a general sense, a mentor is a person the child admires who provides a role model in some area of human endeavor and who stimulates and respects the child. The role varies from hero to colleague but always implies admiration and respect.

From the school's standpoint, mentors for gifted children usually are identified by teachers who wish to extend classroom instruction using key individuals in the community. This assignment of child to community resource person assumes a mentor relationship. If we keep the preceding definition in mind, however, this does not always meet the child's standards for a mentor. The term is used loosely in gifted education. We should think of two dimensions of the term. In the jargon of gifted education, a mentor is a resource person, usually from the community, who can provide supplemental educational experiences in some area of expertise. This person may be a computer analyst, an artist, or an urban geographer. Whether the child perceives this person as a mentor is subject to individual interpretation, but rarely does a community resource person become a true mentor for the child.

We in gifted education must explain the full range of mentor relationships to gifted children. They should understand that a community resource person may be called a mentor for program purposes but that the child has other significant, personal mentors—parent, relative, neighbor, teacher, or other.

The role of mentors in the development of eminent persons has been significant. Research on adult development also stresses the importance of mentors in personal and career success (Goertzel & Goertzel, 1962; Levinson, Darrow, Klein, Levinson, & McKee, 1978). Levinson has pointed out not only the need to have mentors but also the need to understand the amount and kind of mentoring.

What Are the Roles of Mentors?

The role of mentor as discussed here follows the reasoning set forth. The personal mentor could be anyone the gifted student identifies as having a major influence. The resource person is someone a school program might identify to work with a gifted student.

The Personal Mentor

Levinson et al. (1978) provided excellent insights into the role of the personal mentor. The mentor may be a *teacher* who enhances the student's skills and intellectual development. A mentor may be a *sponsor* using influence to facilitate the child's advancement. A mentor may be a *host and guide* into a new world, acquainting the student with values, customs, and resources. "Through his own virtues, achievements, and way of living, the mentor may be an *exemplar* that the protégé can admire and seek to emulate. He may provide *counsel* and moral support in time of stress" (p. 98).

Levinson et al. also discussed the outcomes of the mentor relationship, stating that the student

> may take the admired qualities of the mentor more fully into himself. He may become better able to learn from himself, to listen to the voices from within. His personality is enriched as he makes the mentor a more intrinsic part of himself. The internalization of significant figures is a major source of development in adulthood. (p. 101)

The Resource Mentor

School programs may assign mentors to supplement gifted children's education. These mentors are usually volunteers from the community who invite gifted children to visit their places of work. Boston (1975) defined this role as "the anchoring of the pupil's learning in experience and the mentor's use of the pupil's predilection" (p. 2). Boston (1978) later noted the importance of matching not only the interest of the child to the expertise of the mentor, but also matching the teaching style to the learning style. He described the important characteristics of the mentor as follows:

1. Is usually, but not always an adult
2. Has a special skill, interest, or activity that engages the learner's interest
3. Is able to guide the learner toward personally rewarding experiences
4. Is flexible, helping the learner review and revise activities
5. Is often a role model for the learner, can impart an understanding of life style and attitudes different from those the student might ordinarily meet
6. Is above all interested in the student as a learner and as an individual

These characteristics and roles must be addressed in finding appropriate community mentors for the gifted. Mentorships, both personal and school-based, are essential to fully developing talent and abilities in gifted children.

Another good source of resource mentors for schools is a university or college. A highly developed model was created at Purdue University as the Purdue Mentor Program (Ellingson, Haeger, & Feldhusen, 1986). The students, called "protégés," are selected from a pool of gifted children in order to match their needs with specific mentors from the university community. A ratio of 2 to 4 protégés per mentor is maintained to form a mentoring group. When mentors are selected, they go through a training program to promote a consistent and high quality relationship that will make the mentor sensitive to the needs of the gifted protégés. The program is supervised by graduate assistants who provide evaluation and feedback to correct any problems that may arise.

This model has had excellent results, as evidenced by the comprehensive evaluation reports. The authors concluded that:

> The mentoring process gives youth an opportunity to learn about occupations and helps them make career decisions. Mentoring also motivates youth to pursue interest and activities in fields which fit their talents. It serves an instructional function in that protégés learn valuable information about a field from the mentor. It is also clear that mentors gain valuable understanding and insights about youth through the mentoring experience. (p. 5)

Summary

Teachers, parents, support personnel, and mentors are all critical in the development of the whole child. Utilization of this talent pool is essential to the future of our society. We must continue to educate and expand the cadre of facilitators if we are to realize the contributions of these talented young people.

This chapter by no means offers an exhaustive review of facilitators who might impact the life of a gifted child. As indicated at the outset of the chapter, the possibilities of significant people are many, including but not limited to those discussed here. Grandparents, siblings, friends, and school principals are just a few others who might be important facilitators.

The roles and relationships of facilitators to gifted children must be seen as a collective network that changes over time. In educating gifted children, we must recognize and utilize this network of facilitators in fulfilling our mission.

References

Abraham, W. (1958). *Common sense about gifted children*. New York: Harper & Bros.

Alexander, P., & Muia, J. (1982). *Gifted education*. Rockville, MD: Aspen Systems.

Bishop, W. E. (1968). Successful teachers of the gifted. *Exceptional Children, 34,* 317–325.

Bloom, B. S., & Sosniak, L. (1981). Talent development versus schooling. *Educational Leadership, 39,* 85–94.

Boston, B. O. (1975). *The sorcerer's apprentice*. Reston, VA: ERIC Clearinghouse on Handicapped and Gifted Children.

Boston, B. O. (1978). *Developing a community based mentorship program for gifted and talented*. Washington, DC: U.S. Department of Health, Education and Welfare, Office of Gifted and Talented.

Buescher, T. M. (1987). Counseling gifted adolescents. *Gifted Child Quarterly, 31*(2), 90–94.

Cornell, D. G., & Grossberg, I. N. (1987). Family environment and personality adjustment in gifted program children. *Gifted Child Quarterly, 31*(2), 59–64.

Davis, N. (1954). Teachers of the gifted. *Journal of Teacher Education, 5,* 221–224.

Delp, J. L., & Martinson, R. A. (1975). *The gifted and talented: A handbook for parents.* Ventura, CA: County Superintendent of Schools.

Ellingson, M. K., Haeger, W. W., & Feldhusen, J. F. (1986). The Purdue Mentor Program: A university-based mentorship experience for gifted children. *G/C/T, 9,* 2–5.

Feldhusen, J. (1973). Practicum activities for students and gifted children in a university course. *Gifted Child Quarterly, 17,* 124–129.

Feldhusen, J. F., & Bruch, C. (1985). *Professional training committee reports, 1984.* St. Paul, MN: National Association for Gifted Children.

Gallagher, J. (1960). *Analysis of research on the education of gifted children.* Springfield, IL: Office of Superintendent of Public Instruction.

Gardner, J. (1961). *Excellence: Can we be equal and excellent too?* New York: Harper & Row.

Gear, G. (1979). Teachers of the gifted: A student's perspective. *Roeper Review, 1,* 18–20.

Goertzel, V., & Goertzel, M. (1962). *Cradles of eminence.* Boston: Little, Brown.

Gold, M. (1976). Preparation of teachers for gifted and talented youngsters. *Talents & Gifts, 19,* 22–23.

Gowan, J., & Bruch, C. (1971). What makes a creative person a creative teacher? In J. Gowan & P. Torrance (Eds.), *Educating the ablest* (pp. 165–169). Itasca, IL: F. E. Peacock.

Gowan, J., & Demos, G. D. (1964). *The education of the ablest.* Springfield, IL: Charles C Thomas.

Guy, M. E. (1979, July). *Introductory education for teachers of gifted children in the United States.* Paper presented to Third International Conference on Gifted/Talented Children, Jerusalem.

Hershey, M. (1979). Toward a theory of teacher education for the gifted and talented. *Roeper Review, 1,* 12–14.

Justman, J. (1951). Obstacles to the improvement of teaching in classes for the gifted. *Exceptional Children, 18,* 41–45.

Laird, A. W., & Kowalski, C. J. (1972). Survey of 1,564 colleges and universities on courses offered in the education of the gifted—Teacher training. *Gifted Child Quarterly, 16,* 93–111.

Lazar, A. (1973). Reasons cited by college students in teacher training for taking an elective course on education of the gifted. *Gifted Child Quarterly, 17,* 274–278.

Lazar, A., & Demos, G. (1975, October). *Reasons for taking a course about the gifted.* Long Beach: California State University. (ERIC Document Reproduction Service No. ED 136504)

Levinson, D., Darrow, C. N., Klein, E. B., Levinson, M. H., & McKee, B. (1978). *Seasons of a man's life.* New York: Alfred A. Knopf.

Maker, C. J. (1975). *Training teachers for the gifted and talented: A comparison of models.* Reston, VA: Council for Exceptional Children.

Marland, S. P. (1971). *Education of the gifted and talented* (Vol. 2). Washington, DC: U.S. Office of Education.

Mirman, N. (1964). Teacher qualifications for educating the gifted. *Gifted Child Quarterly, 8,* 123–126.

Newland, T. E. (1962). Some observations on essential qualifications of teachers of the mentally superior. *Exceptional Children, 29,* 111–114.

Newland, T. E. (1976). *The gifted in socio-educational perspective.* Englewood Cliffs, NJ: Prentice-Hall.

Parker, J. P., & Karnes, F. A. (1984). Graduate degree programs in education of the gifted. *Journal for the Education of the Gifted, 7,* 205–216.

Parker, J. P., & Karnes, F. A. (1987a). A current report on graduate programs in gifted and talented education. *Gifted Child Quarterly, 31*(3), 116–117.

Parker, J. P., & Karnes, F. A. (1987b). Graduate degree programs in education of the gifted: Program contents and services offered. *Roeper Review, 9,* 172–175.

Piaget, J. Piaget's theory. (1970). In P. H. Mussen (Ed.), *Carmichael's manual of child psychology* (3rd ed.) (2 vols.). New York: Wiley.

297

Rice, J. (1970) *The gifted: Developing total talent*. Springfield, IL: Charles C Thomas.

Roe, A. (1952). *The making of a scientist*. New York: Dodd, Mead.

Schnur, J. (1977, October). *Description of a teacher training program for the education of the gifted*. Paper presented at the Fifth Annual Conference on Gifted and Talented Education, Ames, IA.

Seeley, K. R. (1979). Competencies for teachers of gifted and talented children. *Journal for the Education of the Gifted, 3,* 7–13.

Seeley, K. R., & Hultgren, H. (1982). *Training teachers of the gifted* (Research monograph). Denver: University of Denver.

Snider, G. (1960). Preservice and inservice education for teachers of the gifted. In B. Shertzer (Ed.), *Working with superior students* (pp. 269–278). Chicago: Science Research Associates.

Stedman, L. C. (1987). It's time we changed the effective schools formula. *Phi Delta Kappan, 69,* 215–224.

Tannenbaum, A. (1979). Pre-Sputnik to post-Watergate concern about the gifted. In A. H. Passow (Ed.), *The gifted and talented: Their education and development* (78th yearbook of the National Society for the Study of Education, Part 1). Chicago: University of Chicago Press.

Teacher training for the gifted and talented is essential. (1978). *Special Education Report, 529,* 1–3.

Terman, L. M. (1954). The discovery and encouragement of exceptional talent. *American Psychologist, 9,* 221–230.

Thomas, S. B. (1973). Neglecting the gifted causes them to hide their talents. *Gifted Child Quarterly, 17,* 193–197.

Torrance, E. P. (1963). *Guiding creative talent*. Englewood Cliffs, NJ: Prentice-Hall.

Ward, V. (1961). *Educating the gifted: An axiomatic approach*. Columbus, OH: Charles E. Merrill.

Waskin, Y. (1979). Filling the gap. *Roeper Review, 1,* 9–11.

Wiener, J. (1960). A study of the relationship between selected variables and attitudes of teachers toward gifted children (Doctoral dissertation, University of California at Los Angeles, 1960). *American Doctoral Dissertations, 54.*

Wilson, F. T. (1953). Preparation for teachers of gifted children. *Exceptional Children, 20,* 78–80.

Wilson, F. (1958). The preparation of teachers for the education of gifted children. In R. Havighurst (Ed.), *Education for the gifted* (57th yearbook of the National Society for the Study of Education, Part 2). Chicago: University of Chicago Press.

Study Questions

1. Does one need to be gifted to teach gifted children?

2. How could we improve teachers' attitudes toward gifted children?

3. How might parents and schools work together more productively to enhance the education of gifted children?

4. How could gifted children serve as facilitators to other gifted learners?

5. Why is the mentor relationship so important to gifted learners' development?

19

Counseling the Gifted

Joyce VanTassel-Baska

The need of gifted learners for counseling is best understood in the context of their differential characteristics in the affective realm. Baska, in chapter 2, already has enumerated several of these, including heightened sensitivity, idealism, unusual drive to excel, and strong sense of justice. Such characteristics, although positive on the face of it, breed problems for the gifted in many arenas. Silverman (1983) documented several of these problems:

> Confusion about the meaning of giftedness
> Feelings of difference
> Feelings of inadequacy
> Relentless self-criticism
> Increased levels of inner conflict
> Lack of understanding from others
> Unrealistic expectations of others
> Hostility of others toward the gifted child's abilities

Taken together, these affective characteristics and concomitant problems of the gifted represent an important basis for a strong counseling intervention as part of their program in schools. Yet in most schools counseling remains the *needed* provision rather than the realized one in programs for the gifted.

299

The literature on successful counseling interventions is rather sparse, except for clinical models (Ogburn-Colangelo, 1979) and applied teacher techniques such as bibliotherapy (Frasier & McCannon, 1981). Most educators of the gifted advocate grouping opportunities that create a nurturing, supportive environment for gifted learners as an underpinning of their social-emotional development (Gowan & Demos, 1964; Silverman, 1983). Furthermore, some would argue the importance of preserving affective differences and strengthening students' awareness of their inner lives so as to enhance their developmental potential in diverse areas (Dabrowski & Piechowski, 1977).

Because the education of the gifted has focused on differential characteristics and needs of the population as a point of departure for any intervention, affective differences can become the focal point for creating special counseling interventions. These interventions may be viewed as critical in three specific areas: psychosocial, academic, and career/life planning. Table 19.1 depicts the relationship between characteristics of a gifted population and the generic counseling approach necessary to address it.

A gifted child who manifests these characteristics to an intense degree is likely to suffer in various ways without appropriate counseling intervention. The nature of such suffering may manifest itself in social isolation, either self-imposed or brought about by peer ostracism; social accommodation, through reversal or homogenization of the gifted characteristics; or social acceptance seeking, through denial that the giftedness exists and by finding ways to channel intellectual energy

TABLE 19.1

Linkage of Characteristics of the Gifted to Counseling Approaches

Characteristics	Counseling Provision
Cluster #1 ability to manipulate abstract symbol systems retention rate quickness to learn and master the environment	Academic program planning that matches learner cognitive needs
Cluster #2 ability to do many things well (multipotentiality) varied and diverse interests internal locus of control (independence)	Life/career planning that presents atypical models
Cluster #3 heightened sensitivity sense of justice perfectionism	Psychosocial counseling that focuses on the preservation of affective differences

that meet the expectations of the social norm. Any of these conditions can result in a deleterious situation for a gifted child with respect to understanding and developing talent. Thus, the nature of giftedness indicates a set of special counseling needs that extend well beyond those required for a more typical learner and individual.

Strategies for Addressing Psychosocial Needs of the Gifted

Just as in the cognitive area, psychosocial needs of the gifted are best addressed through clear recognition and understanding of how the population differs from the norm in the affective area. These differences then can become the basis for systematic intervention. Although many socioemotional needs exist for the gifted, focusing on a few provides a good basis for understanding the concept of optimal match between characteristic and intervention technique. Table 19.2 presents a synthesis of seven key social-emotional needs of the gifted that phenomenologically differ from the needs of more typical students. A strategy for addressing each of the seven also is included for educators and parents to consider for implementation in a counseling setting.

The setting in which these strategies may be used will vary depending on several circumstances, not the least of which is who the provider of the counseling service will be. For many of the suggested interventions, small groups of gifted children work quite well, using a discussion format. Other interventions imply establishing a climate in the home and the classroom that encourages certain kinds of behavior in the individual child. Still others call for clinical intervention or at least one-to-one individual assistance.

Who provides assistance to the gifted child in psychosocial counseling is an open issue. If we think of this type of counseling as a part of the curriculum for the gifted, teachers certainly can be central providers. If we think of these areas of need as primarily clinical, we can turn to school and private counselors for assistance. If we think of these needs as normal developmental issues in rearing gifted children, we see parents as the appropriate providers. Because of the variety of perspectives that exists around the issue of counseling, frequently no one individual role takes responsibility for these needs. Clearly, a partnership model is needed, involving teachers, counselors, and parents integrally in the process. A more complete discussion of this issue occurs at the end of this chapter.

Strategies for Addressing Academic Counseling Needs of the Gifted

Another critical area of counseling need is providing assistance to gifted learners in academic planning no later than sixth grade and consistently throughout the sec-

301

TABLE 19.2

Linkage of Counseling Needs of the Gifted to Strategies for Intervention

Social-Emotional Needs of the Gifted	Strategies to Address the Needs
To understand the ways in which they are different from other children and the ways in which they are the same	Use bibliotheraphy techniques Establish group discussion seminars Hold individual dialogue sessions
To appreciate and treasure their own individuality and the individual differences of others	Promote biography study Honor diverse talents through awards, performance sessions, special seminars, and symposia Encourage contest and competitive entry
To understand and develop social skills that allow them to cope adequately within relationships	Teach creative problem solving in dyads and small groups Create role-playing scenarios Devise appropriate simulation activities
To develop an appreciation for their high-level sensitivity that may manifest itself in humor, artistic endeavors, and intensified emotional experiences	Encourage positive and expressive outlets for sensitivity, such as tutoring, volunteer work, art, music, and drama Promote journal writing that captures feelings about key experiences
To gain a realistic assessment of their ability and talents and how they can be nurtured	Provide for regular testing and assessment procedures Provide for grouping opportunities with others of similar abilities and interests
To develop an understanding of the distinction between "pursuit of excellence" and "pursuit of perfection"	Create a "safe" environment to experiment with failure Promote risk-taking behavior
To learn the art and science of compromise	Provide "cooperation games" Work on goal setting Encourage the development of a philosophy of life

ondary school years. What aspects of academic planning are important to consider for these students? Again, we need to be clear about their needs in this area. Major needs include understanding academic strengths and weaknesses; understanding real-life applications of academic subjects; developing metacognitive strategies; and understanding and evaluating competing choices and opportunities. The following interventions typify a responsive school environment for these learners in respect to the stated needs.

Testing and Assessment Information

Although gifted learners usually score well on standardized tests, they frequently do not have a good understanding of what their scores mean. This is particularly true of students who take the Scholastic Aptitude Test (SAT) as junior high students. Helping students understand how their score results might be interpreted for academic planning purposes is a useful service that a counseling program might provide. VanTassel-Baska (1985) developed recommendations to guide counselors in helping secondary students with academic planning (see Table 19.3).

In addition to providing students with ideas about program options based on test scores, it is also helpful to work with gifted students on an assessment of strengths, weaknesses, interests, and aspirations so that they can set realistic goals for themselves in school and beyond. It is useful to consider having gifted students develop a plan of study every 2–3 years that can be monitored and updated annually.

Applied Academics

Opportunities to experience real-life extensions of academic subjects make the academic planning process more meaningful for gifted learners. Such experiences also provide insight for students into future career possibilities. Yet, at earlier stages of development such as junior high and early high school, these opportunities provide rich experiences for students who seek to make prudent decisions on course-taking directions.

Gifted students in a number of schools are involved in community service, either as part of their course requirements or as volunteer work after school. All of the tenth and eleventh grade students at the High School of Mathematics and Science in Durham, North Carolina, participate in community service, while the twelfth graders have internships and mentorships. Students in PEG, a 5-year combined high school/college program for exceptionally gifted girls at Mary Baldwin College, in Staunton, Virginia, construct a plan for community involvement at a variety of sites, including hospitals, libraries, schools, and community agencies.

303

TABLE 19.3

Ranges of Performance on the SAT and Program Options

LOW			HIGH
200–390 on SATV/SATM	400–520 on SATV or SATM	530–650 on SATM/SATV	600–800 on SATV or SATM
Program Options	Program Options	Program Options	Program Options
Honors-level work in the content area of qualification (math/verbal)	Fast-paced, advanced coursework during academic year in area of strength (algebra or Latin)	Individualized program of study	Individualized program of study
Enrichment seminars	Academic counseling	DP approach in area of strength	DP approach in area of strength
Academic counseling	University summer program	University programs that employ fast-paced model	University programs that employ fast-paced model
		Academic counseling	Academic counseling
		Access to AP early	Access to AP early
		Grade acceleration	Grade acceleration
			Advanced standing at college entrance
			Early admissions
			Mentorships
			Career counseling

Internships

Many high school students do internships in the community through the Executive Internship Program. This program has established sites throughout the country to accommodate gifted high school seniors for a semester in their senior year. Many of these placements are in state government in which students have the opportunity to work with legislators and staff people who are responsible for programs and budgets. Students in Illinois, for example, spend one semester in Springfield, working at the Capitol and attending a seminar 1 day a week at the local high school. In Alexandria, Virginia, the experience is more diversified; students may spend their semester working in the federal government or with other agencies such as hospitals, research labs, and corporations. In an internship, the student works as an apprentice in a professional setting. The student receives high school credit for the experience and gains rich insights into a facet of professional life that may be a potential future career.

Mentorships

A mentorship is a type of program experience in which the student works directly with an individual on a one-to-one basis (also see chapter 18). Mentors may be adults in the community or other students with similar interests and abilities. The mentor model can serve academic planning purposes as well as psychosocial ones, for the mentor also provides an important role model to a young gifted learner. He or she can see in the mentor an idealized self and in that sense realize the possibility for future accomplishments. The mentor also can serve as a guide to making good decisions about academic direction and career path.

Thus, the mentor functions like a tutor or counselor, helping to advance the student's knowledge of a given field; the mentor also provides help and encouragement in considering various challenges and opportunities. The mentor has been found to be a very important factor in a gifted person's life with respect to choices made (Haeger & Feldhusen, 1987; Seeley, 1985). Through setting up mentorships for gifted learners, we can provide them with important access to adult models worthy of emulation.

Organization and Management Skills

For many gifted learners, access to ideas and tips on how to study, how to organize time, and how to take tests can be very useful, especially as they begin the secondary experience. Because elementary school is very easy for the gifted, they never really engage in the study process. When school becomes more difficult and more structured, they are ill prepared to deal with it. Their academic counseling should include attention to these areas. A list of helpful tips on effective study approaches follows:

1. Set up a study schedule that includes long- and short-term deadlines. Prepare such a schedule on a monthly calendar, monitor it weekly, and make a daily study list of what is to be done for homework, long-term projects, and so on. Work backward from deadlines to determine what has to be done on certain days.
2. Set up a study area at home—a place to go regularly to accomplish the schedule. This place should be comfortable, have necessary study tools (reference books, paper, pens) and appropriate lighting. It could be a corner of your room or the kitchen table area or a family room niche. Just be sure it is your area.
3. Set up a study group or find one other student with whom you share interests to study with at least once per week. Quiz each other and review major areas to be learned. This kind of "peer tutoring" is helpful in building study skills that continue over time.
4. Ask for assistance in areas you do not understand. Many times, gifted learners do need help "deciphering" an assignment or a problem or a special project assignment. Be practical and ask for assistance.
5. Try to study or work on projects a little bit every day. Gifted students get into trouble when they procrastinate, letting everything go until the last minute. Frequently, secondary school assignments are too extensive to allow last-minute work to be sufficient. Thus, *daily* application is important in building the self-discipline necessary for successful study habits.
6. When alternatives are available, select outside projects that interest you, and try to be creative in your choice of media to prepare them.

Providing Information About Programs and Course Options

Another essential facet of academic counseling is the selection of appropriate programs. Helping students and families make informed choices is important. Issues of taking Advanced Placement coursework, for example, should be discussed early so that students and parents can plan accordingly. Because the program is available to secondary students at any age and even exclusive of a specific class, this option is important to consider for independent study as well as for a specific curricular offering. The College Board offers 18 courses for students in most academic areas. Major advantages of the program include:

Taking a college-level course while still in high school
Learning good study habits and how to use time
Preparing for competitive colleges
Taking more advanced coursework in a given field
Saving college tuition costs

At a more general level, gifted students are in need of courses that will challenge them and adequately prepare them for high quality college work.

According to a memo from prestigious colleges to secondary school principals, parents, and students (Consortium on Higher Education, 1985), there are several areas of concern regarding lack of preparation by bright students for college. These areas include:

Reading at an analytical and interpretative level
Writing of essays
Solid "discipline study"
Essay exam opportunities
Critical thought and inquiry

Schools can focus on these areas of concern through careful structuring of curriculum opportunities for gifted students. Ensuring that these kinds of experience are a major part of course options for the gifted is an important function of an academic counselor.

Academic advising also implies knowing what preparation colleges are expecting for high-ability students. Background in a foreign language, for example, is a key ingredient in a talented student's profile, and yet many counselors ignore its importance in building programs for talented learners. The following basic program constitutes strong academic preparation for high-ability learners, according to the Consortium on Higher Education:

English (3 years)
Mathematics (3 years)
History (2 years)
Science (1 + years of lab science)
Foreign Language (3 years of *one* language)
The Arts (study of art/music)

Some key areas, then, for academic planning assistance for gifted learners include:

Taking 3 or 4 years of a foreign language
Gifted girls' taking advanced mathematics and science courses
Balancing worthwhile academic courses with specific talent and interest areas
  such as music or art

307

Making decisions about taking outside work during the school year
Taking advantage of available contests and competitions
Preparing to seek scholarship assistance for college
Accessing appropriate summer and academic year program opportunities outside of school

Many of these clearly come under the purview of the school counselor; yet teachers in academic areas also can counsel students and parents effectively on many of these issues.

Strategies for Addressing Career Counseling Needs of the Gifted

Exposure to atypical career models is another area of need for the gifted. Silverman (1983) generated some key prototypes that are worthy of discussion in the classroom:

Delayed decision making
Serial or concurrent careers
Interests as avocations
Multiple options
Synthesizing interests from many fields
Real-life experiences for exploration
Creation of new or unusual careers
Exploration of life themes for career choice

One example from this list, delayed decision making, is important for gifted students to practice. Knowing that many important individuals in various fields did not make career decisions until the end of their undergraduate experience can be meaningful information to students struggling to make a career decision early. The following activities might help students grapple with the issues:

1. Read biographies of five important people in fields you are interested in. Trace the development of their careers.
2. Interview adult family members about the career path they chose. What were important variables in their decision?
3. "Shadow" a professional in a field of interest. What aspects of the job are most interesting and why? Keep a log of your observations.
4. Survey a group of recent high school and college graduates from your geographical area about their career pursuits.

Each of the other career prototype issues for the gifted can be similarly explored by teachers' structuring key activities for the gifted.

VanTassel-Baska (1981) outlined a series of six strands for teachers and counselors to focus on in career planning for gifted students. These strands, from kindergarten to grade 12, highlight the following areas:

Biography reading and discussion
Small-group counseling on special issues and concerns (group dynamics, life planning, coping)
Mentor models and independent study
Individual assessment of abilities, interests, and personality attributes
Academic preparation for high school and college career exploration
Internship opportunities

This scope and sequence of key elements in a gifted and talented career counseling program emphasize the psychosocial needs and the need for planning and decision making among the gifted at each successive stage of development.

Another career counseling need of gifted learners is in the area of life planning. Because the potential for accomplishing many things in various areas is clearly a typical profile for many gifted learners, they have a real need to understand how they might best make decisions at various stages of development. Most adolescents have difficulty "seeing the future" much beyond termination of the schooling process, so it is important for them to examine alternative life models, try them on, and see how they fit. Gifted girls should consider what alternatives exist around having a career and a family and in what order. Specific ideas that could be implemented in a school setting in regard to this issue include:

1. Have students develop a "philosophy of life" paper. What beliefs and values do they espouse about living? How might this relate to setting goals for adulthood?
2. Have students develop five goals they might address during the next 4 years. Have them work out an action plan for implementing them.
3. Use creative problem-solving techniques to work through sample dilemmas in life planning (How might Linda decide whether to get married at 19 or finish college and begin a career first? How might Fred decide between engineering school and medicine?).
4. Study the lives of eminent individuals who were deliberate in their life plans, such as Thomas Jefferson. What factors influenced them at various stages of development?
5. Interview individuals you admire. Structure a questionnaire that examines their lives at critical stages. What events do they consider the most important? Why?

309

Through such focused activities and follow-up discussions, gifted learners can begin to appreciate the need for considering career and life paths at a more global level.

Who Should Counsel the Gifted?

The issue of who should provide counseling for the gifted frequently arises in discussions about providing these types of service. The model that works best is a confluent one in which many individuals take responsibility for a key role in the process. Trained counselors, parents, and teachers all must assume a partnership role in order to provide sufficiently for this population.

The Role of Counselors

Certainly, individuals trained in counseling procedures constitute an important group to provide services to the gifted in the counseling area. Both school and private counselors may be helpful to this population. Many school districts designate one individual as a counselor of the gifted. These individuals usually provide academic planning assistance, some career/college planning help, and occasional individual counseling in the psychosocial area. Because their caseload typically includes many students in addition to the gifted, most of their interventions tend to be group-oriented, except for special cases. Types of intervention frequently conducted by school counselors include group seminars on selective topics; career nights; college visitations; internships in selected career areas; planning of annual courses of study; and clinical counseling on problem areas.

Private counselors can also provide assistance to gifted students. These individuals frequently are used in more serious cases or for more specialized concerns. For example, private counselors may specialize in testing, underachievement cases, or college counseling. Eliciting the services of a private counselor may be judicious if needed services of a specialized nature are not readily available in the school setting. Many times, school counselors refer families to a private counselor if the case warrants it.

The Role of Parents

Many educators view counseling the gifted as mainly the responsibility of the parents. This responsibility, however, may be difficult to discharge. Nevertheless, parents can provide important assistance to their gifted offspring in several key ways. One important role is to *listen* to their problems, their concerns, and their

310

frustrations. Providing quality time with gifted children cannot be overrated as an important function for a parent. Beyond listening, a parent can *discuss* with a child ways of coping with problems, even having a child "pretend" how to act in a given situation. Parents can *ask questions* about how personal and social adjustments are proceeding for their child. Monitoring progress is an important aspect of ensuring that gifted students receive appropriate options throughout school. In these ways, parents can contribute effectively to the counseling process for their children and seek outside assistance when they believe their child needs it.

Moreover, parents can provide a family context that is likely to promote intrinsic motivation in their gifted children rather than set up an environment of reward and punishment in relation to school achievement. Csikszentmihalyi (1987) cited the most important issues for family life that foster intrinsic motivation:

Choice and control of activities
Clarity of rules and feedback
Centering on intrinsic process and rewards
Commitment, involvement, security, trust
Challenging environment with various opportunities for action

The Role of Teachers

Another source of assistance for counseling the gifted is the teacher of the gifted, the individual who sees the behavior of the gifted child on an ongoing basis. Frequently, this individual also is skilled in the nature and needs, both cognitive and affective, of gifted children. Such a person is invaluable in the counseling process in that an individual teacher might undertake all facets of guidance, except clinical intervention. For example, classroom teachers have used techniques such as bibliotherapy very successfully with gifted learners. This technique uses books in which the protagonist is a gifted child with a problem of some kind. Discussion of the book's character and his or her problem provides an instructive but safely removed context for a gifted child to identify and work on a problem area. Secondary teachers also can help with academic counseling and career counseling by including aspects of both in a year's course of study. Using speakers who represent key career areas is one way to help a subject become more meaningful for students. Also, being available to consult on the next level courses in a given area is helpful. Linda Silverman has developed a helpful list of resources (found at the end of this chapter) for teachers who are interested in or involved with counseling the gifted in a classroom context.

Summary

The needs of gifted students for counseling intervention appear great in the key areas of psychosocial development, academic planning, and career education. We must find workable approaches to address these needs that accommodate the current structure of schools and recognize the nature of the constraints within that structure. Thus, parents, teachers, and counselors might cooperatively structure opportunities for affective growth in the gifted, secure in the fact that such interventions are clearly needed and can be implemented in the context of most school settings.

References

Consortium on Higher Education. (1985). *A memo to secondary school principals, parents, and students*. Boston: Author.

Csikszentmihalyi, M. (1987). Presentation to Northwestern University Phi Delta Kappa Research Symposium, Evanston, IL.

Dabrowski, K., & Piechowski, M. (1977). *Theory of levels of emotional development* (2 vols.). Oceanside, NY: Dabor Science.

Frasier, M. M., & McCannon, C. (1981). Using bibliotherapy with gifted children. *Gifted Child Quarterly, 25,* 81–85.

Gowan, J., & Demos, G. (1964). *The education and guidance of the ablest*. Springfield, IL: Charles C Thomas.

Haeger, W., & Feldhusen, J. (1987). *Developing a mentor program*. East Aurora, NY: DOK.

Ogburn-Colangelo, M. K. (1979). Giftedness as multi-level potential: A clinical example. In N. Colangelo & R. Zaffrann, *New voices in counseling the gifted*. Dubuque, IA: Kendall-Hunt.

Seeley, K. (1985). Facilitators for gifted learners. In J. Feldhusen (Ed.), *Toward excellence in gifted education* (pp. 105–134). Denver: Love.

Silverman, L. (1983). Issues in affective development of the gifted. In J. VanTassel-Baska (Ed.), *A practical guide to counseling the gifted in a school setting* (pp. 6–21). Reston, VA: Council for Exceptional Children.

Silverman, L. (1986). What happens to gifted girls? In J. Maker (Ed.), *Critical issues in gifted education* (pp. 43–90). Rockville, MD: Aspen Systems.

Silverman, L. (1988). Affective curriculum for the gifted. In J. VanTassel-Baska, J. Feldhusen, K. Seeley, G. Wheatley, L. Silverman, & W. Foster, *Comprehensive curriculum for the gifted learner* (pp. 335–355). Boston: Allyn & Bacon.

VanTassel-Baska, J. (1981). A comprehensive model of career education for the gifted and talented. *Journal of Career Education, 1,* 325–331.

VanTassel-Baska, J. (1985). The talent search model: Implications for secondary school reform. *National Association of Secondary School Principals Journal, 69*(482), 39–47.

Study Questions

1. Why are affective needs of the gifted as important to attend to as cognitive ones?

2. What are some specific situations that you can name of a gifted child in need of socioemotional support? What happened to the child in such situations in the short term? In the long term?

3. What if you had a child, age 8, who exhibited many of the gifted affective characteristics listed in this chapter? What interventions would you as a parent like the school to provide?

4. Evaluate the appropriateness of viewing counseling interventions for the gifted as part of the curriculum.

5. What aspects of the overall counseling and guidance process might best be undertaken by teachers? What would be the rationale?

6. How might a guidance program for the gifted be implemented at the elementary level? At the secondary level?

Resources for Teachers on Counseling the Gifted

Anderson, J. (1980). *Thinking, changing, rearranging: Improving self-esteem in young people.* Eugene, OR: Timberline Press.

Briggs, D. C. (1970). *Your child's self-esteem: The key to his life.* Garden City, NY: Doubleday.

Brown, G. I. (1971). *Human teaching for human learning: An introduction to confluent education.* New York: Viking Press.

Canfield, J., & Wells, H. C. (1976). *100 ways to enhance self-concept in the classroom: A handbook for teachers and parents.* Englewood Cliffs, NJ: Prentice-Hall.

Carin, A., & Sund, R. B. (1978). *Creative questioning and sensitive listening techniques: A self-concept approach (2nd ed.).* Columbus, OH: Charles E. Merrill.

Eberle, B., & Hall, R. (1979). *Affective direction: Planning and teaching for thinking and feeling.* Buffalo, NY: DOK.

Galbraith, R. E., & Jones, T. (1976). *Moral reasoning: A teaching handbook for adapting Kohlberg to the classroom.* Minneapolis: Free Spirit Press.

Hendricks, G., & Wills, R. (1975). *The centering book: Awareness activities for children, parents, and teachers.* Englewood Cliffs, NJ: Prentice-Hall.

Palmer, P. (1977). *Liking myself.* San Luis Obispo, CA: Impact.

Raths, L. E., Harmin, M., & Simon, S. B. (1978). *Values and teaching: Working with values in the classroom (2nd ed.).* Columbus, OH: Charles E. Merrill.

20

Synthesis

John F. Feldhusen

The major need of gifted and talented youth is for talent-nurturing experiences. Their precocity in an academic area or in a domain of talent can be served best by providing opportunities for growth through interaction with excellent teachers, a high-powered and challenging curriculum, and gifted/talented peers. The goal for those who wish to realize their fullest potential is an occupation in adulthood in which their full creative capacity can be realized and personal-social lives that are rich and fulfilling.

Many gifted and talented youth and their parents will not choose to invest the time, effort, and energy in striving for excellence. They will settle for the less demanding, more comfortable lifestyle of a nice job and a family and not concern themselves with creative achievements. Creative achievement calls for delay of gratification, intense effort, and some tolerance for the isolation associated with long hours of study or practice for advanced levels of employment in creative fields.

The greatest satisfaction in life comes to those who know their own potential, who set goals that are commensurate with their potential, who strive with all their might to attain those goals, and who experience the satisfaction of attaining them. But everyone recognizes that successful attainment of goals is never guaranteed.

Risks of all kinds appear along the way. The striver may have to compromise, settle for less than full success, or fail altogether. Awareness of the risks is surely one of the reasons that many youth, and their parents, will decide to settle for lesser goals that can be more safely attained.

Characteristics and Needs of the Gifted

Gifted and talented youth have special characteristics that in turn evoke special educational needs. The salient characteristics, as presented in chapter 2, are their (1) ability to deal with abstractions, (2) power to concentrate, (3) memory, (4) curiosity, (5) precocity in language development, (6) capacity for independent work, and (7) large store of information in memory. These characteristics give rise to needs for special educational program services.

Some *groups* of potentially gifted youngsters have unique characteristics and additional educational needs. These groups include the disadvantaged, handicapped, girls, underachievers, and minority youth. The first section of this book (chapters 2–7) dealt with these special groups as well as with the process of identifying gifted youth. A philosophical orientation to identification—in which the identification process was viewed as a search for talent rather than a gatekeeping procedure—was stressed.

The second section of the book (chapters 8–11) presented models and systems for programming to meet the needs of the gifted. Models for both elementary and secondary schools are being implemented as articulated programming with K–12 curriculum. The third section of the book (chapters 12–17) presented guidelines for curriculum in all of its critical areas. And models were set forth for the special, higher-level thinking skills that should be integrated into curriculum content. The overall plan for programming and curriculum development stressed challenging cognitive experiences in keeping with the concepts, themes, issues, and challenges of the various fields.

The final section (chapters 18–20) focused on the people who interact with gifted youth in the programs and in implementing the curriculum. Gifted youth need talented, challenging mentors, teachers, and parents who recognize their child's talent, who set high goals or expectations, and who are able and willing to devote the time and effort to help the child achieve excellence.

Social-Emotional Status and Needs of the Gifted

Gifted youth are probably psychologically healthier than the general population of youth (Janos & Robinson, 1985). Yet a perception also exists, especially on the part of parents, that great psychological risks are associated with giftedness. That perception *is* correct if the child is very superior intellectually (Janos & Robinson,

316

1985). Whereas the rate of psychosocial difficulty is about 5%–7% in the moderately gifted (the normal range for the general population), Janos and Robinson (1985), after reviewing a number of studies of the very highly gifted, estimated adjustment difficulties ranging from a low of 21% (Janos, 1983) to a high of 71% (Burks, Jensen, & Terman, 1930).

This research on the psychological health of the gifted clearly suggests that the majority of youth in programs for the gifted in American schools do not have severe problems in social or emotional functioning, but more serious personal problems may beset the highly gifted, so they may need more intensive counseling or psychological therapy. Chapter 19 presented guidelines for counseling the gifted at all levels of giftedness. All gifted students need counseling services that recognize their special cognitive and affective characteristics (as discussed in chapter 2). Special counseling services should focus on self-understanding, peer relationships, family interactions, goal setting, and career aspirations.

Talent Development

Sosniak (1985) summarized findings of the Talent Development Project of Bloom (1985). She concluded that the artists, scientists, and athletes whom Bloom studied who had achieved world class status:

1. Were identified as having special talent at an early age
2. Developed a sense of being special or having special ability
3. Had families who were willing to make sacrifices to help foster the child's talent
4. Had teachers in childhood who fostered talent through playful learning experiences and later had teachers who helped the student strive for excellence
5. Developed much intrinsic motivation for study in the talent area
6. Increasingly embraced short- and long-term career goals in the talent area.

These findings certainly suggest that high-level development of talent calls for long-range commitments on the part of the talented child and his or her family. The child must learn to tolerate long periods of study or practice in relative isolation. Social activities typical of children who have average and low ability may have to be curtailed. Parents will have to contribute a great deal. Many parents will find the demands excessive and will choose *not* to foster their child's talent development (Feldman, 1986).

Other factors in the political, social, and philosophical climate also will affect the development of talent in a highly able child. Feldman (1986) pointed out that receptiveness to the talent domain varies from country to country and from time to time. As examples, computer genius is well received in our current culture, whereas talent for ballet is not currently of high priority.

How Can We Provide a Good Education For Gifted and Talented Youth?

American public schools are programmed to meet the needs of youth with average and low ability. Nevertheless, many American high schools have offered special, fast-paced academic tracks that attempt to serve the needs of fast learners and to prepare them for higher-level professional positions in the arts and sciences. Despite accumulated research evidence that supports special classes for highly able youth (Kulik & Kulik, 1982) and evidence of serious problems of underachievement (Rimm, 1986; Whitmore, 1980), strong opposition to the special tracking provision for gifted or highly able youth has been voiced (Goodlad, 1984). Sizer (1985) also presented a picture of the American high school as lacking in intellectual challenge and emphasizing content teaching only:

> One watches and listens in schoolrooms and sees and hears torrents of facts: formulae, procedures, lists, dates. They pour out of every classroom. Introductory biology classes teach the names of all the central branches of the plant and animal kingdoms. Chemistry labors through the elements. English covers the plots of stories and plays of major writers. Mathematics covers the basic procedures of the generally accepted core of the subject: arithmetic, geometry. History goes from the pharaohs to the latest election. The awesome bulk of a typical world history textbook is deadening and its myriad end-of-chapter questions daunting. Would anyone not in school pick up and read such a weighty tome? (Not students' parents, a point the young poignantly notice.) Who can retain all those facts, usually assembled by a committee of authors, which is evidence enough of the vast scale the volume represents? The exercise of memory and understanding implied by such books chills the hardiest of budding scholars. (p. 93)

Gifted and talented youth should be prepared for higher-level positions as researchers and creators in the basic disciplines, not just for professional-level jobs. The gifted and talented should join the ranks of those who work on the major problems in the disciplines of science and the arts, who make major new discoveries or inventions, and who improve the lot of all humankind by addressing major social, political, and economic problems of our time. This means that these students should be exposed to curricula, to mentors, to counselors, and to teachers who can apprise them of the nature of creative work in the area of their special talent. They should increasingly come to see how their own talents mesh with the demands of the fields of their talent strength, and they should be developing a strong knowledge base in the talent areas ahead of schedule or earlier than less able youth.

Their parents will have to do many things to facilitate their growth. The parents must be constantly supportive, helping their children get to all the higher powered school programs and experiences, fighting for them when school personnel fail to recognize or nurture their talents, providing financial support for special out-of-school programs, and being ever supportive of their emotional development. Beneath it all, parents must provide tender loving care.

318

Teachers must learn to recognize the signs of special talent or giftedness and root out their own prejudices, if they have them, against the gifted and talented. Many teachers believe that the gifted should be able to make it on their own, and some teachers resent the special ability and related personal characteristics of gifted youth. But through special classes and workshops, through development of special curricula, and especially as a result of schoolwide commitment to serve the needs of all youth including the gifted, most teachers can become effective teachers and supporters of the education of gifted children.

Schools need financial support to educate the gifted and talented well. School services for the gifted should be mandated as they are for learning disabled and handicapped children. All states should have special licensure programs for teachers and leaders of programs for the gifted. All schools should offer special classes and opportunities for the gifted, and teachers should have the guidance of curricula that are differentiated and appropriate to meet the needs of gifted and talented youth.

Programs for the gifted and talented are growing in all the states, and many states have mandated that the schools must provide services to meet the needs of these students. Many states have licensure programs for teachers of the gifted. But most elementary programs continue to see severely limited pullout efforts (Cox, Daniel, & Boston, 1985; Gallagher, Weiss, Oglesby, & Thomas, 1983). Elementary programs need strengthening in the areas of the students' academic talents; these programs presently have far too much peripheral enrichment. Higher powered courses often are available in middle school and high school programs, but gifted youth have to wait to take them until their peers of average ability are ready, rather than allowing the gifted to take advanced courses early and when they are ready. Special honors classes, Advanced Placement, seminars, mentoring, and independent study are also good options for the gifted, but these options are often unavailable in school programs.

We need bold new programming and curriculum development efforts to open doors for gifted youth, to let them fly when they are ready, and to provide the challenges that are essential for their intellectual and aesthetic growth. Risks are involved, but the potential payoffs in high-level creative achievement will more than compensate for our occasional failures. Society will benefit, and gifted youth will experience the ecstasy of self-fulfillment.

This book has presented guidelines for identifying the gifted and talented, for understanding their special characteristics and needs, and for developing programs and curricula to meet their needs. The facilitators were identified and their roles delineated in chapters 18 and 19. The remaining task is to synthesize all of the concepts into comprehensive educational services in all the schools.

References

Bloom, B. S. (1985). *Talent development*. New York: Ballantine Books.

Burks, B. S., Jensen, D. W., & Terman, L. M. (1930). *Genetic studies of genius: Vol. 3. The promise of youth: Follow-up studies of a thousand gifted children.* Stanford, CA: Stanford University Press.

Cox, J., Daniel, N., & Boston, B. O. (1985). *Educating able learners, programs and promising practices.* Austin: University of Texas Press.

Feldman, D. H. (1986). *Nature's gambit*. New York: Basic Books.

Gallagher, J. J., Weiss, P., Oglesby, K., & Thomas, T. (1983). *The status of gifted/talented education: United States survey of needs, practices and policies.* Los Angeles: Leadership Training Institute.

Goodlad, J. I. (1984). *A place called school*. New York: McGraw-Hill.

Janos, P. (1983). *The psychosocial adjustment of children of very superior intellectual ability.* Unpublished doctoral dissertation, Ohio State University.

Janos, P. M., & Robinson, N. M. (1985). Psychosocial development in intellectually gifted children. In F. D. Horowitz & M. O'Brian (Eds.), *The gifted and talented: Developmental perspectives* (pp. 149–195). Washington, DC: American Psychological Association.

Kulik, C. C., & Kulik, J. A. (1982). Effects of ability grouping on secondary school students: A meta-analysis of evaluation findings. *American Educational Research Journal, 19,* 415–428.

Rimm, S. B. (1986). *Underachievement syndrome, causes and cures*. Watertown, WI: Apple.

Sizer, T. R. (1985). *Horace's compromise: The dilemma of the American high school* (pp. 93–94). Boston: Houghton Mifflin.

Sosniak, L. A. (1985). Phases of learning. In B. S. Bloom (Ed.), *Developing talent in young people* (pp. 409–438). New York: Ballantine Books.

Whitmore, J. R. (1980). *Giftedness, conflict, and underachievement*. Boston: Allyn & Bacon.

Index

321

323